Hispanic Americans

A Statistical Sourcebook & Guide to Government Data

2009 Edition

Vincennes University
Shake Learning Resources Center
Vincennes, In 47591-9986

Hispanic Americans

A Statistical Sourcebook & Guide to Government Data

2009 Edition

American Profiles Series

Woodside, California

Books from Information Publications

State & Municipal Profiles Series

Almanac of the 50 States

California Cities, Towns & Counties   *Connecticut Municipal Profiles*

Florida Cities, Towns & Counties   *Massachusetts Municipal Profiles*

The New Jersey Municipal Data Book   *North Carolina Cities, Towns & Counties*

American Profiles Series

Asian Americans: A Statistical Sourcebook and Guide to Government Data

Black Americans: A Statistical Sourcebook and Guide to Government Data

Hispanic Americans: A Statistical Sourcebook and Guide to Government Data

Essential Topics Series

Energy, Transportation & the Environment:
A Statistical Sourcebook and Guide to Government Data

Hispanic Americans: A Statistical Sourcebook and Guide to Government Data, 2009
ISBN 978-0-929960-56-2

©2009 Information Publications, Inc.
Printed in the United States of America

Information Publications, Inc.
2995 Woodside Rd., Suite 400-182
Woodside, CA 94062-2446

www.informationpublications.com
info@informationpublications.com

Toll Free Phone 877.544.INFO (4636)
Toll Free Fax 877.544.4635

Direct Dial Phone 650.568.6170
Direct Dial Fax 650.568.6150

Table of Contents

Hispanic Americans: A Statistical Sourcebook 2009

Introduction

(ip)

Essential
Topics
Series

The 2009 edition of *Hispanic Americans: A Statistical Sourcebook and Guide to Government Data* is the 19ᵗʰ edition of this annual reference publication. It is part of Information Publications' **American Profiles** series, which also includes *Asian Americans: A Statistical Sourcebook and Guide to Government Data* and *Black Americans: A Statistical Sourcebook and Guide to Government Data*. While some information on Hispanic Americans is provided in a variety of reference sources, *Hispanic Americans: A Statistical Sourcebook and Guide to Government Data* is a single-volume statistical reference devoted entirely to this important segment of the population.

The overall goal of *Hispanic Americans* is to bring together a variety of diverse information into a single volume and present it in a clear, comprehensible format. It is not intended as a detailed research tool, but rather as a ready reference source that provides a statistical overview and guide to government data on Hispanic Americans.

Hispanic Americans contains an extensive collection of tables providing information on a wide variety of topics. With a few exceptions, each table presents data on the Hispanic population, the White population, and a total for Americans of all races and ethnic groups. The purpose of this approach is not to advance a specific perspective about Hispanic Americans, but to provide a context within which the tabular data can be more fully understood and evaluated.

Presenting data by race and ethnicity puts any publisher at risk of having its motives questioned. While some may view the presentation of such data with suspicion, or perceive a hidden agenda, Information Publications' intent is merely to serve as a reportorial resource and provide access to federal government information. This collection of sometimes difficult to find and hard to understand information serves students, business persons, reporters, social scientists, researchers, and others who need basic data about Hispanic Americans.

It is essential to understand before using this book that 'Hispanic' (as viewed by most federal data collection agencies) is *not* considered a racial category. Hispanics are the only ethnic or cultural group on which the federal government gathers data. Persons of Hispanic origin may be Hispanic and White, or Hispanic and Black, or Hispanic and Asian, etc. As a general guideline, the majority of persons identifying themselves as Hispanic for federal data collection purposes also identify as White, although there are persons who identify as both Black and Hispanic.

The use of the term 'Hispanic' requires some explanation, as it can be controversial. Hispanic Americans have used a number of terms, such as 'Latino' and 'Spanish,' to name themselves. 'Hispanic' is used here solely because it is the word currently used by the federal government in gathering data. Federal usage has changed over the years, and as it continues to change, those changes will be reflected here. In some surveys, data is further broken down into subgroups of the Hispanic population (e.g., Mexican, Cuban, Puerto Rican, etc.). When such information is available, it is presented here.

Whether or not someone is identified as Hispanic can also be a sensitive issue. For federal data-collection and statistical reporting purposes, being Hispanic is based solely on self-identification: Hispanic persons are those who say they are Hispanic (or, in some surveys, Latino or Spanish).

While most agencies of the federal government collect data on Hispanic origin as a supplement to racial categories, some agencies, such as the US Department of Education and the Centers for Disease Control, collect some (but not necessarily all) information on Hispanic origin as if it were a racial category. These agencies count Hispanics separately from non-Hispanic Blacks and non-Hispanic Whites.

Organization

The main portion of this book has been divided into eight chapters:

Chapter 1:	Demographics & Social Characteristics
Chapter 2:	Vital Statistics & Health
Chapter 3:	Education
Chapter 4:	Government & Elections
Chapter 5:	Crime, Law Enforcement & Corrections
Chapter 6:	Labor, Employment & Unemployment
Chapter 7:	Earnings, Income, Poverty & Wealth
Chapter 8:	Special Topics

The tables in each chapter present a comprehensive review of available federal government statistical information on the Hispanic population. Each table presents pertinent information from the source or sources in a clear, comprehensible fashion. The information selected for presentation was chosen for its broad scope and general appeal for a diverse group of readers.

The Sources

All of the information in *Hispanic Americans* is either collected directly or republished by US Government sources. Most of the federal information is from the US Bureau of the Census. Without question, the Census Bureau is the largest data-gathering organization in the nation. It collects information on an exceptionally broad range of topics, not only for its own use and for the use of Congress and the Executive Branch, but also for other federal agencies and departments. The reach of the Census Bureau is wider than most people realize. It encompasses the decennial Census of Population, the Current Population Survey, the Annual Housing Survey, and the American Community Survey. In cooperation with other agencies, the Bureau produces the Consumer Expenditure Survey, the National Crime Survey, the National Family Growth Survey, and many other surveys. The Census Bureau's role in so much of the federal government's data collection adds uniformity to the statistical information published by different agencies and makes the data easier to understand and use. In addition, because of the sheer volume of data it collects, many private data collectors have adopted some of its procedures and terminology, enhancing compatibility between private and public data.

Observant readers will note that the source of many tables found here is a Census Bureau publication, the *Statistical Abstract of the United States*. There are several reasons for this. First, due to budgetary constraints and the huge amount of data collected, much of the information presented in the *Abstract* has never been previously published, or has only been published in part. Second, the *Abstract* presents data that is accessible to many different types of readers. As the preeminent federal data publisher, the Census Bureau has access to a wealth of raw data that it can aggregate and break down by details such as age, sex, race, or geographic region, using its own parameters for publication. Some data has only been published in very fine detail, and the *Abstract* provides an overview that is more accessible to more casual readers.

Types of Information

Data presented here is divided into two categories:

The first is complete count data. For example, questions asked of all Americans by the Census Bureau in its decennial census an attempt a complete count of a given universe.

The second type of data is survey information. When surveying the entire population would be impractical or impossible, a subset of a population is-drawn to represent the entire population or universe. Data on housing units and money income are some of the items in this book based on this type of survey information. Of course, survey information is only as good as the survey itself, so the reader should always consider the accuracy and methods used by the original source. Survey methodology is not discussed here: interested readers should consult the original source materials for a detailed explanation of survey methodology. A full reference to each source appears in every table. Readers should also note that most data collected by government agencies (except for the short form of the Decennial Census) is based on a sample, and that data based on small numbers of individuals is considered statistically unreliable and not presented in the results. In these cases, a note appears in the table.

The Tables

This section details how the tables have been prepared and presented. Table titles are the first source of valuable information. For example:

> **Table 2.02: Fertility, Births, and Birth Rates by Age of the Mother, 1990–2007**

The table number contains the chapter number to the left of the decimal and the location of the table within the chapter to the right of the decimal. Thus Table 2.02 is the second table in Chapter 2. In general, information in tables and across each chapter is presented with the oldest, most general information first, followed by newer, more specific information.

The table title first presents the general topic of the table, followed by the detail presented about the general topic (e.g., the data is presented by age, sex, state of residence, marital status, etc.), and the years for which data is presented. In most cases, the tables retain the original terms used in the source material to make the book compatible with the original sources.

For most tables, the left-most column or columns show data for the Hispanic population, the center column or columns show data for the White population, and the right-hand column or columns show data for all races.

Along the left margin of each table appears a column of line descriptors. Here, after a general heading, subgroups of the heading are shown. In general, counts and quantities appear first, followed by percentages, medians, means, rates, and per capita amounts.

Wherever available and appropriate, a time span of data is presented in order to provide readers with a historical context for the information. However, readers should be cautioned that the years selected have been chosen from no special knowledge of the subject, nor to make any specific point. The fact that there has been an increase or decrease in a given indicator for the period displayed does not mean that the same trend will continue, or that it represents the continuation of a historical trend, or even that which appears to be a trend within this period actually is one. Many apparent changes are merely the result of an agency's redefining its terms: for example, many Census programs have different specifications for Hispanic: 'Hispanics of any race,' 'Hispanic White,' etc. Programs sometimes change the definition that they use, and this may give the appearance of a real change in the population when there was none. For this reason, readers are advised to use caution when comparing figures across different time periods.

Table Notes

The bottom of each table contains three key paragraphs: Source, Notes, and Units. The **Source** paragraph lists the source of the data presented in the table. When more than one source was used, the sources are listed in the same order in which the data itself appears in the table. As all sources are government publications, the issuing agency is listed as the author. Citations provide the table number in the source from which the material was taken. An increasing number of sources are now available on the internet, and in many cases, only on the internet. For tables pulled exclusively from online sources, the URL is listed as the source, along with the date it was accessed.

The **Notes** paragraph includes pertinent facts about the data. One general note will apply to all tabular data: detail (subgroups) may not add to the total shown, due either to rounding or to the fact that only selected subgroups are displayed.

The final paragraph of a table, **Units**, identifies the units used, specifically stating that the quantity is millions of persons, thousands of workers, dollars per capita, etc. Readers are urged to pay special attention to the units when a median, mean, percent, rate, or a per capita amount is provided.

Guide to Sources

Hispanic Americans also presents a complete guide to sources. Sources are listed by chapter and sorted alphabetically by the name of the publication, with the issuing department or group appearing next. Each entry gives a description of the source, including how it was used in the present volume and what information it might present for further research, as well as the online location where the data or report can be accessed.

The Glossary

This book contains definitions for any specialized terms that are needed to understand the data. The tables contain short, clear definitions with only as much background material as necessary to make a term understandable in a general sense. However, for many tables, when it is not possible to adequately define a term in the table notes, the glossary provides a full definition and serves as an important tool in using the tables.

Before drawing any conclusions from the data, it is absolutely vital to understand the meaning of all terms used in a table. Certain terms require some methodological background in order to accurately understand the material presented. The government not only has its own specialized, clearly-defined terms, but it also uses ordinary words in specialized ways. For example, there are real differences between a household and a family, a family and a married couple, the resident population and the civilian non-institutional population, a service industry and a service occupation, and an urban area and a metropolitan area.

Readers requiring detailed definitions and an understating of the technical and methodological detail should refer to the sources for more complete explanations.

The Index

Most key terms from the tables have been indexed. Readers should note that the index provides table numbers as opposed to page numbers.

A Suggestion on How to Use This Book

One way to use this book is by locating a subject of general interest in the **Table of Contents** and turning to that chapter. While the **Table of Contents** is detailed enough to narrow a search, and the index can speed access to specific items, sometimes paging through the dozen or so tables on a given topic uncovers unexpected information that can prove useful. It is just this type of serendipity that has lead to the inclusion of some of the information in this book, and sometimes an unexpected find can greatly enhance a research project.

Disclaimer

Hispanic Americans: A Statistical Sourcebook and Guide to Government Data contains thousands of pieces of information. Every reasonable precaution, along with a good deal of care, was taken in its preparation. Despite our efforts it is possible that some of the information contained in this book may not be accurate. Some errors may be due to errors in the original source materials, others may have been made by the compilers of this volume. An incorrect spelling may occur, a figure may be inverted, or similar mistakes may exist. The compilers, editors, typists, printers and others are all human, and in a work of this magnitude the possibility of error can never be fully eliminated.

The publisher is also aware that some users may apply the data in this book in various remunerative projects. Although we have taken reasonable, responsible measures to insure accuracy, we cannot take responsibility for liability or losses suffered by users of the data. No other guarantees are made or implied.

The publisher assumes no liability for losses incurred by users, and warrants only that diligence and care were used in the production of this volume.

A Final Word

As this book is updated on an annual basis, questions, comments, and criticisms from users are vital to making informed editorial choices about succeeding editions. If you have a suggestion or comment, be assured that it will be both appreciated and carefully considered. If you should find an error here, please let us know so that it may be corrected. Our goal is to provide accurate, easy to use, statistical compendiums that serve our readers' needs. Your help enables us to do our job better. If you know how this book could become more useful to you, please contact us.

The Editors
Information Publications, Inc.
2995 Woodside Road, Suite 400-182
Woodside, CA 94062
www.informationpublications.com
info@informationpublications.com
Toll Free Phone: 877-544-4636
Toll Free Fax: 877-544-4635

Chapter 1

Demographics and Social Characteristics

Chapter One Highlights

This chapter provides information about the demographics and social characteristics of Hispanic persons in the United States, including both the most current data available as well as comparisons of the Hispanic population over time. For almost all tables, corresponding data is provided for the total population of the United States as well as for White persons. This allows for easy comparison between groups. Because 'Hispanic' is not a race or ethnic group, we have included a variety of tables with statistics on some of the ethnic groups that comprise the Hispanic designation (tables 1.04, 1.05, 1.16, 1.17, 1.26, and 1.27).

The chapter includes general population statistics for Hispanic persons organized in a number of different ways, including by age (tables 1.02, 1.04, 1.09, and 1.10), sex (table 1.05), residence (tables 1.06, 1.09, 1.10, 1.12, and 1.19), and educational attainment (table 1.09). In addition, population projections are provided up to the year 2050 (tables 1.11). Since the year 2000, the Hispanic population has increased across the United States, and the latest data on births, deaths, and internal migration is also provided (table 1.03).

In addition, this chapter contains marriage statistics, both for the total population (table 1.13) and divided by gender (tables 1.14 and 1.15). A breakdown of the marital status of a variety of Hispanic ethnic groups is also provided (table 1.16).

Also of note are the tables comparing characteristics such as marital status, residence, and age during 1985, 1990, and 2007. These tables are divided by statistics on households (tables 1.20–1.22) and statistics on family households (tables 1.23–1.25).

This chapter also provides statistics on minors (tables 1.28 and 1.29), in addition to data on childcare arrangements (tables 1.31).

Table 1.01: Resident Population and Median Age, 1980–2007

	Hispanic		White		All Races	
	Total	Median age	Total	Median age	Total	Median age
1980 (April 1)	14,609	23.2	194,713	30.9	226,546	30.0
1985 (July 1)	17,865	NA	202,769	32.4	235,736	31.4
1986 (July 1)	18,523	NA	204,326	32.7	241,096	31.7
1987 (July 1)	19,183	25.1	205,833	33.0	243,400	32.1
1988 (July 1)	19,847	25.8	207,357	33.1	245,807	32.3
1989 (July 1)	20,505	26.1	208,961	33.6	248,240	32.7
1990 (April 1)	22,354	NA	199,686	NA	248,710	32.8
1991 (July 1)	23,350	25.7	210,899	34.1	252,177	33.1
1992 (July 1)	24,238	25.8	212,912	34.4	255,082	33.4
1994 (July 1)	26,077	26.1	216,470	35.0	260,341	34.0
1995 (July 1)	26,994	26.2	218,085	35.3	262,755	34.3
1996 (July 1)	28,269	26.4	219,749	35.7	265,284	34.6
1997 (July 1)	29,348	26.4	221,334	36.0	267,636	34.9
1998 (July 1)	30,250	26.4	223,001	36.3	270,299	35.2
1999 (July 1)	31,337	26.5	224,611	36.6	272,691	35.5
2000 (April 1)	35,306	25.8	228,107*	36.6	281,425*	35.3
2001 (July 1)	36,972	26.2	230,290	36.9	284,797	35.6
2002 (July 1)	38,761	26.8	232,647	30.5	288,369	35.7
2003 (July 1)	39,899	26.7	234,196	37.3	290,810	35.9
2004 (July 1)	41,322	26.9	236,058	37.5	293,655	36.0
2005 (July 1)	42,687	27.2	237,855	37.6	296,410	36.2
2006 (April 1)	44,321	27.4	239,746	37.8	299,398	36.4
2007 (July)	45,504	27.6	241,167	38.0	301,621	36.6

Source: U.S. Bureau of the Census, *Statistical Abstract of the United States, 1989*, table 21; *1990*, table 19; *1991*, table 19; *1993*, tables 12, 14, and 24; *1994*, table 22; *1995*, table 22; *1996*, table 22; *1997*, table 22; *1998*, table 22; *1999*, table 22; *2000*, table 19; *2002*, table 15; *2003*, table 13; *2004–2005*, table 14; *2006*, table 14; *2007*, table 14; *2008*, table 8.

Notes: 'Total' includes races and ethnic groups not shown separately.
* Reflects changes to the Census 2000 population from the Count Question Resolution program and geographic program revisions.

Units: Population in thousands of persons; median age in years.

Table 1.02: Resident Population by Age, Selected Years, 2000–2007

	Hispanic	White	All Races
1998			
Total	*30,250*	*223,001*	*270,299*
Under 5 years old	3,393	15,052	18,966
5–13 years old	5,219	27,907	35,389
14–17 years old	2,122	12,284	15,517
85 years old and older	177	3,666	4,054
2000			
Total	*35,306*	*228,107*	*281,425*
Under 5 years old	3,720	14,657	19,176
5–13 years old	6,186	28,381	37,026
14–17 years old	2,439	12,523	16,093
18–24 years old	4,744	21,197	27,141
65 years and older	1,733	30,964	34,992
85 years old and older	151	3,827	4,240
2007			
Total	*45,504*	*241,167*	*301,621*
Under 5 years old	4,916	15,717	20,724
5–13 years old	7,402	27,454	35,971
14–17 years old	3,101	13,115	17,207
18–24 years old	5,122	22,822	29,492
65 years and older	2,512	32,927	37,888
85 years old and older	280	4,927	5,512

Source: U.S. Bureau of the Census, *Statistical Abstract of the United States, 2008*, table 14; *2009*, table 8.

Notes: 'All races' includes races not shown separately.

Units: Population in thousands of persons.

Table 1.03: Components of Population Change, 2000–2007

	Hispanic	White	All Races
Population on April 1, 2000	35,648,985	228,622,981	281,194,308
+ Births	6,793,383	22,647,264	29,809,472
– Deaths	812,476	14,985,410	17,597,188
+ Net international migration	4,216,935	5,398,422	7,984,271
Net Population Increase	10,197,933	13,060,390	20,196,555
Population on July 1, 2007	45,504,311	241,166,890	301,621,157

Source: U.S. Bureau of the Census, Population Estimates Division, *Cumulative Estimates of the Components of Population Change by Race and Hispanic or Latino Origin for the United States: April 1, 2000 to July 1, 2007* (NC-EST2007-05).
U.S. Bureau of the Census, Population Estimates Division, *Annual Estimates of the Population by Sex, Race and Hispanic or Latino Origin for the United States: April 1, 2000 to July 1, 2007* (NC-EST2007-03).

Notes: 'All Races' includes races not shown separately.
The sum of the components may not add to the total.

Units: Population in number of persons.

Table 1.04: Hispanic Population by Age and Ethnic Group, 2006

	Mexican	Puerto Rican	Cuban	Central American	South American	Other Hispanic	Total Hispanic
Total population	*28,323*	*3,704*	*1,584*	*3,536*	*2,587*	*3,434*	*43,168*
Percent of population:							
Under 5 years old	11.7%	9.3%	7.3%	8.2%	7.5%	9.5%	10.6%
5–9 yrs old	10.2	9.0	5.6	8.1	6.6	7.7	9.3
10–14 yrs old	9.5	9.0	7.4	6.9	7.3	9.6	9.0
15–19 yrs old	8.2	9.0	5.4	7.2	7.3	9.2	8.1
20–24 yrs old	8.7	8.3	5.3	9.2	7.3	7.3	8.4
25–29 yrs old	9.9	8.8	5.6	12.2	8.1	7.0	9.5
30–34 yrs old	8.8	7.3	7.1	11.3	9.4	7.2	8.7
35–44 yrs old	14.2	14.1	17.6	19.3	17.1	15.1	15.0
45–54 yrs old	9.5	11.1	10.9	9.6	13.9	12.6	10.2
55–64 yrs old	5.0	7.5	9.8	4.3	9.0	6.9	5.7
65–74 yrs old	2.5	4.4	8.0	2.5	4.7	4.2	3.2
75–84 yrs old	1.4	1.7	7.6	0.8	1.5	2.8	1.7
85 years and over	0.3	0.5	2.5	0.3	0.3	0.8	0.5

Source: U.S. Bureau of the Census, Current Population Survey, *The Hispanic Population of the United States, 2006*, table 1.2.

Notes: 'Other Hispanic origin' includes Dominicans and persons from Spain and persons identifying themselves generally as Hispanic, Spanish, Spanish-American, Hispano, Latino, etc.

Units: Hispanic population in thousands; percent of total population.

Table 1.05: Hispanic Population by Sex and Ethnic Group, 2003 and 2006

	Male	Female	Both sexes
2003			
Total Hispanic population	*20,190*	*19,193*	*39,384*
Mexican	13,658	12,635	26,293
Puerto Rican	1,856	1,995	3,851
Cuban	734	702	1,436
Central/South American	2,606	2,297	4,905
Other Hispanic	1,336	1,563	2,900
2006			
Total Hispanic population	*22,182*	*20,986*	*43,168*
Mexican	14,722	13,601	28,323
Puerto Rican	1,812	1,893	3,705
Cuban	788	796	1,584
Central American	1,936	1,600	3,536
South American	1,277	1,310	2,587
Other Hispanic	1,648	1,786	3,434

Source: U.S. Bureau of the Census, Current Population Reports, *The Hispanic Population of the United States, 2003*, table 1.2; *2006*, table 1.2.

Notes: 'Other Hispanic' includes Dominicans and persons from Spain and persons identifying themselves generally as Hispanic, Spanish, Spanish-American, Hispano, Latino, etc.

Units: Hispanic population in thousands.

Table 1.06: Resident Population by State, 1980, 1990, and 2007

	1980			1990			2007		
	Hispanic	White	Total	Hispanic	White	Total	Hispanic	White	Total
Alabama	34	2,873	3,894	25	2,976	4,041	125	3,287	4,628
Alaska	9	310	402	18	415	550	40	484	683
Arizona	444	2,241	2,718	688	2,963	3,665	1,878	5,513	6,339
Arkansas	17	1,890	2,286	20	1,945	2,351	150	2,293	2,835
California	4,541	18,031	23,668	7,688	20,524	29,760	13,221	28,082	36,553
Colorado	341	2,571	2,890	424	2,905	3,294	966	4,370	4,862
Connecticut	125	2,799	3,108	213	2,859	3,287	403	2,959	3,502
Delaware	10	488	594	16	535	666	56	644	865
District of Columbia	18	172	638	33	180	607	49	232	588
Florida	585	8,185	9,746	1,574	10,749	12,938	3,756	14,604	18,251
Georgia	61	3,947	5,463	109	4,600	6,478	741	6,259	9,545
Hawaii	71	319	965	81	370	1,108	105	374	1,283
Idaho	37	902	944	53	950	1,007	147	1,421	1,499
Illinois	635	9,233	11,427	904	8,953	11,431	1,920	10,177	12,853
Indiana	87	5,004	5,490	99	5,021	5,544	315	5,593	6,345
Iowa	26	2,839	2,914	33	2,683	2,777	120	2,820	2,988
Kansas	63	2,168	2,364	94	2,232	2,478	244	2,467	2,776
Kentucky	27	3,379	3,661	22	3,392	3,685	95	3,817	4,241
Louisiana	100	2,912	4,206	93	2,839	4,220	137	2,793	4,293
Maine	5	1,110	1,125	7	1,208	1,228	16	1,271	1,317
Maryland	63	3,159	4,217	125	3,394	4,781	356	3,571	5,618
Massachusetts	141	5,363	5,737	288	5,405	6,016	528	5,576	6,450
Michigan	158	7,872	9,262	202	7,756	9,295	403	8,175	10,072
Minnesota	32	3,936	4,076	54	4,130	4,375	206	4,640	5,198
Mississippi	24	1,615	2,521	16	1,633	2,573	60	1,771	2,919
Missouri	52	4,345	4,917	62	4,486	5,117	178	5,001	5,878
Montana	10	740	787	12	741	799	27	868	958
Nebraska	28	1,490	1,570	37	1,481	1,578	134	1,625	1,775

(continued on next page)

Table 1.06: Resident Population by State, 1980, 1990, and 2007

	1980			1990			2007		
	Hispanic	White	Total	Hispanic	White	Total	Hispanic	White	Total
Nevada	54	700	800	124	1,013	1,202	644	2,087	2,565
New Hampshire	5	910	921	11	1,087	1,109	33	1,258	1,316
New Jersey	494	6,127	7,365	740	6,130	7,730	1,382	6,624	8,686
New Mexico	477	978	1,303	579	1,146	1,515	875	1,664	1,970
New York	1,661	13,961	17,558	2,214	13,385	17,990	3,162	14,194	19,298
North Carolina	56	4,458	5,882	77	5,008	6,629	638	6,704	9,061
North Dakota	3	626	653	5	604	639	12	586	640
Ohio	120	9,597	10,798	140	9,522	10,847	284	9,731	11,467
Oklahoma	58	2,598	3,025	86	2,584	3,146	262	2,833	3,617
Oregon	66	2,491	2,633	113	2,637	2,842	396	3,383	3,747
Pennsylvania	154	10,652	11,864	232	10,520	11,882	556	10,640	12,433
Rhode Island	19	897	947	46	917	1,003	119	938	1,058
South Carolina	34	2,147	3,122	31	2,407	3,487	169	3,025	4,408
South Dakota	4	640	691	5	638	696	18	704	796
Tennessee	34	3,835	4,591	33	4,048	4,877	215	4,948	6,157
Texas	2,983	11,198	14,229	4,340	12,775	16,987	8,600	19,742	23,904
Utah	60	1,383	1,461	85	1,616	1,723	307	2,465	2,645
Vermont	3	507	511	4	555	563	8	599	621
Virginia	80	4,230	5,347	160	4,792	6,187	508	5,642	7,712
Washington	121	3,779	4,132	215	4,309	4,867	610	5,473	6,468
West Virginia	13	1,875	1,950	8	1,792	1,856	19	1,714	1,812
Wisconsin	63	4,443	4,706	93	4,513	4,892	272	5,034	5,602
Wyoming	25	446	470	26	427	454	38	492	523

Source: U.S. Bureau of the Census, *Statistical Abstract of the United States, 1972*, tables 12 and 30, *1991*, table 27.
U.S. Bureau of the Census, Population Estimates Division, *Estimates of the Population by Race and Hispanic or Latino Origin for the United States and States: July 1, 2007* (SC-EST2007-04)

Notes: 'Total' includes races and ethnic groups not shown separately.

Units: Population in thousands of persons.

Table 1.07: Population of Cities with 250,000 or More Inhabitants, 2000

	Hispanic	White	All Races
Albuquerque, NM	179.1	321.2	448.6
Anaheim, CA	153.4	179.6	328.0
Anchorage, AK	14.8	188.0	260.3
Arlington, TX	60.8	225.4	333.0
Atlanta, GA	18.7	138.4	416.5
Aurora, CO	54.8	190.3	276.4
Austin, TX	200.6	429.1	656.6
Baltimore, MD	11.1	206.0	651.2
Boston, MA	85.1	320.9	589.1
Buffalo, NY	22.1	159.3	292.6
Charlotte, NC	39.8	315.1	540.8
Chicago, IL	753.6	1,215.3	2,896.0
Cincinnati, OH	4.2	175.5	331.3
Cleveland, OH	34.7	198.5	478.4
Colorado Springs, CO	43.3	291.1	360.9
Columbus, OH	17.5	483.3	711.5
Corpus Christi, TX	150.7	198.7	277.5
Dallas, TX	422.6	604.2	1,188.6
Denver, CO	175.7	362.2	554.6
Detroit, MI	47.2	116.6	951.3
El Paso, TX	431.9	413.1	563.7
Fort Worth, TX	159.4	319.2	534.7
Fresno, CA	170.5	214.6	427.7
Honolulu, HI	16.2	73.1	371.7
Houston, TX	730.9	962.6	1,953.6
Indianapolis, IN	30.6	540.2	781.9
Jacksonville, FL	30.6	474.3	735.6
Kansas City, MO	30.6	267.9	441.5
Las Vegas, NV	113.0	334.2	478.4
Lexington-Fayette, KY	8.6	211.1	260.5
Long Beach, CA	165.1	208.4	461.5
Los Angeles, CA	1,719.1	1,734.0	3,694.8
Louisville, KY	4.8	161.3	256.2
Memphis, TN	19.3	223.7	650.1
Mesa, AZ	78.3	323.7	396.4
Miami, FL	238.4	241.5	362.5
Milwaukee, WI	71.6	298.4	597.0

(continued on next page)

Hispanic Americans: A Statistical Sourcebook 2009

Table 1.07: Population of Cities with 250,000 or More Inhabitants, 2000

	Hispanic	White	All Races
Minneapolis, MN	29.2	249.2	382.6
Nashville-Davidson, TN	25.8	359.6	545.5
New Orleans, LA	14.8	136.0	484.7
New York, NY	2,160.6	3,576.4	8,008.3
Newark, NJ	80.6	72.5	273.5
Oakland, CA	87.5	125.0	399.5
Oklahoma City, OK	51.4	346.2	506.1
Omaha, NE	29.4	305.7	390.0
Philadelphia, PA	128.9	683.3	1,517.6
Phoenix, AZ	450.0	938.9	1,321.0
Pittsburgh, PA	4.4	226.3	334.6
Portland, OR	36.1	412.2	529.1
Raleigh, NC	19.3	174.8	276.1
Riverside, CA	97.3	151.4	255.2
Sacramento, CA	88.0	196.5	407.0
San Antonio, TX	671.4	774.7	1,144.6
San Diego, CA	310.8	736.2	1,223.4
San Francisco, CA	109.5	385.7	776.7
San Jose, CA	270.0	425.0	894.9
Santa Ana, CA	257.1	144.4	338.0
Seattle, WA	29.7	394.9	563.4
St. Louis, MO	7.0	152.7	348.2
St. Paul, MN	22.7	192.4	287.2
Tampa, FL	58.5	194.9	303.4
Toledo, OH	17.1	220.3	313.6
Tucson, AZ	173.9	341.4	486.7
Tulsa, OK	28.1	275.5	393.0
Virginia Beach, VA	17.8	303.7	425.3
Washington, DC	45.0	176.1	572.1
Wichita, KS	33.1	258.9	344.3

Source: U.S. Bureau of the Census, *Statistical Abstract of the United States, 2003*, tables 32 and 33.

Notes: Population as of April 1, 2000. Data refers to boundaries in effect on January 1, 2000.

Units: Population in thousands of persons.

Table 1.08: Population of the 50 Largest Metropolitan Statistical Areas, 2005

	Hispanic	White	All Races
Atlanta, GA	424	3,129	4,918
Austin, TX	421	1,244	1,453
Baltimore, MD	71	1,761	2,656
Birmingham, AL	28	762	1,090
Boston, MA	331	3,749	4,412
Buffalo, NY	36	969	1,148
Charlotte, NC	113	1,104	1,521
Chicago, IL	1,773	7,087	9,443
Cincinnati, OH	31	1,767	2,070
Cleveland, OH	80	1,635	2,126
Columbus, OH	42	1,386	1,709
Dallas, TX	1,491	4,604	5,819
Denver, CO	510	2,075	2,360
Detroit, MI	153	3,234	4,488
Hartford, CT	123	1,002	1,188
Houston, TX	1,703	4,005	5,280
Indianapolis, IN	66	1,349	1,641
Jacksonville, FL	62	910	1,248
Kansas City, MO	125	1,626	1,948
Las Vegas, NV	446	1,349	1,711
Los Angeles, CA	5,625	9,718	12,924
Louisville, KY	28	1,014	1,208
Memphis, TN	39	657	1,261
Miami, FL	2,034	4,090	5,422
Milwaukee, WI	114	1,195	1,513
Minneapolis, MN	134	2,707	3,143
Nashville, TN	66	1,156	1,423
New Orleans, LA	66	765	1,319
New York, NY	3,925	12,968	18,747

(continued on next page)

Table 1.08: Population of the 50 Largest
Metropolitan Statistical Areas, 2005

	Hispanic	White	All Races
Oklahoma City, OK	98	914	1,157
Orlando, FL	406	1,519	1,933
Philadelphia, PA	350	4,276	5,823
Phoenix, AZ	1,124	3,435	3,865
Pittsburgh, PA	21	2,134	2,386
Portland, OR	195	1,844	2,096
Providence, RI	141	1,465	1,623
Richmond, VA	38	771	1,176
Riverside, CA	1,678	3,227	3,910
Rochester, NY	50	882	1,039
Sacramento, CA	358	1,553	2,042
St. Louis, MO	51	2,185	2,779
Salt Lake City, UT	148	955	1,034
San Antonio, TX	989	1,692	1,890
San Diego, CA	864	2,340	2,933
San Francisco, CA	806	2,681	4,153
San Jose, CA	452	1,126	1,755
Seattle, WA	212	2,531	3,203
Tampa, FL	346	2,234	2,648
Virginia Beach, VA	59	1,033	1,647
Washington, DC	581	3,269	5,215

Source: U.S. Bureau of the Census, *Statistical Abstract of the United States*, 2007, table 27.

Notes: As of July 1, 2005. When a Metropolitan Statistical Area contains several cities (i.e., Los Angeles-Long Beach-Santa Ana, CA), only the primary city is shown here.

Units: Population in thousands of persons.

Table 1.09: Age, Educational Attainment, and Residence, 1985 and 1990

1985

	Hispanic	White	All Races
Age			
Persons of all ages	*16,940*	*199,117*	*234,066*
Under 5 years old	1,809	14,610	17,958
5–14 years old	3,355	27,417	33,792
15–44 years old	8,540	93,852	110,948
45–64 years old	2,407	39,033	44,549
65 years old and over	819	24,205	26,818
Years of School Completed			
All persons 25 years old and over	8,455	124,905	143,524
Persons completing:			
0–8 years of school	3,192	16,224	19,893
1–3 years of high school	1,210	14,365	17,553
4 years of high school	2,402	48,728	54,866
1–3 years of college	932	20,652	23,405
4 or more years of college	718	24,935	27,808
Residence			
Northeast	3,144	43,185	49,276
Midwest	1,389	52,280	58,587
South	5,288	63,155	79,165
West	6,964	40,394	46,489

(continued on next page)

Table 1.09: Age, Educational Attainment, and Residence, 1985 and 1990

1990

	Hispanic	White	All Races
Age			
Persons of all ages	*21,405*	*208,611*	*248,644*
Under 5 years old	7,457	51,929	65,049
5–14 years old	2,741	20,383	24,901
15–44 years old	7,139	68,807	81,570
45–64 years old	2,977	40,594	47,032
65 years old and over	1,091	26,898	30,093
Years of School Completed			
All persons 25 years old and over	11,208	136,299	158,694
Did not complete high school	5,455	27,409	34,228
Completed high school, no college	3,285	53,250	61,272
Completed some college, no diploma	1,379	25,358	29,169
Completed college	1,088	30,283	34,025
Residence			
Northeast	3,531	43,727	50,799
Midwest	1,399	52,771	59,914
South	6,598	66,492	85,097
West	9,878	45,622	52,835
Nonfarm	21,297	204,001	243,865
Farm	108	4,610	4,779
Inside metro areas	19,883	159,443	193,052
Outside metro areas	1,522	49,168	55,592

Source: U.S. Bureau of the Census, *Statistical Abstract of the United States, 1987*, table 39; *1990*, table 43.
U.S. Bureau of the Census, Current Population Reports: *Money Income of Households, Families and Persons in the United States, 1984* (Series P-60, #151), table 4; *1988 and 1989* (Series P-60, #171 and 172), tables 4, 20, and 29.

Notes: 'All Races' includes races and ethnic groups not shown separately.

Units: Population in thousands of persons.

Table 1.10: Age and Residence, 2007

	Hispanic	White	All Races
Age			
Persons of all ages	46,026	239,399	299,106
Under 18 years old	15,741	56,685	74,403
18–24 years old	5,011	22,056	28,398
25–34 years old	8,137	31,403	40,146
35–44 years old	6,904	33,476	42,132
45–54 years old	4,887	35,922	43,935
55–59 years old	1,611	15,292	18,371
60–64 years old	1,180	12,726	14,931
65–74 years old	1,530	16,662	19,588
Over 75 years old	1,025	15,177	17,202
Residence			
Northeast	6,190	43,676	54,031
Midwest	4,016	55,700	65,480
South	16,481	83,432	109,710
West	19,339	56,591	69,883

Source: U.S. Bureau of the Census, *Current Population Survey: Annual Social and Economic Supplement, 2008.*

Notes: 'All Races' includes races not shown separately.

Units: Population in thousands of persons.

Table 1.11: Population Projections, Selected Years, 2020–2050

	Hispanic	White	All Races
2020	66,365	266,275	341,387
2025	75,772	276,281	357,452
2030	85,931	286,109	373,504
2035	96,774	295,729	389,531
2040	108,223	305,247	405,655
2045	120,231	314,852	422,059
2050	132,792	324,800	439,010

Source: U.S. Bureau of the Census, Population Division, *Projections of the Population by Sex, Race, and Hispanic Origin for the United States: 2010 to 2050*, table NP2008-T4.

Notes: 'All Races' includes races not shown separately.
Population projections as of July 1 of the year shown.

Units: Estimates of the total population in thousands of persons.

Table 1.12: Nativity by State, 2007

	Hispanic	White	All Races
Alabama	25,548	2,187,800	3,261,251
Alaska	10,811	133,508	263,440
Arizona	803,879	1,470,005	2,180,678
Arkansas	32,398	1,321,043	1,719,723
California	6,856,153	12,112,330	18,949,422
Colorado	470,183	1,659,813	2,009,371
Connecticut	139,572	1,661,469	1,954,752
Delaware	15,158	288,088	393,673
District of Columbia	8,396	28,367	232,332
Florida	837,491	4,129,561	6,058,029
Georgia	158,154	3,234,366	5,218,892
Hawaii	64,160	72,775	695,498
Idaho	45,516	631,732	672,761
Illinois	861,614	6,423,386	8,538,126
Indiana	102,657	3,837,966	4,316,140
Iowa	38,022	2,073,767	2,155,372
Kansas	91,711	1,447,104	1,625,963
Kentucky	19,398	2,729,593	3,013,287
Louisiana	45,014	2,133,083	3,455,166
Maine	4,184	821,388	846,172
Maryland	70,027	1,780,409	2,689,018
Massachusetts	175,004	3,718,049	4,127,399
Michigan	191,685	6,304,443	7,640,459
Minnesota	63,832	3,317,506	3,559,015
Mississippi	10,734	1,141,556	2,096,057
Missouri	55,404	3,311,160	3,881,806
Montana	10,060	448,932	513,453
Nebraska	41,574	1,080,662	1,160,158
Nevada	141,721	408,032	563,983
New Hampshire	7,094	535,738	549,684

(continued on next page)

Table 1.12: Nativity by State, 2007

	Hispanic	White	All Races
New Jersey	430,420	3,485,317	4,552,495
New Mexico	564,482	592,902	1,003,065
New York	1,414,293	9,361,110	12,415,145
North Carolina	134,411	3,676,316	5,301,365
North Dakota	3,237	413,919	449,538
Ohio	121,205	7,397,532	8,602,301
Oklahoma	82,027	1,630,160	2,205,850
Oregon	113,526	1,494,684	1,671,075
Pennsylvania	187,754	8,184,377	9,359,744
Rhode Island	33,647	566,914	630,904
South Carolina	31,610	1,576,462	2,631,604
South Dakota	5,565	455,400	520,947
Tennessee	43,413	2,970,732	3,788,581
Texas	4,929,036	10,184,377	14,240,264
Utah	105,749	1,515,228	1,622,197
Vermont	1,650	318,020	325,941
Virginia	109,921	2,713,226	3,863,834
Washington	206,430	2,567,325	3,001,839
West Virginia	5,637	1,244,305	1,301,712
Wisconsin	102,767	3,667,416	4,015,131
Wyoming	15,846	196,743	216,379

Source: U.S. Bureau of the Census, *American Community Survey 2007*, tables B06004A, B06004B, and C06003.

Notes: Includes the civilian, non-institutional population only.

Units: Population in number of persons.

Table 1.13: Marital Status, Persons Over Age 15, 1990–2008

	Hispanic		White		All Races	
	Number	Percent	Number	Percent	Number	Percent
1990						
Total	*14,576*	*100%*	*163,417*	*100%*	*191,793*	*100%*
Single, never married	4,691	32.2	39,516	24.2	50,223	26.2
Married, spouse present	7,363	50.5	95,337	58.3	106,513	55.3
Married, spouse absent	1,022	7.0	4,191	2.6	6,118	3.2
Widowed	548	3.8	11,731	7.2	13,810	7.2
Divorced	952	6.5	12,643	7.7	15,128	7.9
2000						
Total	*22,793*	*100%*	*177,581*	*100%*	*213*	*100%*
Married, spouse present	11,221	49.2	99,258	55.9	113,002	52.9
Married, spouse absent	666	2.9	1,971	1.1	2,730	1.3
Widowed	881	3.9	11,532	6.5	13,665	6.4
Divorced	1,623	7.1	16,547	9.3	19,881	9.3
Seperated	845	3.7	2,976	1.7	4,479	2.1
Never married	7,558	33.2	45,297	25.5	60,016	28.1
2008						
Total	*32,677*	*100%*	*192,842*	*100%*	*237,993*	*100%*
Never married	12,021	36.8	52,917	27.4	71,479	30.0
Married, spouse present	15,002	45.9	102,956	53.4	120,258	50.5
Married, spouse absent	1,109	3.4	2,432	1.3	3,413	1.4
Widowed	1,068	3.3	11,870	6.2	14,314	6.0
Divorced	2,330	7.1	19,116	9.9	23,346	9.8
Seperated	1,147	3.5	3,551	1.8	5,183	2.2

Source: U.S. Bureau of the Census, Current Population Reports, *Marital Status and Living Arrangements, 1990* (Series P-20, #450), table 1.
Current Population Reports, *America's Families and Living Arrangements: 2000,* (Series P-20, #537), table A1.
Current Population Survey, *Annual Social and Econmic Supplement, 2008,* table A1.

Notes: 'All Races' includes races not shown seperately.
For 2008 data, 'White' as shown is equivalent to 'White Alone.'
Percents may not add to 100.

Units: Number of persons over age 15 in thousands; percent of total.

Table 1.14: Marital Status, Men Over Age 15, 1990–2008

	Hispanic		White		All Races	
	Number	Percent	Number	Percent	Number	Percent
1990						
Total	*9,948*	*100%*	*78,908*	*100%*	*91,033*	*100%*
Single, never married	4,319	43.4	22,078	28.0	27,422	30.1
Married, spouse present	3,862	38.8	47,700	60.4	52,924	58.1
Married, spouse absent	627	6.3	1,842	2.3	2,360	2.6
Widowed	338	3.4	1,930	2.4	2,282	2.5
Divorced	802	8.1	5,359	6.8	6,045	6.6
2000						
Total	*11,327*	*100%*	*86,443*	*100%*	*103,114*	*100%*
Married, spouse present	5,550	49.0	49,672	57.5	56,501	54.8
Married, spouse absent	402	3.5	979	1.1	1,365	1.3
Widowed	170	1.5	2,196	2.5	2,604	2.5
Divorced	669	5.9	7,246	8.4	8,572	8.3
Seperated	288	2.5	1,237	1.4	1,818	1.8
Never married	4,249	37.5	25,113	29.1	32,253	31.3
2008						
Total	*16,832*	*100%*	*94,707*	*100%*	*115,599*	*100%*
Never married	6,955	41.3	29,517	31.2	38,685	33.5
Married, spouse present	7,445	44.2	51,618	54.5	60,129	52.0
Married, spouse absent	820	4.9	1,421	1.5	1,944	1.7
Widowed	228	1.4	2,450	2.6	2,916	2.5
Divorced	945	5.6	8,193	8.7	9,782	8.5
Seperated	438	2.6	1,507	1.6	2,144	1.9

Source: U.S. Bureau of the Census, *Current Population Reports, Marital Status and Living Arrangements, 1990* (Series P-20, #450), table 1.
Current Population Reports, *America's Families and Living Arrangements: 2000,* (Series P-20, #537), table A1.
Current Population Survey, *Annual Social and Econmic Supplement, 2008*, table A1.

Notes: 'All Races' includes races not shown seperately.
For 2008 data, 'White' as shown is equivalent to 'White Alone.'
Percents may not add to 100.

Units: Number of men over age 15 in thousands; percent of total.

Table 1.15: Marital Status, Women Over Age 15, 1990–2008

	Hispanic		White		All Races	
	Number	Percent	Number	Percent	Number	Percent
1990						
Total	*11,966*	*100%*	*84,508*	*100%*	*99,838*	*100%*
Single, never married	4,416	36.9	17,438	20.6	22,718	22.8
Married, spouse present	3,757	31.4	47,637	56.4	53,256	53.3
Married, spouse absent	1,056	8.8	2,349	2.8	3,541	3.5
Widowed	1,392	11.6	9,800	11.6	11,477	11.5
Divorced	1,344	11.2	7,284	8.6	8,845	8.9
2000						
Total	*14,167*	*100%*	*91,138*	*100%*	*110,660*	*100%*
Married, spouse present	4,097	28.9	49,586	54.4	56,501	51.1
Married, spouse absent	223	1.6	992	1.1	1,365	1.2
Widowed	1,367	9.6	9,336	10.2	11,061	10.0
Divorced	1,670	11.8	9,301	10.2	11,309	10.2
Seperated	803	5.7	1,739	1.9	2,661	2.4
Never married	6,008	42.4	20,184	22.1	27,763	25.1
2008						
Total	*15,845*	*100%*	*98,134*	*100%*	*122,394*	*100%*
Never married	5,066	32.0	23,399	23.8	32,794	26.8
Married, spouse present	7,557	47.7	51,338	52.3	60,129	49.1
Married, spouse absent	288	1.8	1,011	1.0	1,470	1.2
Widowed	839	5.3	9,419	9.6	11,398	9.3
Divorced	1,385	8.7	10,923	11.1	13,564	11.1
Seperated	709	4.5	2,043	2.1	3,039	2.5

Source: U.S. Bureau of the Census, Current Population Reports, *Marital Status and Living Arrange-ments, 1990* (Series P-20, #450), table 1.
Current Population Reports, *America's Families and Living Arrangements: 2000*, (Series P-20, #537), table A1.
Current Population Survey, *Annual Social and Econmic Supplement, 2008*, table A1.

Notes: All Races' includes races not shown seperately.
For 2008 data, 'White' as shown is equivalent to 'White Alone.'
Percents may not add to 100.

Units: Number of women over age 15 in thousands; percent of total.

Table 1.16: Marital Status of Hispanic Population by Ethnic Group, 2003 and 2006

	Mexican	Puerto Rican	Cuban	Central/ South American	Other Hispanic	Total Hispanic
2003						
Total population, 15 years old and over:						
Married	9,547	1,137	662	1,920	976	14,242
Widowed	537	99	93	99	89	917
Divorced	1,098	261	112	199	228	1,898
Separated	626	129	43	142	88	1,028
Never married	6,266	1,075	277	1,494	753	9,865

2006	Mexican	Puerto Rican	Cuban	Central American	South American	Other Hispanic	Total Hispanic
Total population, 15 years old and over:	19,427	2,693	1,262	2,714	2,033	2,512	30,640
Married	10,283	1,047	698	1,309	1,058	1,147	15,542
Widowed	603	97	97	50	58	103	1,008
Divorced	1,220	281	135	175	179	257	2,247
Separated	604	120	26	106	66	110	1,065
Never married	6,717	1,147	305	1,073	640	896	10,778

Source: U.S. Bureau of the Census, Current Population Reports, *The Hispanic Population of the United States, 2003*, table 1.2; *2006*, table 1.2.

Notes: 'Other Hispanic' includes Dominicans and persons from Spain and persons identifying themselves generally as Hispanic, Spanish, Spanish-American, Hispano, Latino, etc.

Units: Total Hispanic population 15 years old and older in thousands.

Table 1.17: Hispanic Married Couple Households by Type of Origin of the Husband and Wife, 1993

	Mexican	Puerto Rican	Cuban	Central/ South American	Other Hispanic	Total Hispanic
By Origin of the Wife						
Total Hispanic population	*85.1%*	*81.4%*	*82.9%*	*84.4%*	*65.7%*	*83.1%*
By Origin						
Mexican	82.8	2.7	1.7	4.3	1.4	53.6
Puerto Rican	0.1	70.7	2.1	2.1	1.4	6.7
Cuban	0.1	1.2	77.1	2.8	0.7	5.5
Central/South American	1.6	3.7	1.3	74.8	2.1	12.1
Other Hispanic	0.5	3.0	0.8	0.4	60.1	5.2
Not Hispanic	14.9	18.6	17.1	15.6	34.3	16.9
By Origin of the Husband						
Total population	4.5%	0.6%	0.4%	1.0%	0.5%	7.1%
Total Hispanic population	55.7	7.3	5.4	12.3	5.1	85.8
By Origin						
Mexican	85.6	0.4	0.2	1.0	0.2	87.3
Puerto Rican	0.9	69.3	1.5	3.3	1.2	76.1
Cuban	1.3	1.7	79.7	6.5	0.9	90.1
Central/South American	7.4	2.3	0.6	77.4	1.2	88.9
Other Hispanic	4.2	3.8	0.8	0.8	64.9	74.4
Not Hispanic	0.7	0.1	0.1	0.2	0.2	1.3

Source: U.S. Bureau of the Census, Current Population Reports, *The Hispanic Population in the United States: March, 1993*, table A.

Notes: 'Other Hispanic' includes Dominicans and persons from Spain and persons identifying themselves generally as Hispanic, Spanish, Spanish-American, Hispano, Latino, etc.

Units: Percent of total Hispanic population.

Table 1.18: Characteristics of Married and Unmarried Male-Female Couples: March 2000

	Unmarried couples	Married couples
Both Hispanic	332	4,739
Neither Hispanic	3,268	50,015
One Hispanic and one non-Hispanic	222	1,743

Source: U.S. Bureau of the Census, Current Population Reports, *America's Families and Living Arrangements*, June 2001 (Series P20, #537), table 8.

Units: Thousands of couples.

Table 1.19: Living Arrangements Married and Unmarried-Partner Households in Which Only One Partner is Hispanic, 2000

	Same-Sex Male	Same-Sex Female	Opposite-Sex Unmarried	Opposite-Sex Married
United States	6.9%	5.4%	6.4%	3.1%
By Region:				
Northeast	5.9%	4.3%	5.2%	2.1%
Midwest	3.8	3.0	4.0	1.7
South	5.8	4.3	5.2	2.7
West	11.1	9.2	11.2	6.1
By State:				
Alabama	1.5%	1.2%	1.9%	0.9%
Alaska	5.4	6.0	4.9	3.6
Arizona	10.7	10.3	12.3	6.6
Arkansas	2.1	1.8	2.7	1.2
California	12.8	10.5	12.7	7.2
Colorado	11.5	9.1	11.5	6.2
Connecticut	5.2	3.9	6.6	2.3
Delaware	4.0	3.5	3.9	1.7
District of Columbia	9.4	4.1	3.9	2.9
Florida	8.5	6.7	7.3	4.1
Georgia	3.8	2.6	3.1	1.6
Hawaii	7.9	8.9	12.6	6.2
Idaho	4.9	5.4	6.7	3.0
Illinois	6.7	4.3	5.7	2.6
Indiana	2.5	2.3	3.4	1.5
Iowa	2.2	2.7	3.6	1.2
Kansas	3.7	4.2	6.9	2.8
Kentucky	1.6	1.6	1.8	0.8
Louisiana	3.7	2.9	2.9	1.8
Maine	1.5	1.5	1.1	0.7
Maryland	3.5	3.2	2.9	1.9
Massachusetts	4.6	3.5	4.4	1.5
Michigan	3.5	2.8	4.2	1.8
Minnesota	3.4	2.6	3.3	1.2
Mississippi	1.7	1.1	1.5	0.8

(continued on next page)

Table 1.19: Living Arrangements Married and Unmarried-Partner Households in Which Only One Partner is Hispanic, 2000

	Same-Sex Male	Same-Sex Female	Opposite-Sex Unmarried	Opposite-Sex Married
Missouri	2.7	2.9	2.7	1.4
Montana	4.0	3.3	4.3	1.9
Nebraska	3.1	4.4	5.9	2.0
Nevada	9.1	8.3	10.7	6.2
New Hampshire	2.1	2.3	2.0	1.0
New Jersey	6.6	5.2	7.5	3.1
New Mexico	17.6	14.7	18.4	11.2
New York	8.0	6.0	6.7	3.0
North Carolina	2.1	2.2	3.0	1.4
North Dakota	0.6	1.7	2.3	0.8
Ohio	2.4	2.0	2.9	1.2
Oklahoma	3.3	4.5	5.8	2.6
Oregon	5.6	4.6	6.4	3.0
Pennsylvania	3.1	2.2	3.2	1.1
Rhode Island	3.9	2.8	4.3	1.5
South Carolina	1.4	1.7	2.3	1.1
South Dakota	1.8	0.9	2.8	1.0
Tennessee	1.8	1.8	2.2	1.0
Texas	10.7	8.0	11.2	5.4
Utah	6.4	6.5	10.0	3.8
Vermont	1.7	0.9	1.4	0.9
Virginia	4.2	3.5	3.6	2.1
Washington	5.9	5.4	6.6	3.2
West Virginia	0.9	0.9	1.0	0.5
Wisconsin	3.3	3.0	3.9	1.4
Wyoming	5.6	5.8	8.7	4.0

Source: U.S. Bureau of the Census, *Married-Couple and Unmarried-Partner Households: 2000* (special tabulation from Summary File 1, 2000), table 5.

Notes: 'Hispanic' refers to persons identifying themselves generally as Hispanic, Spanish, Spanish-American, Hispano, Latino, etc.

Units: Percent of households in which only one member of a couple is Hispanic.

Table 1.20: Selected Characteristics of Households, 1985

	Hispanic	White	All Races
Total households	*4,883*	*75,328*	*86,789*
By Marital Status and Sex of Householder			
Male householder	3,357	53,868	60,025
Married, wife present	2,638	43,444	47,683
Married, wife absent	129	1,013	1,416
Widowed	84	1,386	1,620
Divorced	162	3,078	3,535
Single, never married	344	4,947	5,772
Female householder	1,526	21,461	26,763
Married, husband present	186	2,199	2,667
Married, husband absent	351	1,668	2,497
Widowed	313	8,304	9,728
Divorced	334	5,203	6,265
Single, never married	342	4,087	5,606
By Age of the Householder			
15–24 years old	489	4,626	5,438
25–34 years old	1,363	17,010	20,013
35–44 years old	1,184	15,024	17,481
45–54 years old	743	10,792	12,628
55–64 years old	606	11,471	13,073
65 years old and over	497	16,406	18,155
By Housing Tenure			
Own housing unit	2,007	50,611	55,845
Rent housing unit	2,876	24,667	30,943

(continued on next page)

Table 1.20: Selected Characteristics of Households, 1985

	Hispanic	White	All Races
By Size of the Household			
One person	756	17,876	20,602
Two persons	1,026	24,558	27,289
Three persons	995	13,336	15,465
Four persons	959	11,795	13,631
Five persons	576	5,061	6,108
Six persons	297	1,819	2,299
Seven or more persons	275	882	1,296
Persons per household	2.96	2.64	2.69
By Residence			
Northeast	1,017	16,244	18,348
Midwest	376	19,599	21,697
South	1,553	24,283	29,581
West	1,937	15,202	17,163

Source: U.S. Bureau of the Census, Current Population Reports, *Money Income of House-holds, Families, and Persons in the United States, March 1984* (Series P-60, #151), table 4.

U.S. Bureau of the Census, Current Population Reports: *Household & Family Characteristics, March 1985* (Series P-20, #411), table 22.

Units: 'All Races' includes races and ethnic groups not shown separately.

Notes: Number of households in thousands; average persons per household.

Table 1.21: Selected Characteristics of Households, 1990

	Hispanic	White	All Races
Total households	*5,933*	*80,163*	*93,347*
By Marital Status and Type of Householder			
Family households	4,840	56,590	66,090
Married couple families	3,395	46,981	52,317
Male householder, no wife present	329	2,303	2,884
Female householder, no husband present	1,116	7,306	10,890
Non-family households	1,093	23,573	27,257
Male householder	587	9,951	11,606
Living alone	415	7,718	9,049
Female householder	506	13,622	15,651
Living alone	442	12,161	13,950
By Age of the Householder			
15–24 years old	542	4,222	5,121
25–34 years old	1,721	17,137	20,472
35-44 years old	1,405	17,395	20,554
45–54 years old	930	12,404	14,514
55–64 years old	664	10,862	12,529
65 years old and over	671	18,144	20,156
By Housing Tenure			
Own housing unit	2,443	54,094	59,846
Rent housing unit	3,383	24,685	31,895

(continued on next page)

Table 1.21: Selected Characteristics of Households, 1990

	Hispanic	White	All Races
By Size of the Household			
One person	856	19,879	22,999
Two persons	1,292	26,714	30,114
Three persons	1,139	13,585	16,128
Four persons	1,172	12,399	14,456
Five persons	752	5,104	6,213
Six persons	386	1,615	2,143
Seven or more persons	336	877	1,295
Persons per household	3.48	2.58	2.63
By Residence			
Northeast	1,037	16,773	19,127
Midwest	398	20,339	22,760
South	1,953	26,155	32,262
West	2,544	16,896	19,197
Inside metropolitan areas	5,479	61,155	72,331
Outside metropolitan areas	454	19,009	21,016
Nonfarm	8,897	78,556	91,710
Farm	36	1,608	1,637

Source: U.S. Bureau of the Census, Current Population Reports, *Money Income of Households Families and Persons in the United States: 1988 and 1989* (Series P-60, #172), table 1.

Notes: 'All Races' includes races and ethnic groups not shown separately.

Units: Number of households in thousands; average persons per household.

Table 1.22: Selected Characteristics of Households, 2007

	Hispanic	White	All Races
All households	*13,339*	*95,112*	*116,783*
By Marital Status and Sex of Householder			
Family households	10,394	63,566	77,873
Married couple families	6,888	50,247	58,370
Male householder, no wife present	983	3,892	5,100
Female householder, no husband present	2,522	9,427	14,404
Non-family households	2,945	31,545	38,910
Male householder	1,654	14,540	17,872
Living alone	1,138	11,204	13,870
Female householder	1,291	17,006	21,038
Living alone	1,065	14,735	18,297
By Age of Householder			
15–24 years old	1,182	4,973	6,554
25–34 years old	3,401	14,985	19,225
35–44 years old	3,385	17,688	22,448
45–54 years old	2,480	19,893	24,536
55–64 years old	1,497	16,627	19,909
65 years old and over	1,394	20,946	24,113
By Size of Household			
One person	2,203	25,939	32,167
Two persons	3,033	32,716	38,737
Three persons	2,529	14,661	18,522
Four persons	2,678	12,793	15,865
Five persons	1,712	5,908	7,332
Six persons	727	2,067	2,694
Seven or more persons	457	1,027	1,467
Persons per household	3.34	2.53	2.56

(continued on next page)

Table 1.22: Selected Characteristics of Households, 2007

	Hispanic	White	All Races
By Residence			
Northeast	1,954	17,525	21,351
Midwest	1,097	22,694	26,266
South	4,944	33,329	43,062
West	5,344	21,564	26,105
Inside metropolitan areas	12,377	78,137	97,591
Outside metropolitan areas	961	16,975	19,192

Source: U.S. Bureau of the Census, Current Population Reports: *Annual Social and Economic Supplement 2008*, household income table HINC-01.

Notes: 'All Races' includes races not shown separately.
'White' as shown is equivalent to 'White alone.'

Units: Number of households in thousands of households.

Table 1.23: Selected Characteristics of Family Households, 1985

	Hispanic	White	All Races
Total families	*3,939*	*54,400*	*62,706*
By Type of Family			
Married couple families	2,824	45,643	50,350
Male householder, no wife present	210	1,816	2,228
Female householder, no husband present	905	6,941	10,129
By Size of Family			
Two persons	962	22,711	25,349
Three persons	948	12,743	14,804
Four persons	936	11,517	13,259
Five persons	552	4,894	5,894
Six persons	276	1,704	2,175
Seven or more persons	266	831	1,225
Average per family	3.88	3.16	3.23
By Number of Related Children under 18 Years Old			
No children	1,337	28,169	31,594
One child	904	11,174	13,108
Two children	865	9,937	11,645
Three children	481	3,695	4,486
Four children	215	1,049	1,329
Five children	87	261	373
Six or more children	50	115	171
Average per family	1.44	0.88	0.92
Average per family with children	2.18	1.83	1.85

(continued on next page)

Table 1.23: Selected Characteristics of Family Households, 1985

	Hispanic	White	All Races
By Number of Earners			
No earners	599	7,674	9,221
One earner	1,290	15,219	17,949
Two earners	1,485	23,303	26,160
Three earners	370	5,317	6,029
Four earners or more	161	2,263	2,570
By Housing Tenure			
Own housing unit	1,772	40,865	45,015
Rent housing unit	2,167	13,535	17,691
By Residence			
Northeast	808	11,631	13,149
Midwest	313	14,309	15,839
South	1,273	17,953	21,781
West	1,545	10,507	11,938

Source: U.S. Bureau of the Census, Current Population Reports: *Money Income of Households, Families, and Persons in the United States, 1984* (Series P-60, #151), table 21.
U.S. Bureau of the Census, Current Population Reports: *Household & Family Characteristics, March 1985* (Series P-20, #437), tables 1 and 22.

Notes: 'All Races' includes races not shown separately.
'Number of earners' excludes families with members in the armed forces.

Units: Number of family households in thousands; average persons and children per family.

Table 1.24: Selected Characteristics of Family Households, 1990

	Hispanic	White	All Races
All families	*4,840*	*56,590*	*66,090*
By Type of Family			
Married couple families	3,395	46,981	52,317
Male householder, no wife present	329	2,303	2,884
Female householder, no husband present	1,116	7,306	10,890
By Size of Family			
Two persons	1,226	24,438	27,606
Three persons	1,114	12,937	15,353
Four persons	1,146	12,048	14,036
Five persons	714	4,882	5,938
Six persons	347	1,505	1,997
Seven or more persons	293	781	1,170
Average per family	3.83	3.11	3.17
By Number of Related Children Under 18 Years Old			
No children	1,790	29,872	33,801
One child	1,095	11,186	13,530
Two children	1,036	10,342	12,263
Three children	579	3,853	4,650
Four children	232	970	1,279
Five children	73	247	379
Six or more children	35	121	188
Average per family	1.34	0.86	0.89
Average per family with children	2.12	1.82	1.83

(continued on next page)

Table 1.24: Selected Characteristics of Family Households, 1990

	Hispanic	White	All Races
By Number of Earners			
No earners	615	7,816	9,439
One earner	1,554	14,970	18,146
Two earners	1,860	25,737	29,235
Three earners	541	5,832	6,724
Four earners or more	271	2,236	2,546
By Housing Tenure			
Own housing unit	3,448	42,588	47,142
Rent housing unit	2,678	14,003	18,948
By Residence			
Northeast	815	11,837	13,494
Midwest	330	14,370	16,059
South	1,596	18,746	23,244
West	2,101	11,638	13,293
Nonfarm	4,813	55,225	64,701
Farm	28	1,365	1,390
Inside metropolitan areas	6,256	42,592	50,619
Outside metropolitan areas	1,215	13,999	15,471

Source: U.S. Bureau of the Census, Current Population Reports, *Money Income of House-holds, Families, and Persons in the United States: 1988 and 1989 (Series P-60, #172)*, tables 1, 13, and 18.
Current Population Reports, *Household & Family Characteristics: March 1990 and 1989 (Series P-20, #447)*, tables 1 and 2.

Notes: 'All Races' includes races not shown separately.
'Number of earners' excludes families with members in the armed forces.

Units: Number of family households in thousands; average children and persons per family.

Table 1.25: Selected Characteristics of Family Households, 2006

	Hispanic	White	All Races
All families	*10,155*	*64,120*	*78,454*
By Type of family			
Married couple families	6,764	50,747	58,964
Male householder, no wife present	945	3,809	5,067
Female householder, no husband present	2,446	9,563	14,424
By Size of family			
Two persons	2,677	29,604	35,102
Three persons	2,413	13,919	17,566
Four persons	2,515	12,420	15,400
Five persons	1,500	5,413	6,718
Six persons	664	1,895	2,456
Seven or more persons	386	868	1,213
By Number of earners			
No earner	967	9,152	11,185
One earner	3,825	19,450	25,013
Two earners	3,993	28,423	33,808
Three earners	1,015	5,379	6,377
Four earners or more	355	1,715	2,070
By Residence			
Northeast	1,449	11,634	14,197
Midwest	850	15,350	17,706
South	3,720	22,778	29,142
West	4,136	14,358	17,409

Source: U.S. Bureau of the Census, Current Population Reports, *Annual Social and Economic Supplement 2007*, family income table FINC-01.

Notes: 'All Races' includes races not shown separately. 'White' as shown is equivalent to 'White alone.'
'Number of earners' excludes families with members in the armed forces.

Units: Number of family households in thousands.

Table 1.26: Type and Tenure of Hispanic Households by Ethnic Group, 2003 and 2006

	Mexican	Puerto Rican	Cuban	Central/ South American	Other Hispanic	Total Hispanic
2003						
Total households	7,126	1,256	551	1,462	944	11,339
Family households	5,832	964	415	1,198	681	9,090
Percent by tenure						
Owner-occupied	49.8%	38.4%	61.6%	41.0%	44.0%	47.5%
Renter-occupied	50.2	61.6	38.4	59.0	56.0	52.5

	Mexican	Puerto Rican	Cuban	Central American	South American	Other Hispanic	Total Hispanic
2006							
Total households	7,702	1,239	587	1,026	806	1,159	12,519
Family households	6,239	900	429	819	630	845	9,862
Percent by tenure							
Owner-occupied	34.8%	24.8%	40.8%	23.6%	29.7%	44.4%	33.8%
Renter-occupied	65.2	75.2	59.2	76.4	70.3	55.6	66.2

Source: U.S. Bureau of the Census, Current Population Reports, *The Hispanic Population of the United States, 2003*, table 16.2; *2006*, table 16.2.

Notes: 'Other Hispanic origin' includes Dominicans and persons from Spain and persons identifying themselves generally as Hispanic, Spanish, Spanish-American, Hispano, Latino, etc.

Units: Number of households in thousands; percent of all households by tenure.

Table 1.27: Type and Size of Family Households by Hispanic Origin and Race, 2006

	Hispanic	Non-Hispanic White	Other Non-Hispanic	All Races
Total families	*9,862*	*54,257*	*13,283*	*77,402*
Two persons	2,636	26,629	5,189	34,454
Three persons	2,286	11,801	3,438	17,525
Four persons	2,383	10,084	2,607	15,075
Five or more persons	2,556	5,743	2,049	10,349
Married couples	*6,642*	*44,116*	*7,421*	*58,179*
Two persons	1,459	20,877	2,494	24,830
Three persons	1,354	8,952	1,701	12,006
Four persons	1,788	9,053	1,808	12,649
Five or more persons	2,041	5,235	1,418	8,694
Male householder, no spouse present	*969*	*3,003*	*1,158*	*5,130*
Two persons	419	1,881	643	2,942
Three persons	259	754	279	1,292
Four persons	153	234	127	514
Five or more persons	139	134	108	381
Female householder, no spouse present	*2,252*	*7,138*	*4,703*	*14,093*
Two persons	758	3,871	2,052	6,681
Three persons	674	2,095	1,457	4,226
Four persons	443	797	672	1,912
Five or more persons	376	375	522	1,273

Source: U.S. Bureau of the Census, Current Population Reports, *The Hispanic Population of the United States, 2006*, table 5.1.

Notes: 'All Races' includes races not shown separately.
Numbers exclude family members in the armed forces.

Units: Population in thousands.

Table 1.28: Family Structure and Living Arrangements, Children Under 17, 1990–2008

	Hispanic			White			All Races		
	Married Parents	Mother Only	Father Only	Married Parents	Mother Only	Father Only	Married Parents	Mother Only	Father Only
1990	67%	27%	3%	81%	15%	3%	73%	22%	3%
1991	66	27	3	80	15	3	72	22	3
1992	65	28	4	79	16	3	71	23	3
1993	65	28	4	79	16	3	71	23	3
1994	63	28	4	79	16	3	69	23	3
1995	63	28	4	78	16	3	69	23	4
1996	62	29	4	77	16	4	68	24	4
1997	64	27	4	77	17	4	68	24	4
1998	64	27	4	76	16	5	68	23	4
1999	63	27	5	77	16	4	68	23	4
2000	65	25	4	77	16	4	69	22	4
2001	65	25	5	78	16	4	69	22	4
2002	65	25	5	77	16	4	69	23	5
2003	65	25	6	77	16	4	68	23	5
2004	65	25	5	77	16	4	68	23	5
2005	65	25	5	76	16	5	67	23	5
2006	66	25	4	76	16	5	67	23	5
2007	66	24	2	74	17	3	68	23	3
2008	64	24	2	73	17	4	67	23	4

Source: U.S. Census Bureau, Current Population Survey, *Families and Living Arrangements 2008*, table C3.

Notes: After 2003, 'White' as used here refer to persons who indicated only one racial identity within the racial categories presented; however, before 2003 'White' may also refer to persons who selected more than one racial category.

Units: Percentages are of total family household for each category.

Table 1.29: Living Arrangements of Children
Under 18 Years of Age, 2000 and 2006

	Hispanic Children	White Children	All Children
2000			
Living with both parents	7,561	42,497	49,795
Living with mother only	2,919	9,765	16,162
Living with father only	506	2,427	3,058
Living with neither parent	626	1,752	2,981
2006			
Living with both parents	9,686	41,599	49,661
Living with mother only	3,674	10,090	17,161
Living with father only	603	2,603	3,458
Living with neither parent	734	2,040	3,383

Source: U.S. Bureau of the Census, Current Population Reports, *America's Families and Living Arrangements: 2000* (Series P-20, #537), table C2; *2006*, table C2.

Notes: 'All Children' includes children of races not shown separately.
For 2006 data, 'White' is equivalent to 'White Alone.'

Units: Number of children in thousands.

Table 1.30: Single Parents Living With Own Children Under 18 Years Old, 2000 and 2008

	Hispanic	White	All Races
2000			
Single Mothers			
With own children under 18	1,565	6,216	9,681
With own children under 12	1,190	4,558	7,337
With own children under 6	720	2,519	4,115
With own children under 3	409	1,396	2,319
With own children under 1	141	499	824
Single Fathers			
With own children under 18	313	1,622	2,044
With own children under 12	260	1,145	1,441
With own children under 6	189	647	819
With own children under 3	129	393	511
With own children under 1	51	152	196
2008			
Single Mothers			
With own children under 18	1,957	6,628	10,404
With own children under 12	1,501	4,661	7,438
With own children under 6	887	2,678	4,350
With own children under 3	533	1,551	2,467
With own children under 1	169	515	830
Single Fathers			
With own children under 18	423	1,914	2,501
With own children under 12	318	1,252	1,683
With own children under 6	224	691	952
With own children under 3	144	411	575
With own children under 1	57	165	227

Source: U.S. Bureau of the Census, Current Population Reports, *America's Families and Living Arrangements: 2000*, table FG-5; *2008*, table FG-4.

Notes: 'All Races' includes other races not shown separately. For 2008 data, 'White' as shown is equivalent to 'White Alone.'

Units: Thousands of fathers or mothers.

Table 1.31: Primary Child Care Arrangements Used for Preschoolers by Families With Employed Mothers, Winter 2002 and Spring 2005

	Hispanic Children	White Children	All Children
Winter 2002			
All preschoolers with employed mothers	*1,502*	*7,699*	*9,823*
Designated parent	2.8%	3.6%	3.3%
Other parent	15.4	19.0	18.2
Sibling	1.4	0.5	1.0
Grandparent	24.4	18.5	19.4
Other relative	10.9	4.6	5.4
Daycare center	15.4	18.6	19.0
Nursery/preschool	3.4	5.0	5.3
Head start	1.7	0.7	0.8
Family day care	4.0	9.5	9.2
Other non-relative	10.1	9.6	9.0
Spring 2005			
All preschoolers with employed mothers	*1,761*	*8,739*	*11,334*
Designated parent	3.5%	4.9%	4.6%
Other parent	15.0	19.3	18.2
Sibling	3.5	1.1	1.5
Grandparent	27.7	20.2	20.5
Other relative	9.7	4.8	5.4
Daycare center	11.7	18.1	19.1
Nursery/preschool	2.3	5.2	5.3
Head start	1.0	0.5	0.8
Family day care	4.0	8.5	7.8
Other non-relative	10.7	9.5	9.0
School	4.3	2.2	2.6
No regular arrangement	10.3	11.4	10.5

Source: U.S. Bureau of the Census, Current Population Reports, *Who's Minding the Kids? Child Care Arrangements: Winter 2002*, table 2B; *Spring 2005*, table 2B.

Notes: 'All Children' includes children of races not shown separately.
Because of multiple arrangements, numbers and percentages may exceed the total number of children. 'Designated parent' is selected in households where both parents are present to report child care arrangements for each child.

Units: Thousands of children living in family households; percent of total with the given child-care arrangement.

Table 1.32: Average Weekly Child Care Expenditures of Families with Employed Mothers, Winter 2002 and Spring 2005

	Hispanic	White	All Races
Winter 2002			
Families with children under 5 years	*581*	*3,522*	*4,475*
Average weekly child care expenditures	$119	$127	$122
Average monthly family income	$4,525	$5,648	$5,598
Percent of family's monthly income spent on child care	11.4%	9.8%	9.5%
Average monthly mother's income	$2,198	$2,531	$2,577
Ratio of child care expenditures to mother's income	23.4	21.8	20.5
Families with children 5 to 14 years	*653*	*4,351*	*5,372*
Average weekly child care expenditures	$81	$85	$84
Average monthly family income	$4,146	$5,941	$5,762
Percent of family's monthly income spent on child care	8.5%	6.2%	6.3%
Average monthly mother's income	$2,198	$2,874	$2,796
Ratio of child care expenditures to mother's income	16.0	12.8	13.0
Spring 2005			
Families with children under 5 years	*733*	*3,565*	*4,599*
Average weekly child care expenditures	$99	$129	$128
Average monthly family income	$4,091	$6,880	$6,482
Percent of family's monthly income spent on child care	10.5%	8.2%	8.6%
Average monthly mother's income	$2,072	$3,418	$3,199
Ratio of child care expenditures to mother's income	20.7	16.4	17.4
Families with children 5 to 14 years	*857*	*4,279*	*5,379*
Average weekly child care expenditures	$84	$94	$97
Average monthly family income	$5,023	$8,443	$7,749
Percent of family's monthly income spent on child care	7.3%	4.8%	5.4%
Average monthly mother's income	$2,475	$4,108	$3,803
Ratio of child care expenditures to mother's income	14.7	9.9	11.1

Source: U.S. Bureau of the Census, Current Population Reports, *Who's Minding the Kids? Child Care Arrangements: Winter 2002*, table 6; *Spring 2005*, table 6.

Notes: 'All Races' includes races not shown separately. Race designation is based on race of mother.

Units: Families in thousands; monthly income; expenditures per week; percent of income; ratio of expenditures to income.

Chapter 2

Vital Statistics and Health

Chapter Two Highlights

This chapter provides vital statistics and information about the health of Hispanic persons in the United States, including both the most current data available as well as comparisons of the Hispanic population over time. For almost all tables, corresponding data is provided for the total population of the United States as well as for White persons, allowing easy comparison between groups.

This chapter includes information about birth rates (tables 2.02–2.04), as well as information about infant mortality and its causes (tables 2.10–2.12). In addition, we have provided data on low birth weight (2.03) and low birth weight by ethnic group (2.07). Statistics on abortion are also included (table 2.09).

Information about children's health is provided, including data on health status (table 2.14), health care access (table 2.14), and vaccinations (table 2.15).

The chapter also contains statistics about death rates and causes of death, including heart disease (table 2.18), cancer (table 2.20), motor vehicle accidents (table 2.21), homicide (table 2.22), and suicide (table 2.23). Data on HIV transmission and AIDS rates are also included (tables 2.25–2.27).

The chapter also contains statistics on a variety of physical conditions, such as injuries, migraines, and hearing and vision trouble (tables 2.30–2.33).

Also of note are statistics on body mass, including statistics about obese, overweight, and underweight persons (tables 2.39 and 2.40). Information is provided for adults, adolescents, and children (table 2.41). We have also included data on time spent engaging in leisure–time physical exercise (tables 2.42 and 2.43).

The chapter includes statistics on smoking, alcohol consumption, and other substances organized in a number of ways, including by sex (table 2.45) and by age (table 2.46).

We have also provided data on feelings of emotional distress in adults (table 2.47) and suicide attempts by teenagers (table 2.48).

The chapter contains statistics on health insurance coverage by type of coverage (tables 2.50 and 2.51) and statistics on persons lacking coverage (table 2.49). In addition, we have included data on heath care visits (table 2.52), including dental visits (table 2.53) and hospitalization rates (table 2.54).

Table 2.01: Self-Assessment of Health, 1995-2007

	Hispanic	White	All Races
1995			
Fair or poor	15.1%	9.7%	10.6%
2000			
Fair or poor	12.8%	8.2%	9.0%
2003			
Fair or poor	13.9%	8.5%	9.2%
2005			
Excellent	28.5%	36.8%	35.8%
Very good	28.4	31.5	31.0
Good	29.8	23.0	24.0
Fair or poor	13.2	8.6	9.2
2006			
Excellent	29.2%	36.4%	35.5%
Very good	27.4	31.5	30.8
Good	30.4	23.4	24.4
Fair	10.1	6.7	7.2
Poor	2.9	2.0	2.1
2007			
Excellent	29.3%	36.8%	36.2%
Very good	27.4	31.2	30.3
Good	30.3	23.1	24.0
Fair	10.1	6.6	7.2
Poor	2.9	2.2	2.4

Source: U.S. Department of Health and Human Services, National Center for Health Statistics, *Health, United States, 1991*, table 61; *1992*, table 63; *2001*, table 58; *2002*, table 59; *2003*, table 57; *2004*, table 57; *2005*, table 60.
U.S. Department of Health and Human Services, *National Health Interview Survey: Summary Health Statistics, 2005*, table 2; *2006*, table 2.

Notes: 'All Races' includes races not shown separately.
Data is age-adjusted.
Data starting in 1997 is not strictly comparable with data for earlier years due to the 1997 questionnaire redesign.

Units: Percent of the population.

Table 2.02: Fertility, Births and Birth Rates, by Age of the Mother, 1990–2007

	Hispanic Mothers	White Mothers	All Mothers
1990			
Births	NA	NA	NA
Fertility rate	107.7	68.3	70.9
Birth rate per 1,000 by age group			
15–19 years old	100.3	50.8	59.9
20–24 years old	181.0	109.8	116.5
25–29 years old	153.0	120.7	120.2
30–34 years old	98.3	81.7	80.8
35–39 years old	45.3	31.5	31.7
40–44 years old	10.9	5.2	5.5
2000			
Births	NA	NA	NA
Fertility rate	95.9	65.3	65.9
Birth rate per 1,000 by age group			
15–19 years old	87.3	43.2	47.7
20–24 years old	161.3	106.6	109.7
25–29 years old	139.9	116.7	113.5
30–34 years old	97.1	94.6	91.2
35–39 years old	46.6	40.2	39.7
40–44 years old	11.5	7.9	8.0
2005			
Births	985,505	2,279,768	4,138,349
Fertility rate	99.4	58.3	66.7
Birth rate per 1,000 by age group			
Total	23.1	11.5	14.0
10–14 years old	1.3	0.2	0.7
15–19 years old	81.7	25.9	40.5
20–24 years old	170.0	81.4	102.2
25–29 years old	149.2	109.1	115.5
30–34 years old	106.8	96.9	95.8
35–39 years old	54.2	45.6	46.3
40–44 years old	13.0	8.3	9.1
45–54 years old	0.8	0.5	0.6

(continued on next page)

Table 2.02: Fertility, Births and Birth Rates, by Age of the Mother, 1990–2007

	Hispanic Mothers	White Mothers	All Mothers
2006			
Births	1,039,077	2,309,833	4,265,996
Fertility rate	101.5	59.5	68.5
Birth rate per 1,000 by age group			
Total	23.4	11.6	14.2
10–14 years old	1.3	0.2	0.6
15–19 years old	83.0	26.6	41.9
20–24 years old	177.0	83.4	105.9
25–29 years old	152.4	109.2	116.8
30–34 years old	108.5	98.1	97.7
35–39 years old	55.6	46.3	47.3
40–44 years old	13.3	8.4	9.4
45–54 years old	0.8	0.6	0.6
2007 (Preliminary)			
Births	1,061,970	2,312,473	4,317,119
Fertility rate	102.1	11.5	14.3
Birth rate per 1,000 by age group			
Total	23.3	60.1	69.5
10–14 years old	1.2	0.2	0.6
15–19 years old	81.7	27.2	42.5
20–24 years old	178.5	83.3	106.4
25–29 years old	155.6	108.8	117.5
30–34 years old	110.8	99.7	99.9
35–39 years old	56.4	45.8	47.5
40–44 years old	13.4	8.6	9.5
45–54 years old	0.8	0.6	0.6

Source: U.S. Department of Health and Human Services, *Births: Final Data for 2005*, table 1.
U.S. Department of Health and Human Services, *Births: Preliminary Data for 2007*, tables 1 and 2.

Notes: 'All Races' includes races not shown separately.
Data based on race of the mother.
Fertility rate is the total number of births, regardless of age of mother, per 1,000 women aged 15–44 years.

Units: Live births in number of births; rates as shown.

Table 2.03: Selected Characteristics of Live Births, 1980–2005

	Hispanic Births	White Births	All Births
1980			
Birth weight under 2,500 grams	6.12%	5.72%	6.84%
Birth weight under 1,500 grams	2.48	0.90	1.15
Mother under 18 years old	7.4	4.5	5.8
Mother 18–19 years old	11.6	9.0	9.8
Births to unmarried mothers	23.6	11.2	18.4
Mother with less than 12 years of school	51.1	20.8	23.7
Mother with 16 years or more of school	4.2	15.5	14.0
Prenatal care began in 1st trimester	60.2	79.2	76.3
Prenatal care began in 3rd trimester or no prenatal care	12.0	4.3	5.1
1990			
Birth weight under 2,500 grams	6.06%	5.70%	6.97%
Birth weight under 1,500 grams	2.92	0.95	1.27
Mother under 18 years old	6.6	3.6	4.7
Mother 18–19 years old	10.2	7.3	8.1
Births to unmarried mothers	36.7	20.4	28.0
Mother with less than 12 years of school	53.9	22.4	23.8
Mother with 16 years or more of school	5.1	19.3	17.5
Prenatal care began in 1st trimester	60.2	79.2	75.8
Prenatal care began in 3rd trimester or no prenatal care	12.0	4.9	6.1
2000			
Birth weight under 2,500 grams	6.41%	6.55%	7.57%
Birth weight under 1,500 grams	3.07	1.14	1.43
Mother under 18 years old	6.3	3.5	4.1
Mother 18–19 years old	9.9	7.1	7.7
Births to unmarried mothers	42.7	27.1	33.2
Mother with less than 12 years of school	48.9	21.4	21.7
Mother with 16 years or more of school	7.6	26.3	24.7
Prenatal care began in 1st trimester	74.4	85.0	83.2
Prenatal care began in 3rd trimester or no prenatal care	6.3	3.3	3.9

(continued on next page)

Table 2.03: Selected Characteristics of Live Births, 1980–2005

	Hispanic Births	White Births	All Births
2004			
Birth weight under 2,500 grams	6.79%	7.07%	8.08%
Birth weight under 1,500 grams	1.20	1.20	1.48
Mother under 18 years old	5.4	3.0	3.4
Mother 18–19 years old	8.9	6.4	6.8
Births to unmarried mothers	46.4	30.5	35.8
Mother with less than 12 years of school	48.4	22.7	22.2
Mother with 16 years or more of school	8.0	28.0	26.9
Prenatal care began in 1st trimester	77.5	85.4	83.9
Prenatal care began in 3rd trimester or no prenatal care	5.4	3.2	3.6
2005			
Birth weight under 2,500 grams	6.88%	7.16%	8.19%
Birth weight under 1,500 grams	1.20	1.20	1.49
Mother under 18 years old	5.3	2.9	3.4
Mother 18–19 years old	8.8	6.3	6.8
Births to unmarried mothers	48.0	31.7	36.9
Mother with less than 12 years of school	6.2	7.3	8.5
Mother with 16 years or more of school	6.7	6.5	7.3
Prenatal care began in 1st trimester	57.0	75.6	72.8
Prenatal care began in 3rd trimester or no prenatal care	10.8	5.0	6.0

Source: U.S. Department of Health and Human Services, National Center for Health Statistics, *Health United States, 2008*, tables 7, 9, 10, 12, and 13.

Notes: Data based on race of the mother.
For 2004 and 2005, data for prenatal care was only reported by 7 states, so caution should be used when making comparisons between this data and data for previous years.
For 2004 and 2005, data for education was reported by only 37 states, so caution should be used when making comparisons between this data and data for previous years.

Units: Percent of all live births.

Table 2.04: Birth Rates by Live Birth Order, 2005–2007

	Hispanic Mothers	White Mothers	All Mothers
2005			
All live births	99.4	66.3	66.7
First child	35.5	26.3	26.5
Second child	30.5	21.7	21.5
Third child	19.5	11.4	11.3
Fourth child	8.6	4.4	4.5
Fifth child	3.2	1.5	1.6
Sixth and Seventh child	1.7	0.8	0.9
Eighth child and over	0.4	0.3	0.3
2006			
All live births	101.5	68.0	68.5
First child	36.3	27.1	27.4
Second child	30.9	22.0	21.9
Third child	19.9	11.6	11.6
Fourth child and over	14.4	4.6	4.7
2007			
All live births	102.1	60.1	69.5
First child	36.4	25.2	27.9
Second child	30.8	19.9	22.1
Third child	20.2	9.5	11.7
Fourth child and over	14.7	5.5	7.8

Source: U.S. Department of Health and Human Services, *Births: Preliminary Data for 2007*, table 5.
U.S. Department of Health and Human Services, *Births: Final Data for 2005*, table 3.

Notes: Data based on race of the mother.
Data for 2006 and 2007 is preliminary.

Units: Births per 1,000 women aged 15–44 years.

Table 2.05: Nonmarital Childbearing, 1980–2005

	Hispanic Women	White Women	All Women
Live births per 1,000 to unmarried mothers			
1980	NA	18.1	29.4
1985	NA	22.5	32.8
1990	89.6	32.9	43.8
1995	88.7	37.0	44.3
2000	87.2	38.2	44.0
2001	87.8	38.5	43.8
2002	87.9	38.9	43.7
2003	92.2	40.4	44.9
2004	95.7	41.6	46.1
2005	100.3	43.0	47.5
Percent of live births to unmarried mothers			
1980	23.6%	11.2%	18.4%
1985	29.5	14.7	22.0
1990	36.7	20.4	28.0
1995	40.8	25.3	32.2
2000	42.7	27.1	33.2
2001	42.5	27.7	33.5
2002	43.5	28.5	34.0
2003	45.0	29.4	34.6
2004	46.4	30.5	35.8
2005	48.0	31.7	36.9

Source: U.S. Department of Health and Human Services, Centers for Disease Control and Prevention, National Center for Health Statistics, *Health, United States, 2006*, table 10.
U.S. Department of Health and Human Services, Centers for Disease Control and Prevention, National Vital Statistics Reports, *Births: Final Data for 2005*, table 18.

Notes: 'All women' includes women of races not shown separately.

Units: Live births per 1,000 unmarried women 15–44 years of age.

Table 2.06: Projected Fertility Rates, Women 10–49 years old, 2010

	Hispanic women	White women	All women
Total fertility rate	*2,818*	*2,098*	*2,123*
Birth Rates by Age			
10–14 years old	2.3	0.9	1.3
15–19 years old	95.7	54.3	60.2
20–24 years old	175.2	112.6	115.8
25–29 years old	146.7	118.5	115.7
30–34 years old	91.6	90.0	87.8
35–39 years old	41.9	36.6	36.7
40–44 years old	9.9	7.1	7.3
45–49 years old	0.6	0.3	0.3

Source: U.S. Bureau of the Census, *Statistical Abstract of the United States, 2006*, table 78.

Notes: 'All women' includes women of races not shown separately.
The total fertility rate is the number of births that 1,000 women would have in their lifetime if, at each year of age, they experienced the birth rates occurring in the specified year. Projections are based on middle fertility assumptions.

Units: Total fertility rate and birth rate in births per 1,000 women.

Table 2.07: Low-Birthweight Live Births by Ethnic Group, 2000–2005

	Low Birthweight	Very Low Birthweight
2000		
Total Hispanic	*6.41%*	*1.14%*
Mexican	6.01	1.03
Puerto Rican	9.30	1.93
Cuban	6.49	1.21
Central/South American	6.34	1.20
Other Hispanic	7.84	1.42
White	6.55	1.14
All Races	7.57	1.43
2004		
Total Hispanic	*6.79%*	*1.20%*
Mexican	6.44	1.13
Puerto Rican	9.82	1.96
Cuban	7.72	1.30
Central/South American	6.70	1.19
Other Hispanic	7.78	1.27
White	7.07	1.20
All Races	8.08	1.48
2005		
Total Hispanic	*6.88%*	*1.20%*
Mexican	6.49	1.12
Puerto Rican	9.92	1.87
Cuban	7.64	1.50
Central/South American	6.78	1.19
Other Hispanic	8.27	1.36
White	7.16	1.20
All Races	8.19	1.49

Source: U.S. Department of Health and Human Services, *Health United States, 2008*, table 12

Notes: Excludes live births with unknown birthweight.
'Low Birthweight' indicates less than 2,500 grams.
'Very Low Birthweight' indicates less than 1,500 grams.

Units: Percent of live births with known birthweight.

Table 2.08: Contraceptive Use for Women 15–44 Years of Age by Method of Contraception, 1995 and 2002

	Hispanic Women	White Women	All Women
1995			
All methods	*59.0%*	*66.2%*	*64.2%*
Female sterilization	36.6	24.5	27.8
Male sterilization	4.0*	13.7	10.9
Birth control pill	23.0	28.7	27.0
Intrauterine device	NA	0.7	0.8
Diaphragm	NA	2.3	1.9
Condom	21.2	22.5	23.4
2002			
All methods	*59.0%*	*64.6%*	*61.9%*
Female sterilization	33.8	23.9	27.0
Male sterilization	4.7	12.9	10.2
Birth control pill	22.1	34.9	31.0
Intrauterine device	5.3	1.7	2.2
Diaphragm	NA	NA	0.6
Condom	24.1	21.7	23.8

Source: U.S. Department of Health and Human Services, Centers for Disease Control and Prevention, National Center for Health Statistics, *Health, United States, 2005*, table 17.

Notes: 'All women' includes women of races not shown separately. 'White' includes women who are not of Hispanic or Latino origin only. Data is based on household interviews of samples of women in the childbearing ages.
'NA' means that estimates are considered unreliable.
* Indicates data with a relative standard error of 20–30%.

Units: Percent of women using contraception; individual methods as a percent of all women using some form of contraception.

Table 2.09: Abortions, 1992–2004

	Hispanic Women	White Women	All Women
1992	30.7	23.6	33.5
1993	28.9	23.1	33.4
1994	27.8	21.7	32.1
1995	27.1	20.3	31.1
1996	27.6	20.2	31.4
1997	26.8	19.4	30.6
1998	27.3	18.9	26.4
1999	26.1	17.7	25.6
2000	22.5	16.7	24.5
2001	23.0	16.5	24.6
2002	23.3	16.4	24.6
2003	22.8	16.5	24.1
2004	21.1	16.1	22.5

Source: U.S. Department of Health and Human Services, Centers for Disease Control and Prevention, National Center for Health Statistics, *Health, United States, 2006*, table 16.
U.S. Department of Health and Human Services, Centers for Disease Control and Prevention, *Morbidity and Mortality Weekly Report, vol. 56, no. SS-9*, "Abortion Surveillance–United States, 2004," table 9.

Notes: 'All women' includes women of races not shown separately. For 1989 and later, 'White' includes women of Hispanic ethnicity.
The following states did not report abortion data in the years given: Alaska (1998–2002), California (1998–2004), New Hampshire (1998–2004), Oklahoma (1998–1999), and West Virginia (2004–2004). Data for these years exclude those states.

Units: Abortions per 100 live births.

Table 2.10: Infant Mortality Rates, 2000–2005

	Hispanic Mothers	White Mothers	All Mothers
2000			
Infant mortality rate	5.6	5.7	6.9
Neonatal mortality rate	3.8	3.8	4.6
Post neonatal mortality rate	1.8	1.9	2.3
2001			
Infant mortality rate	5.4	5.7	6.8
Neonatal mortality rate	3.6	3.8	4.5
Post neonatal mortality rate	1.8	1.9	2.3
2002			
Infant mortality rate	5.6	5.8	7.0
Neonatal mortality rate	3.8	3.9	4.7
Post neonatal mortality rate	1.8	1.9	2.3
2003			
Infant mortality rate	5.6	5.7	6.8
Neonatal mortality rate	3.9	3.9	4.6
Post neonatal mortality rate	1.7	1.9	2.2
2004			
Infant mortality rate	5.5	5.7	6.8
Neonatal mortality rate	3.8	3.8	4.5
Post neonatal mortality rate	1.7	1.9	2.3
2005			
Infant mortality rate	5.6	5.7	6.9
Neonatal mortality rate	3.9	3.8	4.5
Post neonatal mortality rate	1.8	2.0	2.3

Source: U.S. Department of Health and Human Services, National Center for Health Statistics, *Health, United States, 2008*, table 18.

Notes: 'All Mother's includes mothers of races not shown separately.
Data based on race of the mother.
Infant mortality rate is the number of deaths of infants under one year; neonatal deaths occur within 28 days of birth; post-neonatal deaths occur 28 days to 11 months after birth.

Units: All rates per 1,000 live births, as shown.

Table 2.11: Infant Mortality Rates, Leading Causes of Death, 2004

	Hispanic	White	All Races
2004			
All causes	*400.2*	*564.8*	*676.3*
Congenital malformations	136.3	132.2	136.6
Disorders related to short gestation and low birth rate	87.7	84.4	113.8
Sudden infant death syndrome	25.5	41.9	51.2
Newborn affected by maternal complications of pregnancy	28.3	31.1	41.4
Newborn affected by complications of placenta, cord and membranes	18.4	20.3	24.2

Source: U.S. Department of Health and Human Services, Centers for Disease Control and Prevention, National Vital Statistics Reports, *Deaths: Preliminary Data for 2004*, table 8.

Notes: Preliminary data for 2004.
'All Races' includes races not shown separately.

Units: Deaths per 100,000 live births.

Table 2.12: Infant Mortality Rate by State, 2003–2005

	Hispanic Infants	White Infants	All Infants
United States	3.9	3.7	4.6
Alabama	*4.4	4.0	5.4
Alaska	*	*2.6	3.2
Arizona	4.8	4.0	4.5
Arkansas	*3.8	4.3	5.1
California	3.5	3.0	3.5
Colorado	5.3	3.8	4.6
Connecticut	6.1	2.8	4.0
Delaware	*4.4	4.5	6.4
District of Columbia	*	*	8.6
Florida	3.5	3.5	4.7
Georgia	3.8	3.9	5.6
Hawaii	*5.7	*3.1	4.7
Idaho	*3.8	4.0	3.9
Illinois	4.3	4.1	5.1
Indiana	4.9	4.6	5.3
Iowa	*3.7	3.2	3.4
Kansas	3.4	4.4	4.6
Kentucky	*5.5	3.7	4.0
Louisiana	*	4.0	5.8
Maine	*	4.3	4.4
Maryland	3.8	3.7	5.8
Massachusetts	4.9	3.0	3.7
Michigan	5.1	4.3	5.6
Minnesota	*2.9	2.9	3.2
Mississippi	*	3.5	6.2
Missouri	4.6	4.4	5.1
Montana	*	3.4	3.5
Nebraska	*3.6	3.3	3.7
Nevada	2.6	3.6	3.7

(continued on next page)

Table 2.12: Infant Mortality Rate by State, 2003–2005

	Hispanic Infants	White Infants	All Infants
New Hampshire	*	3.6	3.9
New Jersey	3.7	2.6	3.8
New Mexico	3.3	4.1	3.6
New York	3.8	3.4	4.2
North Carolina	4.7	4.2	6.0
North Dakota	*	4.5	4.8
Ohio	4.8	4.2	5.3
Oklahoma	4.0	4.3	4.6
Oregon	3.8	3.7	3.8
Pennsylvania	5.5	4.0	5.2
Rhode Island	*5.8	3.5	4.8
South Carolina	4.7	4.2	6.1
South Dakota	*	4.1	4.3
Tennessee	5.0	4.0	5.7
Texas	3.8	3.7	4.2
Utah	4.2	3.1	3.4
Vermont	*	3.7	3.8
Virginia	4.0	3.9	5.2
Washington	3.7	2.9	3.4
West Virginia	*	4.7	4.8
Wisconsin	4.4	3.5	4.3
Wyoming	*	4.6	4.6

Source: U.S. Department of Health and Human Services, National Center for Health Statistics, *Health, United States, 2008*, table 23.

Notes: Infant deaths are defined as occurring prior to 1 year of age.
* Estimates are considered unreliable.
Rates preceded by an asterisk are based on fewer than 50 deaths.
Rates not shown are based on fewer than 20 deaths.

Units: Infant deaths per 1,000 live births.

Table 2.13: Maternal Mortality Rates,
by Age of the Mother, 1990–2005

	Hispanic Mothers	White Mothers	All Mothers
1990			
Number of deaths	47	177	343
All ages, age-adjusted rate	7.4	5.1	7.6
2000			
Number of deaths	81	240	396
All ages, age-adjusted rate	9.0	6.2	8.2
2002			
Number of deaths	62	190	357
All ages, age-adjusted rate	6.0	4.8	7.6
2004			
Number of deaths	80	300	540
All ages, age-adjusted rate	7.3	7.5	11.3
2005			
Number of deaths	95	360	623
All ages, age-adjusted rate	8.2	7.5	9.6

Source: U.S. Department of Health and Human Services, Centers for Disease Control and Prevention, National Center for Health Statistics, *Health, United States, 2007*, table 43.

Notes: 'All mothers' include mothers of races not shown separately.
Data for maternal mortality for complications of pregnancy, childbirth, and the puerperium.

Units: Number of maternal deaths; deaths of mothers per 100,000 live births.

Table 2.14: Health Status and Health Care Access for Children, 2006 and 2007

	Hispanic Children	White Children	All Children
2006			
Respondent-Assessed Health Status			
All children under 18	*14,815*	*55,881*	*73,493*
Excellent	6,372	30,773	39,501
Very good	4,427	15,878	20,621
Good	3,627	8,284	11,933
Fair/poor	389	912	1,398
Selected Measures of Health Care Access			
All children under 18	*14,815*	*55,866*	*73,492*
Uninsured for health care	2,850	5,250	6,921
Unmet medical need	472	1,327	1,792
Delayed care due to cost	704	2,309	2,942
2007			
Respondent-Assessed Health Status			
All children under 18	*15,350*	*55,646*	*73,728*
Excellent	6,951	31,364	41,054
Very good	4,120	15,341	19,838
Good	3,800	8,208	11,519
Fair/poor	478	713	1,297
Selected Measures of Health Care Access			
All children under 18	15,349	55,721	73,727
Uninsured for health care	2,340	5,138	6,602
Unmet medical need	467	1,311	1,726
Delayed care due to cost	546	1,940	2,450

Source: U.S. Department of Health and Human Services, *National Health Interview Survey: Summary Health Statistics for U.S. Children, 2005*, tables 5 and 15; *2006*, tables 5 and 15; *2007*, tables 5 and 15.

Notes: 'All children' includes races and ethnic groups not shown separately.

Units: Number in thousands of children under 18 years of age.

Table 2.15: Vaccinations of Children 19–35 Months of Age for Selected Diseases, 2000 and 2006

	Hispanic	White	All Races
2000			
Ccombined series (4:3:1:3)	73%	79%	76%
DTP (4 doses or more)	79	84	82
Polio (3 doses or more)	88	91	90
Measles-containing	90	92	91
Hib (3 doses or more)	91	95	93
Hepatitis B (3 doses or more)	88	91	90
Varicella	70	66	68
2006			
Combined series (4:3:1:3)	77%	78%	77%
DTP (4 doses or more)	85	87	85
Polio (3 doses or more)	93	93	93
Measles-containing	92	93	92
Hib (3 doses or more)	94	94	93
Hepatitis B (3 doses or more)	94	94	93
Varicella	90	89	89

Source: U.S. Department of Health and Human Services, Centers for Disease Control and Prevention, National Center for Health Statistics, *Health, United States, 2007*, table 83.

Notes: 'All Races' includes races not shown separately. 'White' excludes White Hispanics. Data excludes cases of residents of U.S. Territories. The 4:3:1:3 combined series consists of 4 doses of diphtheria-tetanus-pertussis (DTP) vaccine, 3 doses of polio vaccine, 1 dose of a measles-containing vaccine, and 3 doses of *Haemophilus influenza* type b (Hib) vaccine. DTP is the Diphtheria-tetanus-pertussis vaccine. Hib is the *Haemophilus influenza* type b (Hib) vaccine.

Units: Percent of children 19–35 months of age receiving vaccinations.

Table 2.16: Death Rates, by Selected Causes of Death, 2003 and 2005

	Hispanic	White	All Races
2003			
Heart disease			
Men	206.8	282.9	286.6
Women	145.8	185.4	190.3
Cerebrovascular diseases			
Men	43.0	51.7	54.1
Women	38.1	50.5	52.3
Suicide			
Men	9.7	19.6	18.0
Women	1.7	4.6	4.2
HIV (human immunodeficiency virus)			
Men	9.2	4.2	7.1
Women	2.7	0.9	2.4
Malignant neoplasms			
Men	156.5	230.1	233.3
Women	105.9	160.2	160.9
2005			
Heart disease			
Men	192.4	258.0	260.9
Women	129.1	168.2	172.3
Cerebrovascular diseases			
Men	38.0	44.7	46.9
Women	33.5	44.0	45.6
Suicide			
Men	9.4	19.6	18.0
Women	1.8	4.9	4.4
HIV (human immunodeficiency virus)			
Men	7.5	3.6	6.2
Women	1.9	0.8	2.3
Malignant neoplasms			
Men	152.7	222.3	225.1
Women	101.9	155.2	155.6

Source: U.S. Department of Health and Human Services, Centers for Disease Control and Prevention, National Center for Health Statistics, *Health, United States, 2007*, tables 36–38, 42, and 46.

Notes: Age-adjusted rates for all ages.
'All Races' includes races not shown separately.

Units: Deaths per 100,000 population.

Table 2.17: Death Rates by Age and Sex, 1985–2005

	Hispanic		White		All Races	
	Male	Female	Male	Female	Male	Female
1985						
All ages, age-adjusted	*889.2*	*546.1*	*1,249.8*	*764.3*	*1,278.1*	*784.5*
All ages, crude	*374.6*	*251.9*	*963.6*	*840.1*	*948.6*	*809.1*
Under 1 year old	1,044.6	791.4	1,056.5	799.3	1,219.9	950.6
1–4 years old	53.8	42.3	52.8	40.0	58.5	44.8
5–14 years old	23.0	16.0	30.1	19.5	31.8	21.0
15–24 years old	147.5	36.2	134.2	48.1	138.9	49.6
25–34 years old	202.1	56.3	158.8	59.4	179.6	69.4
35–44 years old	290.1	100.0	243.1	121.9	278.9	138.7
45–54 years old	495.7	251.3	611.7	341.7	671.6	375.2
55–64 years old	1,129.4	619.7	1,625.8	869.1	1,711.4	925.6
65–74 years old	2,484.9	1,449.5	3,770.7	2,027.1	3,856.3	2,096.9
75–84 years old	5,696.1	3,551.8	8,486.1	5,111.6	8,501.6	5,162.1
85 years old and over	12,156.2	10,228.6	18,980.1	14,745.4	18,614.1	14,553.9
1990						
All ages, age-adjusted	*886.4*	*537.1*	*1,165.9*	*728.8*	*1,202.8*	*750.9*
All ages, crude	*411.6*	*285.4*	*930.9*	*846.9*	*918.4*	*812.0*
Under 1 year old	921.8	746.6	896.1	690.0	1,082.8	855.7
1–4 years old	53.8	42.1	45.9	36.1	52.4	41.0
5–14 years old	26.0	17.3	26.4	17.9	28.5	19.3
15–24 years old	159.3	40.6	131.3	45.9	147.4	49.0
25–34 years old	234.0	62.9	176.1	61.5	204.3	74.2
35–44 years old	341.8	109.3	268.2	117.4	310.4	137.9
45–54 years old	533.9	253.3	548.7	309.3	610.3	342.7
55–64 years old	1,123.7	607.5	1,467.2	822.7	1,553.4	878.8
65–74 years old	2,368.2	1,453.8	3,397.7	1,923.5	3,491.5	1,991.2
75–84 years old	5,369.1	3351.3	7,844.9	4,839.1	7,888.6	4,883.1
85 years old and over	12,272.1	10,098.7	18,268.3	14,400.6	18,056.6	14,274.3

(continued on next page)

Table 2.17: Death Rates by Age and Sex, 1985–2005

	Hispanic		White		All Races	
	Male	**Female**	**Male**	**Female**	**Male**	**Female**
2000						
All ages, age-adjusted	*818.1*	*546.0*	*1,029.4*	*715.3*	*1,053.8*	*731.4*
All ages, crude	*331.3*	*274.6*	*887.8*	*912.3*	*853.0*	*855.0*
Under 1 year old	637.1	553.6	667.6	550.5	806.5	663.4
1–4 years old	31.5	27.5	32.6	25.5	35.9	28.7
5–14 years old	17.9	13.4	19.8	14.1	20.9	15.0
15–24 years old	107.7	31.7	105.8	41.1	114.9	43.1
25–34 years old	120.2	43.4	124.1	55.1	138.6	63.5
35–44 years old	211.0	100.5	233.6	125.7	255.2	143.2
45–54 years old	439.0	223.8	496.9	281.4	542.8	312.5
55–64 years old	965.7	548.4	1,163.3	730.9	1,230.7	772.2
65–74 years old	2,287.9	1423.2	2,905.7	1,868.3	2,979.6	1,921.2
75–84 years old	5,395.3	3624.5	6,933.1	4,785.3	6,972.6	4,814.7
85 years old and over	13,086.2	11202.8	17,716.4	14,890.7	17,501.4	14,719.2
2005						
All ages, age-adjusted	*717.0*	*485.3*	*933.2*	*666.5*	*951.1*	*677.6*
All ages, crude	*334.4*	*278.2*	*864.5*	*882.8*	*827.2*	*824.6*
Under 1 year old	670.2	555.4	640.0	515.3	762.3	619.4
1–4 years old	33.2	24.5	30.9	22.9	33.4	25.1
5–14 years old	15.3	12.0	17.1	12.8	18.6	13.9
15–24 years old	120.4	36.6	110.4	41.5	117.8	42.7
25–34 years old	115.5	41.1	130.8	58.0	143.4	64.1
35–44 years old	182.0	90.6	228.5	130.4	243.0	143.6
45–54 years old	417.4	216.4	509.3	291.1	547.8	319.9
55–64 years old	875.8	493.9	1,068.1	663.9	1,131.0	698.5
65–74 years old	2,029.4	1,291.6	2,552.7	1,700.4	2,612.2	1,736.3
75–84 years old	4,856.8	3,365.8	6,343.2	4,519.4	6,349.8	4,520.0
85 years old and over	10,140.5	9,068.4	15,156.5	13,498.3	14,889.4	13,297.7

Source: U.S. Department of Health and Human Services, Centers for Disease Control and Prevention, National Center for Health Statistics, *Health, United States, 2006*, table 35; *2007*, table 35.

Notes: 'All Races' includes races not shown separately. 'All ages' includes ages not stated.

Units: Rates per 100,000 of population in specified age groups, as shown.

Table 2.18: Death Rates for Heart Disease, 1990–2005

	Hispanic		White		All Races	
	Male	Female	Male	Female	Male	Female
1990						
All ages, age-adjusted rate	413.6	177.2	409.2	250.9	412.4	257.0
All ages, crude rate	336.5	79.4	312.7	298.4	297.6	281.8
45–54 years old	172.8	43.5	170.6	50.2	183.0	61.0
55–64 years old	521.3	153.2	516.7	192.4	537.3	215.7
65–74 years old	1,243.4	460.4	1,230.5	583.6	1,250.0	616.8
75–84 years old	3,007.7	1,259.7	2,983.4	1,874.3	2,968.2	1,893.8
85 years old and over	7,663.4	4,440.3	7,558.7	6,563.4	7,418.4	6,478.1
2000						
All ages, age-adjusted rate	286.9	163.7	316.7	205.6	320.0	210.9
All ages, crude rate	282.9	71.5	265.8	274.5	249.8	255.3
45–54 years old	129.8	28.2	130.7	40.9	140.2	49.8
55–64 years old	317.7	111.2	351.8	141.3	371.7	159.3
65–74 years old	767.3	366.3	877.8	445.2	898.3	474.0
75–84 years old	2,049.9	1,169.4	2,247.0	1,452.4	2,248.1	1,475.1
85 years old and over	5,821.0	4,605.8	6,560.8	5,801.4	6,430.0	5,720.9
2005						
All ages, age-adjusted rate	192.4	129.1	258.0	168.2	260.9	172.3
All ages, crude rate	72.1	66.2	234.9	235.5	221.1	218.9
45–54 years old	77.9	26.2	121.3	40.8	131.5	49.2
55–64 years old	219.3	92.6	288.2	114.5	306.9	129.1
65–74 years old	561.5	305.9	671.9	351.8	692.3	372.7
75–84 years old	1,469.2	973.4	1,831.8	1,193.3	1,829.4	1,210.5
85 years old and over	3,534.2	3,341.2	5,288.4	4,691.0	5,143.4	4,610.8

Source: U.S. Department of Health and Human Services, Centers for Disease Control and Prevention, National Center for Health Statistics, *Health, United States, 2007*, table 36.

Notes: 'All Races' includes races not shown separately.

Units: Rate is the number of deaths per 100,000 resident population, by age group.

Table 2.19: Death Rates for Cerebrovascular Disease, by Sex and Age, 2000 and 2005

	Hispanic		White		All Races	
	Male	Female	Male	Female	Male	Female
2000						
All ages, age-adjusted	*50.5*	*43.0*	*59.8*	*57.3*	*62.4*	*59.1*
All ages, crude	*15.8*	*19.4*	*48.4*	*76.9*	*46.9*	*71.8*
45–54 years old	18.1	12.4	13.6	11.2	17.5	14.5
55–64 years old	48.8	31.9	39.7	30.2	47.2	35.3
65–74 years old	136.1	95.2	133.8	107.3	145.0	115.1
75–84 years old	392.9	311.3	480.0	434.2	490.8	442.1
85 years old and over	1,029.9	1,108.9	1,490.7	1,646.7	1,484.3	1,632.0
2005						
All ages, age-adjusted	*38.0*	*33.5*	*44.7*	*44.0*	*46.9*	*45.6*
All ages, crude	*14.4*	*17.7*	*39.7*	*61.6*	*38.8*	*57.8*
45–54 years old	17.8	12.1	12.8	10.5	16.5	13.6
55–64 years old	40.3	27.1	31.7	23.8	38.5	27.9
65–74 years old	106.2	75.8	103.0	83.2	113.6	90.5
75–84 years old	294.0	262.6	364.8	342.9	372.9	349.5
85 years old and over	692.4	762.5	1,033.7	1,208.5	1,023.3	1,196.1

Source: U.S. Department of Health and Human Services, Centers for Disease Control and Prevention, National Center for Health Statistics, *Health, United States, 2007*, table 37.

Notes: 'All Races' includes races not shown separately.
Excludes deaths of nonresidents of the United States.

Units: Rate is the number of deaths per 100,000 resident population.

Table 2.20: Female Death Rates for Malignant Neoplasms of the Breast by Age, 1990–2005

	Hispanic women	White women	All women
1990			
All ages, age–adjusted rate	*19.5*	*33.2*	*33.3*
All ages, crude rate	*11.5*	*35.9*	*34.0*
35–44 years old	11.7	17.1	17.8
45–54 years old	32.8	44.3	45.4
55–64 years old	45.8	78.5	78.6
65–74 years old	64.8	113.3	111.7
75–84 years old	67.2	148.2	146.3
85 years old and over	102.8	198.0	196.8
2000			
All ages, age–adjusted rate	*16.1*	*26.3*	*26.8*
All ages, crude rate	*9.8*	*30.7*	*29.2*
35–44 years old	9.1	11.3	12.4
45–54 years old	21.0	31.2	33.0
55–64 years old	38.8	57.9	59.3
65–74 years old	48.4	89.3	88.3
75–84 years old	70.8	130.2	128.9
85 years old and over	114.8	205.5	205.7
2005			
All ages, age-adjusted rate	*15.0*	*23.4*	*24.1*
All ages, crude rate	*9.4*	*28.3*	*27.3*
35–44 years old	8.0	10.2	11.3
45–54 years old	20.0	26.2	28.7
55–64 years old	34.7	52.4	54.5
65–74 years old	46.9	79.3	79.2
75–84 years old	73.3	120.7	119.2
85 years old and over	95.1	179.1	177.9

Source: U.S. Department of Health and Human Services, Centers for Disease Control and Prevention, National Center for Health Statistics, *Health, United States, 2007*, table 40.

Notes: 'All women' includes women of races not shown separately.
Data excludes deaths of nonresidents of the United States.
Age-adjusted rates may differ from those shown in previous editions of *Health, United States*.

Units: Rate is the number of deaths per 100,000 resident female population, by age group.

Hispanic Americans: A Statistical Sourcebook 2009

Table 2.21: Death Rates for Motor Vehicle Accidents by Sex and Age, 2000 and 2005

| | Hispanic | | White | | All Races | |
	Male	Female	Male	Female	Male	Female
2000						
All ages, age-adjusted	*21.3*	*7.9*	*21.8*	*9.8*	*21.7*	*9.5*
All ages, crude	*20.1*	*7.2*	*21.6*	*10.0*	*21.3*	*9.7*
1–14 years old	4.4	3.9	4.8	3.7	4.9	3.7
15–24 years old	34.7	10.6	39.6	17.1	37.4	15.9
25–34 years old	24.9	6.5	25.1	8.9	25.5	8.8
35–44 years old	21.6	7.3	21.8	8.9	22.0	8.8
45–64 years old	21.7	8.3	19.7	8.7	20.2	8.7
65 years old and over	28.9	13.4	29.4	16.2	29.5	15.8
2005						
All ages, age-adjusted	*21.3*	*7.8*	*22.2*	*9.2*	*21.7*	*8.9*
All ages, crude	*20.7*	*7.4*	*22.3*	*9.5*	*21.7*	*9.1*
1–14 years old	4.7	3.3	4.1	3.1	4.1	3.1
15–24 years old	40.3	13.4	39.1	15.8	36.5	14.7
25–34 years old	26.3	7.2	27.3	9.3	26.9	8.8
35–44 years old	20.2	7.4	22.4	8.9	22.2	8.6
45–64 years old	20.1	7.5	21.7	8.6	21.6	8.5
65 years old and over	26.6	11.1	28.7	14.4	28.5	14.0

Source: U.S. Department of Health and Human Services, Centers for Disease Control and Prevention, National Center for Health Statistics, *Health, United States, 2007*, table 44.

Notes: 'All Races' includes races not shown separately. Excludes deaths of nonresidents of the United States.
Age-adjusted rates may differ from those shown in previous editions of *Health, United States*.

Units: Rate is the number of deaths per 100,000 resident population.

Table 2.22: Death Rates for Assault (Homicide) by Sex and Age, 2000 and 2005

	Hispanic		White		All Races	
	Male	Female	Male	Female	Male	Female
2000						
All ages, age-adjusted	*11.8*	*2.8*	*5.2*	*2.1*	*9.0*	*2.8*
All ages, crude	*13.4*	*2.8*	*5.2*	*2.1*	*9.3*	*2.8*
Under 1 year	6.6	7.4	8.2	5.0	10.4	7.9
1–14 years old	1.7	1.0	1.2	0.8	1.5	1.1
15–24 years old	28.5	3.7	9.9	2.7	20.9	3.9
25–44 years old	17.2	3.7	7.4	2.9	13.3	4.0
45–64 years old	9.1	2.9	4.1	1.8	6.0	2.1
65 years old and over	4.4	2.4	2.5	1.6	3.3	1.8
2005						
All ages, age-adjusted	*12.1*	*2.4*	*5.3*	*1.9*	*9.6*	*2.5*
All ages, crude	*13.6*	*2.5*	*5.4*	*1.9*	*9.8*	*2.5*
Under 1 year	6.3	6.6	6.7	5.5	8.2	6.6
1–14 years old	1.5	1.0	1.0	0.8	1.4	1.1
15–24 years old	31.0	3.6	10.6	2.3	22.0	3.4
25–44 years old	18.0	3.4	8.0	2.8	14.9	3.7
45–64 years old	8.2	1.9	4.3	1.5	6.2	1.9
65 years old and over	4.4	*	2.2	1.6	3.0	1.7

Source: U.S. Department of Health and Human Services, Centers for Disease Control and Prevention, National Center for Health Statistics, *Health, United States, 2007*, table 45.

Notes: 'All Races' includes races not shown separately. Excludes deaths of nonresidents of the United States.
*Data is based on fewer than 20 deaths, and is not shown.
Age-adjusted rates may differ from those shown in previous editions of *Health, United States*.

Units: Rate is the number of deaths per 100,000 resident population.

Table 2.23: Death Rates for Suicide by Sex and Age, 2000 and 2005

	Hispanic		White		All Races	
	Male	Female	Male	Female	Male	Female
2000						
All ages, age-adjusted	*10.3*	*1.7*	*19.1*	*4.3*	*17.7*	*4.0*
All ages, crude	*8.4*	*1.5*	*18.8*	*4.4*	*17.1*	*4.0*
15–24 years old	10.9	2.0	17.9	3.1	17.1	3.0
25–44 years old	11.2	2.1	22.9	6.0	21.3	5.4
45–64 years old	12.0	2.5	23.2	6.9	21.3	6.2
65 years old and over	19.5	*	33.3	4.3	31.1	4.0
2005						
All ages, age-adjusted	*9.4*	*1.8*	*19.6*	*4.9*	*18.0*	*4.4*
All ages, crude	*8.3*	*1.7*	*19.7*	*5.0*	*17.7*	*4.5*
15–24 years old	12.1	2.7	17.3	3.7	16.2	3.5
25–44 years old	11.2	2.2	23.5	6.5	21.6	5.8
45–64 years old	10.7	2.1	26.6	8.1	24.0	7.2
65 years old and over	14.1	2.0	32.1	4.2	29.5	4.0

Source: U.S. Department of Health and Human Services, Centers for Disease Control and Prevention, National Center for Health Statistics, *Health, United States, 2007*, table 46.

Notes: 'All Races' includes races not shown separately. Excludes deaths of nonresidents of the United States.
*Indicates data based on fewer than 20 deaths.
Age-adjusted rates may differ from those shown in previous editions of *Health, United States*.

Units: Rate is the number of deaths per 100,000 resident population.

Table 2.24: Death Rates for Firearm-Related Injuries, 2000 and 2005

	Hispanic		White		All Races	
	Male	Female	Male	Female	Male	Female
2000						
All ages	*13.6*	*1.8*	*15.9*	*2.7*	*18.1*	*2.8*
1–14 years	1.0	NA	1.0	NA	1.1	0.3
15–24 years	30.8	2.9	19.6	2.8	29.4	3.5
25–44 years	17.3	2.5	18.0	3.9	22.0	4.2
45–64 years	12.0	2.2	17.4	3.5	17.1	3.4
65 years and over	12.2	*	28.2	2.4	26.4	2.2
2005						
All ages	*13.3*	*1.6*	*15.7*	*2.6*	*18.3*	*2.7*
1–14 years	0.7	NA	0.8	NA	1.0	0.4
15–24 years	33.0	2.6	18.2	2.3	28.7	3.0
25–44 years	18.8	2.7	17.9	3.7	23.1	3.9
45–64 years	9.1	1.2	19.0	3.6	18.3	3.3
65 years and over	9.8	*	27.1	2.3	25.1	2.1

Source: U.S. Department of Health and Human Services, Centers for Disease Control and Prevention, National Center for Health Statistics, *Health, United States, 2007*, table 47.

Notes: 'All Races' includes other races not shown separately. Excludes residents of U.S. Territories.
* Data is based on fewer than 20 deaths, and is not shown here.
NA = data not collected.
Age-adjusted rates may differ from those shown in previous editions of *Health, United States*.

Units: Death rate per 100,000 population.

Table 2.25: Death Rates for Human Immunodeficiency Virus (HIV) Infection by Sex, 1987–2005

	Hispanic		White		All Races	
	Male	Female	Male	Female	Male	Female
1987	18.8	2.1	8.7	0.6	10.4	1.1
1990	28.8	3.8	15.7	1.1	18.5	2.2
1995	40.8	8.8	20.4	2.5	27.3	5.3
1997	14.0	3.3	5.9	1.0	9.6	2.6
1998	10.2	2.8	4.5	0.8	7.6	2.2
1999	10.9	3.0	4.9	1.0	8.2	2.5
2000	10.6	2.9	4.6	1.0	7.9	2.5
2001	9.7	2.7	4.4	0.9	7.5	2.5
2002	9.1	2.6	4.3	0.9	7.4	2.5
2003	9.2	2.7	4.2	0.9	7.1	2.4
2004	8.2	2.4	3.8	0.9	6.6	2.4
2005	7.5	1.9	3.6	0.8	6.2	2.3

Source: U.S. Department of Health and Human Services, Centers for Disease Control and Prevention, National Center for Health Statistics, *Health, United States, 2007*, table 42.

Notes: 'All Races' includes races not shown separately. Data excludes residents of U.S. Territories.
Age-adjusted rates may differ from those shown in previous editions of *Health, United States*.

Units: Number of deaths per 100,000 population known to the Centers for Disease Control.

Table 2.26: AIDS (Acquired Immunodeficiency Syndrome) Cases by Sex and Age, 1985–2006

	Hispanic	White	All Races
All years*			
Children under 13 years old	1,748	1,599	9,144
Persons over 13 years old			
Male	129,540	353,945	783,786
Female	30,218	38,478	189,566
1985			
Children under 13 years old	18	26	131
Persons over 13 years old			
Male	992	4,746	7,504
Female	98	143	524
1990			
Children under 13 years old	169	157	725
Persons over 13 years old			
Male	4,743	20,825	36,179
Female	726	1,228	4,544
1995			
Children under 13 years old	135	117	745
Persons over 13 years old			
Male	9,111	26,028	56,689
Female	2,236	3,042	12,978
2000			
Children under 13 years old	30	32	189
Persons over 13 years old			
Male	5,275	11,314	30,135
Female	1,462	1,859	9,958
2001			
Children under 13 years old	26	30	170
Persons over 13 years old			
Male	5,318	11,054	30,663
Female	1,543	1,993	10,617

(continued on next page)

Hispanic Americans: A Statistical Sourcebook 2009

Table 2.26: AIDS (Acquired Immunodeficiency Syndrome) Cases by Sex and Age, 1985–2006

	Hispanic	White	All Races
2002			
Children under 13 years old	18	14	106
Persons over 13 years old			
Male	5,269	9,523	28,067
Female	1,424	1,696	9,959
2003			
Children under 13 years old	10	12	70
Persons over 13 years old			
Male	5,511	9,363	28,079
Female	1,581	1,573	10,389
2004			
Children under 13 years old	9	7	53
Persons over 13 years old			
Male	5,330	9,347	27,532
Female	1,432	1,711	10,141
2005			
Children under 13 years old	8	4	53
Persons over 13 years old			
Male	5,305	9,120	26,787
Female	1,509	1,552	9,713
2006			
Children under 13 years old	3	4	53
Persons over 13 years old			
Male	5,388	9,267	26,989
Female	1,516	1,659	9,801

Source: U.S. Department of Health and Human Services, National Center for Health Statistics, *Health, United States, 2008*, table 51.

Notes: 'All Races' includes other races not shown separately.
'White' excludes white Hispanics.
Data excludes residents of U.S. Territories.
Historic data is revised continually on an ongoing basis.
*'All years' includes cases prior to 1985. Data for all years has been updated through June 30, 2007 to include temporarily delayed case reports and may differ from previous editions of *Health, United States*.

Units: Number of cases known to the Centers for Disease Control.

Table 2.27: Estimated Number of AIDS (Acquired Immunodefiency Syndrome) Cases by Transmission Category, 2000–2006

	Hispanic	White	All cases
Cumulative			
All transmission categories	*177,163*	*375,154*	*944,306*
Adults and Adolescents	175,035	373,542	NA
Male adult or adolescent	140,923	337,771	NA
Male-to-male sexual contact	66,390	256,079	NA
Injection drug use	48,938	33,906	NA
Male-to-male sexual contact and injection drug use	10,774	30,624	NA
High-risk heterosexual contact	13,249	9,344	NA
Female adult or adolescent	34,112	35,770	NA
Injection drug use	13,579	15,566	NA
High-risk heterosexual contact	19,611	17,888	NA
Children under 13	2,128	1,612	NA
Perinatal	1,989	1,253	NA
2000			
All transmission categories	*7,957*	*11,378*	*39,513*
Adults and Adolescents	7,939	11,367	NA
Male adult or adolescent	6,090	9,669	NA
Male-to-male sexual contact	2,887	6,955	NA
Injection drug use	1,838	1,243	NA
Male-to-male sexual contact and injection drug use	422	820	NA
High-risk heterosexual contact	888	522	NA
Female adult or adolescent	1,849	1,698	NA
Injection drug use	614	696	NA
High-risk heterosexual contact	1,195	961	NA
Children under 13	18	11	NA
Perinatal	18	11	NA

(continued on next page)

Table 2.27: Estimated Number of AIDS (Acquired Immunodefiency Syndrome) Cases by Transmission Category, 2000–2006

	Hispanic	White	All cases
2002			
All transmission categories	7,907	11,604	40,267
Adults and Adolescents	7,886	11,589	NA
Male adult or adolescent	6,156	9,869	NA
Male-to-male sexual contact	3,161	7,115	NA
Injection drug use	1,584	1,203	NA
Male-to-male sexual contact and injection drug use	342	813	NA
High-risk heterosexual contact	1,017	635	NA
Female adult or adolescent	1,730	1,720	NA
Injection drug use	462	654	NA
High-risk heterosexual contact	1,227	1,026	NA
Children under 13	21	14	NA
Perinatal	19	14	NA
2006			
All transmission categories	*7,732*	*10,978*	*37,852*
Adults and Adolescents	7,728	10,974	NA
Male adult or adolescent	5,957	9,307	NA
Male-to-male sexual contact	3,337	6,691	NA
Injection drug use	1,211	1,020	NA
Male-to-male sexual contact and injection drug use	357	750	NA
High-risk heterosexual contact	1,001	776	NA
Female adult or adolescent	1,771	1,667	NA
Injection drug use	439	561	NA
High-risk heterosexual contact	1,281	1,075	NA
Children under 13	3	4	NA
Perinatal	3	4	NA

Source: U.S. Department of Health and Human Services, Centers for Disease Control, *Cases of HIV Infection and AIDS in the United States, by Race/Ethnicity, 2000–2004*, table 4.

Notes: 'Cumulative' includes all cases with a diagnosis of AIDS since the beginning of the epidemic.

'High-risk heterosexual contact' includes heterosexual contact with a person who is HIV-positive, a male who engages in sex with other males, a person who injects drugs, has hemophelia or another coagulation disorder, or is a transplant or transfusion recipient.

'Other' includes hemophilia, blood transfusions, perinatal exposure (for adults), and other factors not identified.

Totals are based on estimates, and may not equal the sum of the subroups.

Units: Estimated cases of AIDS.

Table 2.28: Cancer Incidence Rates, Selected Cancer Sites, by Sex, 1990, 2000, and 2005

	Hispanic		White		All Races	
	Male	**Female**	**Male**	**Female**	**Male**	**Female**
1990						
All sites	414.9	318.3	590.5	421.0	583.7	410.9
Lung/bronchus	59.2	25.8	94.2	48.4	95.0	47.2
Colon/rectum	47.5	34.2	72.9	49.8	72.2	50.2
Oral cavity/pharynx	10.8	3.9	17.9	7.4	18.5	7.3
Stomach	20.2	10.8	12.8	5.7	14.6	6.7
Pancreas	10.7	9.8	12.7	9.8	13.0	10.0
Urinary bladder	21.9	5.7	40.7	9.9	37.2	9.5
Non-Hodgkin's lymphoma	17.4	13.3	23.7	15.4	22.6	14.5
Leukemia	12.0	8.4	17.9	10.2	17.1	9.8
Prostate	118.1	NA	168.3	NA	166.7	NA
Breast	NA	88.2	NA	134.2	NA	129.2
Cervix uteri	NA	21.3	NA	11.2	NA	11.9
Corpus uteri	NA	17.3	NA	26.0	NA	24.2
Ovary	NA	12.2	NA	16.4	NA	15.5
2000						
All sites	425.0	310.3	565.7	428.6	560.5	411.1
Lung/bronchus	44.3	23.7	76.3	50.8	77.5	48.5
Colon/rectum	49.1	32.9	62.2	45.5	62.4	45.9
Oral cavity/pharynx	8.9	3.6	15.6	6.2	15.7	6.2
Stomach	16.1	10.7	10.7	5.0	12.5	6.1
Pancreas	12.1	9.0	12.6	9.6	12.8	9.8
Urinary bladder	19.7	5.6	40.7	9.9	36.7	9.0
Non-Hodgkin's lymphoma	20.0	13.2	24.7	16.8	23.4	15.8
Leukemia	12.5	7.5	17.3	10.6	16.3	9.9
Prostate	145.5	NA	173.0	NA	177.0	NA
Breast	NA	93.6	NA	140.6	NA	133.5
Cervix uteri	NA	17.0	NA	8.9	NA	8.8
Corpus uteri	NA	14.9	NA	25.2	NA	23.3
Ovary	NA	10.7	NA	15.0	NA	14.1

(continued on next page)

Table 2.28: Cancer Incidence Rates, Selected Cancer Sites, by Sex, 1990, 2000, and 2005

	Hispanic		White		All Races	
	Male	**Female**	**Male**	**Female**	**Male**	**Female**
2005						
All sites	390.1	309.2	517.2	411.5	510.1	396.7
Lung/bronchus	39.7	20.7	68.1	50.2	68.7	48.3
Colon/rectum	43.3	31.3	52.5	39.4	52.8	40.3
Oral cavity/pharynx	9.1	3.4	14.7	5.8	14.4	6.0
Stomach	14.4	9.7	9.3	4.5	11.0	5.5
Pancreas	11.4	10.3	12.8	10.1	13.0	10.3
Urinary bladder	18.4	5.6	39.2	9.4	35.5	8.8
Non-Hodgkin's lymphoma	18.3	13.9	24.7	17.0	23.6	15.9
Leukemia	11.7	7.7	16.2	9.5	15.1	9.0
Prostate	122.2	NA	142.1	NA	147.1	NA
Breast	NA	89.7	NA	126.8	NA	121.5
Cervix uteri	NA	13.5	NA	7.6	NA	7.7
Corpus uteri	NA	18.3	NA	24.4	NA	23.1
Ovary	NA	11.1	NA	13.3	NA	12.6

Source: U.S. Department of Health and Human Services, National Center for Health Statistics, *Health, United States, 2008,* table 52.

Notes: 'All Races' includes races not shown separately.

Units: Number of new cases per 100,000 population.

Table 2.29: Sexual Contact for People Ages 15–44, by Sex and Number of Lifetime Partners, 2002

	Hispanic		White		All Races	
	Male	**Female**	**Male**	**Female**	**Male**	**Female**
Total people	*10,188*	*9,107*	*38,738*	*39,498*	*61,147*	*61,561*
By Number of Partners						
Any partners	*91.8%*	*89.5%*	*90.3%*	*92.1%*	*90.3%*	*91.4%*
1	13.7	34.6	13.4	21.0	12.8	22.5
2	8.6	14.9	8.3	10.6	8.1	10.8
3–6	32.8	27.2	27.1	32.1	27.5	32.6
7–14	18.6	8.2	19.2	18.2	19.3	16.3
More than 15	18.1	4.6	22.3	10.2	22.6	9.2
Median number of partners	4.5	1.7	5.3	3.6	5.4	3.3

Source: U.S. Census Bureau, *Statistical Abstract of the United States: 2008*, table 91.

Notes: Includes opposite-sex partners only. Same-sex contact was assessed using different questions, and results are not shown here.
Median number of partners excludes people who have have had no opposite-sex partners.
'All Races' includes races not shown here. 'White' excludes Hispanics, who may be of any race.

Units: Number of people age 15–44 in thousands; percent of total; median number of sexual partners.

Table 2.30: Medical Injury and Poisoning Episodes, 2004 and 2007

	Hispanic	White	All Races
2004			
All persons	*40,753*	*234,601*	*288,252*
All episodes	*2,472*	*27,975*	*31,173*
Fall	991	10,524	12,030
Struck by person or object	*219	3,293	3,852
Transportation	335	2,843	3,690
Over-exertion	292	3,987	4,763
Cutting / piercing instrument	*236	2,516	2,844
Other causes	387	4,551	5,619
Poisoning	†	*261	375
2007			
All persons	*45,206*	*236,959*	*296,905*
All episodes	*2,785*	*29,483*	*34,347*
Fall	1,163	11,035	12,874
Struck by person or object	*567	4,172	4,653
Transportation	*231	3,100	3,779
Over-exertion	*218	3,337	3,773
Cutting / piercing instrument	*261	2,706	3,050
Other causes	346	4,754	5,753
Poisoning	†	*380	*464

Source: U.S. Department of Health and Human Services, *National Health Interview Survey: Summary Health Statistics, 2004*, tables 8 and 9; *Vital and Health Statistics, 2007*, tables 8 and 9.

Notes: 'All Races' includes races not shown separately.
Based on a question in survey that asked all respondents whether they had been poisoned and/or injured seriously enough in the past 3 months to seek medical advice or treatment.
* Estimates have a relative standard error between 30 and 50 percent, and should be used with caution.
† Estimates have a relative standard error over 50 percent, and are not reported.

Units: Number of persons or incidents in thousands.

Table 2.31: Injuries by Selected Characteristics, 2004 and 2007

	Hispanic	White	All Races
2004			
All episodes	*2,472*	*27,975*	*33,173*
By Activity Engaged			
Driving	*216	1,839	2,534
Working at paid job	412	4,753	5,324
Working around house or yard	*263	4,414	4,831
Attending school	*93	791	1,069
Sports	324	4,432	5,103
Leisure activities (non-sports)	806	7,500	8,935
By Place of Occurrence			
Home, inside	560	7,218	8,567
Home, outside	515	5,772	6,701
School/childcare center	213	2,036	2,598
Hospital	†	450	554
Street or highway	466	3,481	4,449
Recreational area	339	3,638	4,003
Industrial place	*176	1,676	1,766
Service area	†	1,112	1,314

(continued on next page)

Table 2.31: Injuries by Selected Characteristics, 2004 and 2007

	Hispanic	White	All Races
2007			
All episodes	*2,785*	*29,483*	*34,347*
By Activity Engaged			
Driving	*226	1,953	2,417
Working at paid job	662	4,669	5,773
Working around house or yard	*188	3,847	4,433
Attending school	*185	619	760
Sports	*465	5,530	6,250
Leisure activities (non-sports)	646	6,987	7,815
By Place of Occurrence			
Home, inside	457	7,981	9,390
Home, outside	*381	5,188	5,826
School/childcare center	*351	1,965	2,483
Hospital	†	703	958
Street or highway	529	3,248	3,753
Recreational area	*521	4,742	5,275
Industrial place	†	1,677	2,040
Service area	*190	1,225	1,478

Source: U.S. Department of Health and Human Services, *National Health Interview Survey,*
          2004, tables 8, 11, and 13; *2007*, tables 8, 11, and 13.

Notes: 'All Races' includes other races not shown separately.
          Based on a question in survey that asked all respondents whether they had been
             poisoned and/or injured seriously enough in the past 3 months to seek medical
             advice or treatment.
          * Estimates have a relative standard error between 30 and 50 percent, and should be
             used with caution.
          † Estimates have a relative standard error over 50 percent, and are not reported.

Units: Number of persons who had a medically attended injury episode in thousands.

Table 2.32: Migraines and Pain in the Neck, Lower Back, Face, and Jaw, 2007

	Hispanic	White	All Races
Total adults	*29,857*	*180,815*	*223,181*
Migraine or severe headache	3,462	22,241	27,364
Neck pain	3,321	24,727	29,019
Lower back pain	6,851	47,523	57,070
Face or jaw pain	970	7,532	9,062
Percent of Total			
Migraine or severe headache	11.4%	12.5%	12.3%
Neck pain	12.5	13.4	13.0
Lower back pain	24.3	26.0	25.6
Face or jaw pain	3.4	4.2	4.1

Source: U.S. Department of Health and Human Services, *National Health Interview Survey: Summary Health Statistics for U.S. Adults, 2007*, tables 9 and 10.

Notes: Respondents were asked, in separate questions, whether during the past three months, they had experienced: a severe headache or migraine, meck pain, lower back pain, and facial or jaw pain.
Respondents were instructed to report only pain that had lasted a whole day or more, and not fleeting or minor aches and pains.
Respondents may have answered 'yes' to more than one question.

Units: Number of adults 18 years of age and older in thousands; percent of total.

Table 2.33: Hearing Trouble, Vision Trouble, and Absence of Teeth, 2007

	Hispanic	White	All Races
Total adults	*29,857*	*180,815*	*223,181*
Hearing trouble	2,290	29,618	33,318
Vision trouble	2,481	18,358	22,378
Absence of all natural teeth	1,404	13,997	16,997
Percent of Total			
Hearing trouble	10.8%	15.7%	14.7%
Vision trouble	9.9	9.9	9.9
Absence of all natural teeth	7.4	7.5	7.6

Source: U.S. Department of Health and Human Services, *National Health Interview Survey: Summary Health Statistics for U.S. Adults, 2007*, tables 11 and 12.

Notes: Respondents were asked, in separate questions, whether they had trouble hearing without a hearing aid, whether they had trouble seeing without glasses or contact lenses, and whether they had lost all of their upper and lower natural (permanent) teeth.
Respondents may be represented in more than one column.
Percentages are age-adjusted.

Units: Number of adults 18 years of age and older in thousands; percent of total.

Table 2.34: Limitation of Activity, 2004 and 2007

	Hispanic	White	All Races
Physical activities that are very difficult or cannot be done at all:			
2004			
Any physical difficulty	15.2%	14.5%	14.7%
Walk a quarter of a mile	7.3	6.7	7.0
Climb up to 10 steps without resting	6.9	5.0	5.3
Stand for 2 hours	9.0	8.3	8.6
Sit for 2 hours	4.1	3.1	3.1
Stoop, bend or kneel	8.9	8.4	8.5
Reach over one's head	3.5	2.4	2.4
Grasp or handle small objects	2.5	1.8	1.8
Lift or carry 10 pounds	6.4	4.0	4.3
Push or pull large objects	8.3	6.3	6.5
2007			
Any physical difficulty	13.3%	14.2%	14.5%
Walk a quarter of a mile	6.7	6.9	7.2
Climb up to 10 steps without resting	5.6	5.0	5.4
Stand for 2 hours	7.9	8.2	8.5
Sit for 2 hours	3.4	3.1	3.1
Stoop, bend or kneel	7.8	8.6	8.8
Reach over one's head	3.1	2.3	2.4
Grasp or handle small objects	1.9	1.6	1.6
Lift or carry 10 pounds	4.8	3.6	3.9
Push or pull large objects	7.0	5.9	6.2

Source: U.S. Department of Health and Human Services, *National Health Interview Survey: Summary Health Statistics for U.S. Adults, 2004*, table 19; *2007*, table 19.

Notes: 'All Races' includes other races not shown separately.
Heavy object is defined as something as heavy as 10 pounds (such as a full bag of groceries).

Units: Percent of the population of 18 years of age and over.

Table 2.35: Selected Characteristics of Persons With a Work Disability, 2007

	Hispanic	White	All Races
Persons with a work disability by age:			
Total	2,247	15,097	19,963
16–24 years old	218	1,038	1,499
25–34 years old	318	1,666	2,272
35–44 years old	462	2,536	3,431
45–54 years old	593	4,372	5,748
55–64 years old	656	5,485	7,012
Work disabled as a percent of total population, by age:			
16–24 years old	3.3%	3.6%	4.0%
25–34 years old	3.9	5.4	5.7
35–44 years old	6.9	7.5	8.1
45–54 years old	12.8	12.3	13.3
55–64 years old	24.9	20.2	21.8
Percent of work disabled:			
Receiving Social Security Income	24.8%	34.9%	33.7%
Receiving Food Stamps	23.8	15.9	19.1
Covered by Medicaid	54.3	68.2	65.4
Residing in public housing	7.7	5.1	6.8
Residing in subsidized housing	5.0	2.6	3.6

Source: U.S. Bureau of the Census, *Statistical Abstract of the United States, 2009*, table 541.

Notes: 'All Races' includes other races not shown separately.

Covers the civilian noninstitutional population and members of the armed forces living off post or with members of their families on post.

Persons are classified as having a work disability if they (1) have a health problem or disability which prevents them from or which limits the kind or amount of work they can do; (2) have a service disability or ever retired or left a job for health reasons; (3) did not work in survey reference week or previous year because of long-term illness or disability; or, (4) are under age 65 and are covered by Medicare or receive Supplemental Security Income.

Units: Persons with a work disability in thousands of persons; work disabled as a percent of total population in percent; characteristics as a percent of the work disabled.

Table 2.36: Work-Loss Days, 2004–2007

	Hispanic	White	All Races
2004			
All persons	*26,798*	*178,552*	*215,191*
Bed days in the past 12 months	68,113	728,668	872,431
Days per person	2.6	4.1	4.1
All employed persons	*19,155*	*125,757*	*151,650*
Work-loss days in the past 12 months	55,596	476,176	578,319
Days per person	2.9	3.8	3.9
2005			
All persons	*27,770*	*180,477*	*217,774*
Bed days in the past 12 months	89,483	810,240	1,001,761
Days per person	3.3	4.6	4.7
All employed persons	*20,495*	*128,151*	*154,265*
Work-loss days in the past 12 months	60,798	542,535	652,984
Days per person	3.0	4.3	4.3
2006			
All persons	*28,664*	*179,456*	*220,267*
Bed days in the past 12 months	85,094	852,537	1,022,637
Days per person	3.0	4.8	4.7
All employed persons	*21,253*	*126,980*	*156,295*
Work-loss days in the past 12 months	71,034	528,519	637,465
Days per person	3.4	4.2	4.1
2007			
All persons	*21,827*	*180,815*	*223,181*
Bed days in the past 12 months	72,373	789,021	991,962
Days per person	3.4	4.5	4.5
All employed persons	*29,857*	*127,900*	*157,912*
Work-loss days in the past 12 months	106,393	502,317	627,639
Days per person	3.6	4.0	4.0

Source: U.S. Department of Health and Human Services, *National Health Interview Survey: Summary Health Statistics for U.S. Adults, 2004*, table 17; *2005*, table 17; *2006*, table 17; *2007*, table 17.

Notes: 'All Races' includes other races not shown separately.
Respondents were asked how many times in the last 12 months an injury or illness caused them to miss a day of work or had kept them in bed more than half a day.

Units: Number of persons and employed persons in thousands; average (mean) work-loss days and bed-days per person.

Table 2.37: Learning Disabilities and Attention Deficit Hyperactivity Disorder for Children Age 3 to 17, 2005 and 2006

	Hispanic	White	All Races
2005			
Total children	11,600	47,287	61,192
Learning disability	807	3,233	4,244
ADHD	533	3,123	3,998
Percent of total			
Learning disability	7.1%	6.8%	6.9%
ADHD	4.7	6.6	6.5
2006			
Total children	12,014	46,885	61,354
Learning disability	753	3,736	4,748
ADHD	602	3,553	4,545
Percent of total			
Learning disability	6.4%	8.0%	7.7%
ADHD	5.1	7.6	7.4

Source: U.S. Census Bureau, *Statistical Abstract of the United States: 2008*, table 178.
U.S. Department of Health and Human Services, Centers for Disease Control and Prevention, *National Health Interview Survey: Summary Health Statistics for U.S. Children, 2006*, table 3.

Notes: Questions measure whether children have been told by a doctor or school or health professional that they had a learning disorder or Attention Deficit Hyperactivity Disorder.

Units: Number of children age 3-17 in thousands; percent of total.

Table 2.38: Asthma in Children, 2005-2007

	Hispanic	White	All Races
2005			
Total children under 18	*14,423*	*56,761*	*73,376*
Ever told they had asthma	1,780	6,558	9,287
Still have asthma	1,237	4,519	6,531
Percent of total			
Ever told they had asthma	12.6%	11.6%	12.7%
Still have asthma	8.7	8.0	8.9
2006			
Total children under 18	*14,815*	*55,881*	*73,493*
Ever told they had asthma	1,901	7,100	9,876
Still have asthma	1,328	4,816	6,819
Percent of total			
Ever told they had asthma	13.2%	12.8%	13.6%
Still have asthma	9.2	8.7	9.4
2007			
Total children under 18	*15,350*	*55,646*	*73,728*
Ever told they had asthma	1,937	6,278	9,605
Still have asthma	1,422	4,263	6,703
Percent of total			
Ever told they had asthma	12.9%	11.3%	13.1%
Still have asthma	9.4	7.7	9.7

Source: U.S. Department of Health and Human Services, *National Health Interview Survey: Summary Health Statistics for U.S. Children, 2005*, table 1; *2006*, table 1; *2007*, table 1.

Notes: Respondents were asked if their child has ever been diagnosed with asthma by a doctor or other health professional, and if the child still has asthma.

Units: Number of children under 18 years old in thousands; percent of total.

Table 2.39: Obese, Overweight, and Underweight Adults, 2006 and 2007

	Hispanic	White	All Races
2006			
Total number	*28,664*	*179,456*	*220,267*
Obese	7,244	43,311	54,050
Overweight	10,678	60,240	73,285
Healthy weight	8,986	64,196	78,705
Underweight	278	2,763	3,618
Frequency			
Obese	27.4%	25.1%	25.5%
Overweight	39.6	35.1	34.9
Healthy weight	32.0	38.2	37.9
Underweight	1.0	1.7	1.8
2007			
Total number	*29,857*	*180,815*	*223,181*
Obese	7,843	43,935	55,382
Overweight	11,117	61,191	74,625
Healthy weight	8,782	63,142	77,605
Underweight	416	3,011	3,923
Frequency			
Obese	27.5%	25.4%	25.9%
Overweight	40.3	35.4	35.1
Healthy weight	30.8	37.4	37.1
Underweight	1.5	1.8	1.9

Source: U.S. Department of Health and Human Services, National Health Interview Survey: Summary Health Statistics for U.S. Adults, 2005, tables 30 and 31; 2006, tables 30 and 31; 2007, tables 30 and 31.

Notes: Weight categories are measured using the Body Mass Index (BMI), based on weight and height.
'Overweight' is indicated by a BMI of greater than or equal to 25.0 and less than 30.0.
'Obese' is indicated by at BMI over 30.0.
'Healthy weight' is indicated by a BMI between 18.5 and 25.0.
'Underweight' is indicated by a BMI less than 18.5.
'All Races' includes other races not shown separately.

Units: Number of adults over 18 in thousands; percent of total adults.

Table 2.40: Overweight, Obesity, and Healthy Weight Among Adults 20 Years of Age or Older, 1988–1994, 2001–2004, and 2003–2006

	Mexican		White		All Races	
	Male	Female	Male	Female	Male	Female
1988–1994						
Overweight	69.4%	69.6%	61.6%	47.2%	61.0%	51.2%
Obese	24.4	36.1	20.7	23.3	20.6	36.0
Healthy Weight	29.8	29.0	37.4	49.2	37.9	45.3
2001–2004						
Overweight	75.8%	73.2%	71.1%	57.1%	70.7%	61.4%
Obese	30.5	40.3	31.0	31.5	30.2	34.0
Healthy Weight	24.2	26.3	27.8	40.2	28.1	36.2
2003–2006						
Overweight	75.8%	73.9%	71.8%	57.9%	72.1%	61.3%
Obese	29.5	41.8	32.4	31.6	32.4	34.3
Healthy Weight	23.8	25.1	26.8	39.6	26.6	36.5

Source: U.S. Department of Health and Human Services, National Center for Health Statistics, *Health, United States, 2006*, table 73; *2007*, table 75.

Notes: Weight categories are measured using the Body Mass Index (BMI), based on weight and height.
'Overweight' is indicated by a BMI of greater than or equal to 25.0 and less than 30.0.
'Obese' is indicated by at BMI over 30.0.
'Healthy weight' is indicated by a BMI between 18.5 and 25.0. '
All Races' includes other races not shown separately.

Units: Percent of total adults over age 20 in the U.S.

Table 2.41: Overweight Children and Adolescents 6 to 19 Years of Age, 1976–1980, 1988–1994, 2001–2004, and 2003–2006

	Mexican		White		All Races	
	Boys	**Girls**	**Boys**	**Girls**	**Boys**	**Girls**
1976–1980						
6–11 years of age	13.3%	9.8%	6.1%	5.2%	6.6%	6.4%
12–19 years of age	7.7	8.8	3.8	4.6	4.8	5.3
1988–1994						
6–11 years of age	11.0%	15.3%	10.7%	*9.8%	11.6%	11.0%
12–19 years of age	14.1	*13.4	11.6	8.9	11.3	9.7
2001–2004						
6–11 years of age	25.6%	16.6%	16.9%	15.6%	18.7%	16.3%
12–19 years of age	20.0	17.1	17.9	14.6	17.9	16.0
2003–2006						
6–11 years of age	27.5%	19.7%	15.5%	14.4%	18.0%	15.8%
12–19 years of age	22.1	19.9	17.3	14.5	18.2	16.8

Source: U.S. Department of Health and Human Services, National Center for Health Statistics, *Health, United States, 2006*, table 74; *2007*, table 76.

Notes: 'Overweight' is defined as a Body Mass Index (BMI) at or above the sex- and age-specific 95th percentile, based on 2000 CDC growth charts.
* Estimate has a relative standard error between 20 and 30 percent and is considered unreliable.

Units: Percent of total children and adolescents in U.S.

Table 2.42: Leisure-Time Physical Exercise by Frequency, 2006 and 2007

	Hispanic	White	All Races
2006			
Total adults	*28,664*	*179,456*	*220,267*
Frequency of vigorous leisure-time physical activity per week:			
Never	71.9%	60.7%	61.7%
Less than 1	1.7	2.7	2.6
1 or 2	8.7	11.9	11.6
3 or 4	9.7	13.4	13.1
5 or more	8.0	11.3	11.0
2007			
Total adults	*29,857*	*180,815*	*223,181*
Frequency of vigorous leisure-time physical activity per week:			
Never	71.8%	60.0%	61.3%
Less than 1	2.1	2.8	2.8
1 or 2	8.0	12.0	11.6
3 or 4	9.2	13.3	12.9
5 or more	8.9	11.9	11.4

Source: U.S. Department of Health and Human Services, *National Health Interview Survey: Summary Health Statistics for U.S. Adults, 2005*, tables 28 and 29; *2006*, tables 28 and 29; *2007*, tables 28 and 29.

Notes: Activity is defined as vigorous activity lasting at least 10 minutes that causes heavy sweating and large increases in breathing or heart rates.
'All races' includes races not shown separately.

Units: Thousands of adults age 18 or over, percent of total adults.

Table 2.43: Percent of Adults Engaging in Leisure-Time Physical Activity, Selected Years 1997–2005

	Hispanic	White	All Races
1997			
No participation in physical activity	36.6%	27.6%	29.5%
Participates in regular, sustained activity	17.1	20.3	19.6
Participates in regular, vigorous activity	8.6	14.0	12.9
1998			
No participation in physical activity	38.4%	26.7%	28.7%
Participates in regular, sustained activity	17.4	21.6	20.8
Participates in regular, vigorous activity	11.4	14.0	13.6
2000			
Persons who are physically inactive	41.0%	24.2%	27.6%
Persons with insufficient activity	37.9	48.3	46.2
Persons who meet recommended activity	21.1	27.5	26.2
2003			
Persons who are physically inactive	36.0%	20.9%	24.3%
Persons not meeting recommended activity	62.5	51.0	54.0
Persons who meet recommended activity	37.5	49.0	46.0
2005			
Persons who are physically inactive	37.4%	21.4%	25.1%
Persons not meeting recommended activity	57.9	49.1	51.7
Persons who meet recommended activity	42.1	50.9	48.3

Source: U.S. Bureau of the Census, *Statistical Abstract of the United States, 1999*, table 248; *2000*, table 232; *2002*, table 191; *2004*, table 195; *2008*, table 200.

Notes: 'All Races' includes races not shown separately.
'Recommended activity' is physical activity at least 30 minutes of activity 5 times per week, or 20 minutes of vigorous activity 3 times per week. 'Regular, sustained activity' is any type or intensity of activity that occurs 5 or more times per week and 30 minutes or more per occasion. 'Regular, vigorous activity' is rhythmic contraction of large muscle groups performed 3 times per week or more for at least 20 minutes per occasion.

Units: Percent of persons 18 years of age and over.

Table 2.44: Smoking and Alcohol Consumption among Adults, 2007

	Hispanic	White	All Races
Total adults	*29,857*	*180,815*	*223,181*
Smoking			
All current smokers	12.8%	20.3%	19.7%
Everyday smokers	7.7	15.9	15.3
Some day smokers	5.1	4.5	4.4
Former smokers	16.1	22.6	21.2
Non-smokers	71.0	57.0	59.1
Alcohol			
Lifetime abstainer	35.5%	21.1%	24.0%
Former infrequent	7.9	8.0	8.3
Former regular	5.6	6.4	6.3
Current infrequent	12.5	12.4	12.4
Current regular	38.0	51.6	48.6

Source: U.S. Department of Health and Human Services, *National Health Interview Survey: Summary Health Statistics for U.S. Adults, 2007*, tables 24–27.

Notes: 'Current smokers' have smoked at least 100 cigarettes in their lifetime and curently smoke.
'Everyday smokers' are current smokers who smoke every day.
'Some day smokers' are current smokers who smoke on some days.
'Former smokers' have smoked at least 100 cigarettes in their lifetime, but currently do not smoke at all.
'Non-smokers' have smoked fewer than 100 cigarettes in their lifetime.
'Lifetime abstainers' have had fewer than 12 drinks in their lifetime.
'Former drinkers' have had at least 12 drinks in any one year and no drinks in the last year.
'Current infrequent drinkers' have had at least 12 drinks in their lifetime and fewer than 12 drinks in the past year.
'Current regular drinkers' have had at least 12 drinks in the past year.
Drinkers whose frequency or amount of drinking was not known are not included.

Units: Thousands of adults 18 years or age and over; percent of total adults.

Table 2.45: Current Cigarette Smoking Among Adults by Sex, 1990–1992, 1995–1998 and 2004–2006

	Hispanic		White		All Races	
	Male	Female	Male	Female	Male	Female
1990–1992	25.7%	15.8%	27.4%	24.3%	27.9%	23.7%
1995–1998	24.4	13.7	26.4	22.9	26.5	22.1
2004–2006	19.0	10.5	23.3	19.1	23.3	18.4

Source: U.S. Department of Health and Human Services, National Center for Health Statistics, *Health, United States, 2008*, table 65.

Notes: All rates are age-adjusted.
Data prior to 1997 is not strictly comparable to later data due to survey redesign.

Units: Percent of persons 18 years or older who are current cigarette smokers.

Table 2.46: Use of Selected Substances by Persons 12 Years and Older, 2000 and 2006

	Hispanic	White	All Races
2000			
Any illicit drug	5.3%	6.4%	6.3%
Marijuana	3.6	4.9	4.8
Psychotherapeutic drug	1.7	1.8	1.7
Alcohol	39.8	50.7	46.6
Binge alcohol	22.7	21.2	20.6
Any tobacco	22.2	31.0	29.3
Cigarettes	20.7	25.9	24.9
Cigars	3.5	5.0	4.8
2006			
Any illicit drug	*6.9%*	*8.5%*	*8.3%*
Marijuana	4.1	6.4	6.0
Psychotherapeutic drug	2.9	3.0	2.8
Alcohol	41.8	55.8	50.9
Binge alcohol	23.9	24.1	23.0
Any tobacco	24.4	31.4	29.6
Cigarettes	22.4	26.1	25.0
Cigars	4.8	5.7	5.6

Source: U.S. Department of Health and Human Services, National Center for Health Statistics, *Health, United States, 2003*, tables 62 and 63; *2008*, table 66.

Notes: Data is based on household interviews with a sample of the civilian noninstitutionalized population. '
All Races' includes races not shown separately.
'White' excludes Hispanic persons.
Use of selected substances in the past month by person 12 years of age and over.
'Any illicit drug' includes marijuana/hashish, cocaine, heroin, hallucinogens, or any psychotherapeutic drug for nonmedical use.
'Psychotherapeutic drug' includes non-medical use of prescription-type pain relievers, tranquilizers, stimulants, or sedatives; does not include over-the-counter drugs.
'Binge Alcohol' refers to consuming five or more drinks on the same occasion at least once in the past month.

Units: Percent of population using selected substance.

Table 2.47: Feelings of Emotional Distress in Adults, 2007

	Hispanic	White	All Races
Sadness			
All or most of the time	4.9%	2.6%	2.8%
Some of the time	7.5	6.8	7.0
Hopelessness			
All or most of the time	3.1%	2.0%	1.9%
Some of the time	4.3	3.6	3.7
Worthlessness			
All or most of the time	2.6%	1.8%	1.7%
Some of the time	2.6	2.9	3.0
Everything is an effort			
All or most of the time	4.8%	4.4%	4.8%
Some of the time	6.2	7.7	7.7
Nervousness			
All or most of the time	4.5%	3.8%	3.7%
Some of the time	7.8	9.9	9.6
Restlessness			
All or most of the time	5.1%	5.1%	4.8%
Some of the time	7.4	10.5	10.2

Source: U.S. Department of Health and Human Services, *National Health Interview Survey: Summary Health Statistics for U.S. Adults, 2007*, tables 14 and 16.

Notes: Respondents were asked, in separate questions, how often in the past 30 days they felt: so sad that nothing could cheer them up, hopeless, worthless, that everything was an effort, nervous, or restless. Respondents could choose from among five response categories: 'all of the time,' 'most of the time,' 'some of the time,' 'a little of the time,' or 'none of the time.' Here, 'all' and 'most' are combined, and 'some' is shown separately.

Units: Percent of adults 18 years of age or older.

Table 2.48: Suicidal Ideation and Suicide Attempts Among High School Students by Sex, 1991–2007

	Hispanic		White		All Races	
	Male	Female	Male	Female	Male	Female
Seriously considered suicide						
1991	18.0%	34.6%	21.7%	38.6%	20.8%	37.2%
1993	17.9	34.1	19.1	29.7	18.8	29.6
1995	15.7	34.1	19.1	31.6	18.3	30.4
1997	17.1	30.3	14.4	26.1	15.1	27.1
1999	13.6	26.1	12.5	23.2	13.7	24.9
2001	12.2	26.5	14.9	24.2	14.2	23.6
2003	12.9	23.4	12.0	21.2	12.8	21.3
2005	11.9	24.2	12.4	21.5	12.0	21.8
2007	10.7	21.1	10.2	17.8	10.3	18.7
Attempted suicide						
1991	3.7%	11.6%	3.3%	10.4%	3.9%	10.7%
1993	7.4	19.7	4.4	11.3	5.0	12.5
1995	5.8	21.0	5.2	10.4	5.6	11.9
1997	7.2	14.9	3.2	10.3	4.5	11.6
1999	6.6	18.9	4.5	9.0	5.7	10.9
2001	8.0	15.9	5.3	10.3	6.2	11.2
2003	6.1	15.0	3.7	10.3	5.4	11.5
2005	7.8	14.9	5.2	9.3	6.0	10.8
2007	6.3	14.0	3.4	7.7	4.6	9.3
Suicide attempt requiring medical attention						
1991	0.5%	2.7%	1.0%	2.3%	1.0%	2.5%
1993	2.0	5.5	1.4	3.6	1.6	3.8
1995	2.9	6.6	2.1	2.9	2.2	3.4
1997	2.1	3.8	1.5	2.6	2.0	3.3
1999	1.4	4.6	1.6	2.3	2.1	3.1
2001	2.5	4.2	1.7	2.9	2.1	3.1
2003	4.2	5.7	1.1	2.4	2.4	3.2
2005	2.8	3.7	1.5	2.7	1.8	2.9
2007	1.8	3.9	0.9	2.1	1.5	2.4

Source: U.S. Department of Health and Human Services, *Health, United States, 2008*, table 62.

Notes: 'White' excludes White Hispanics.
Responses are for the 12 months preceding the survey.

Units: Percent of students in grades 9–12.

Table 2.49: People Lacking Health Insurance Coverage, 2000–2006

	Hispanic	White	Total
2000			
All people	32.0%	12.9%	14.0%
Children under 18	24.9	10.9	11.6
2001			
All people	33.2%	13.6%	14.6%
Children under 18	24.1	11.0	11.7
2002			
All people	32.4%	14.2%	15.2%
Children under 18	22.7	11.1	11.6
2003			
All people	32.7%	14.6%	15.6%
Children under 18	21.0	7.4	11.4
2004			
All people	32.7%	14.9%	15.7%
Children under 18	21.1	7.6	11.2
2005			
All people	32.7%	15.0%	15.9%
Children under 18	21.9	7.2	11.2
2006			
All people	34.1%	14.9%	15.8%
Children under 18	22.1	7.3	11.7

Source: U.S. Bureau of the Census, Current Population Reports, *Income, Poverty, and Health Insurance Coverage in the United States: 2003*, table 5 and figure 7; *2004*, table 7 and figure 7; *2005*, table C-1 and figure 8; *2006*, tables C-1 and C2, and figure 8.
U.S. Bureau of the Census, Current Population Reports, *Health Insurance Coverage: 2000*, figures 2 and 4; *2001*, figures 2 and 4; *2002*, figures 2 and 4.

Notes: 'Total' includes races and ethnic groups not shown separately. 'White' as shown is equivalent to 'White Alone.' People identifying as 'Hispanic' can be of any race.
Figures may have been adjusted since their initial publication, and may not match current estimates.

Units: Percent of all people, and children under 18, not covered by government or private health insurance.

Table 2.50: Health Care Coverage for Persons Under 65 Years of Age by Type of Coverage, 1995 and 2000–2004

	Hispanic	White	All Races
1995			
Private insurance	46.4%	74.5%	71.3%
Obtained through workplace	43.4	68.4	65.4
Medicaid or other public assistance	21.9	8.9	11.5
No health insurance coverage	31.4	15.5	16.1
2000			
Private insurance	47.8%	75.7%	71.5%
Obtained through workplace	45.0	70.6	66.7
Medicaid or other public assistance	15.5	7.1	9.5
No health insurance coverage	35.6	15.4	17.0
2001			
Private insurance	46.1%	75.1%	71.2%
Obtained through workplace	43.8	70.2	66.7
Medicaid or other public assistance	17.5	8.0	10.4
No health insurance coverage	35.0	14.9	16.4
2002			
Private insurance	44.4%	73.4%	69.4%
Obtained through workplace	41.9	68.7	65.0
Medicaid or other public assistance	20.8	9.3	11.8
No health insurance coverage	33.9	15.5	16.8

(continued on next page)

Table 2.50: Health Care Coverage for Persons Under 65 Years of Age by Type of Coverage, 1995 and 2000–2004

	Hispanic	White	All Races
2003			
Private insurance	41.9%	71.5%	68.9%
Obtained through workplace	38.9	65.6	63.3
Medicaid or other public assistance	21.8	10.4	12.3
No health insurance coverage	34.7	16.0	16.5
2004			
Private insurance	41.7%	71.4%	68.8%
Obtained through workplace	39.0	65.8	63.5
Medicaid or other public assistance	22.5	10.4	12.5
No health insurance coverage	34.4	16.1	16.4

Source : U.S. Department of Health and Human Services, Centers for Disease Control and Prevention, National Center for Health Statistics, *Health, United States, 2006*, tables 133-135.

Notes: 'All Races' includes other races not shown separately.
'Medicaid' includes persons receiving AFDC (Aid to Families with Dependent Children) or SSI (Supplemental Security Income), or those with a current Medicaid card.
Data is age-adjusted. The questionnaire changed in 1997 compared with previous years. Beginning in quarter 3 of the 2004 NHIS, persons under 65 years with no reported coverage were asked explicitly about Medicaid coverage. Estimates shown here were calculated with this additional information.

Units: Percent of the population under 65 years of age.

Table 2.51: Health Care Coverage for Persons 65 Years of Age and Over by Type of Coverage, 1992–2006

	Hispanic	White	All Races
1992			
Employer-sponsored plan	20.7%	45.9%	42.8%
Medicare HMO	*	3.6	3.9
Medicaid	39.0	5.6	9.4
Medigap	15.8	37.2	33.9
Other	18.3	7.7	9.9
1995			
Employer-sponsored plan	16.9%	41.3%	38.6%
Medicare HMO	15.5	8.4	8.9
Medicaid	40.5	5.4	9.6
Medigap	10.1	36.2	32.5
Other	17.1	8.7	10.5
2000			
Employer-sponsored plan	15.8%	38.6%	35.2%
Medicare HMO	27.5	18.4	19.3
Medicaid	28.7	5.1	9.0
Medigap	11.3	28.3	25.0
Other	16.7	9.6	11.5
2006			
Employer-sponsored plan	17.1%	37.1%	34.1%
Medicare HMO	37.0	17.2	19.2
Medicaid	23.4	5.9	9.4
Medigap	8.9	26.7	23.5
Other	13.6	13.1	13.9

Source: U.S. Department of Health and Human Services, *Health United States, 2008*, table 141.

Notes: 'All Races' includes races not shown separately.
Medicare HMO enrollees are listed regardless of other insurance.
Medicaid enrollees exclude those also enrolled in a Medicare HMO.
'Medigap' includes supplemental insurance plans purchased privately or through organizations such as AARP or professional organizations.
'Other' includes Medicare fee-for-service only or other public plans besides Medicaid.
Data is age-adjusted.
The questionnaire changed in 1997 compared with previous years.
* Sample size is 50 or lower.

Units: Percent of the population.

Table 2.52: Number of Health Care Visits in the Past 12 Months, 2003–2006

	Hispanic	White	All Races
2003			
None	25.3%	15.7%	15.8%
1–3 visits	42.9	45.6	45.8
4–9 visits	20.3	25.1	24.8
10 or more visits	11.5	13.6	13.6
2004			
None	26.7%	16.0%	16.1%
1–3 visits	41.8	45.4	45.8
4–9 visits	20.6	24.8	24.6
10 or more visits	10.9	13.8	13.5
2005			
None	24.0%	15.2%	15.6%
1–3 visits	42.4	46.0	46.2
4–9 visits	21.7	24.9	24.6
10 or more visits	11.9	14.0	13.7
2006			
None	27.1%	17.2%	17.2%
1–3 visits	43.0	46.2	46.9
4–9 visits	19.6	23.4	23.1
10 or more visits	10.3	13.2	12.7

Source: U.S. Department of Health and Human Services, *Health United States, 2002*, table 72; *2006*, table 80; *2007*, table 82; *2008*, table 83.

Notes: 'All Places' includes visits to physician offices and hospital outpatient and emergency departments.
'Health care visits' includes ambulatory and home health care visits during a 12-month period.

Units: Percent of persons visiting doctor's offices, emergency departments, and home visit within 12 months.

Table 2.53: Dental Visits in the Past Year
by Age and Poverty Status, 2000 and 2006

	Hispanic	White	All Races
2000			
Poor			
Age 2 and older	41.3%	52.0%	47.6%
2-17 years	53.9	63.0	61.8
18-64 years	38.1	52.1	46.7
65 years and older	31.4	34.4	30.3
Non-Poor			
Age 2 and older	62.5%	75.0%	73.1%
2-17 years	69.1	82.5	80.1
18-64 years	61.3	73.8	72.0
65 years and older	54.3	68.3	66.7
2006			
Poor			
Age 2 and older	46.6%	55.1%	51.5%
2-17 years	63.1	71.6	67.5
18-64 years	36.7	50.6	44.8
65 years and older	29.7	41.4	36.9
Non-Poor			
Age 2 and older	60.5%	73.4%	71.7%
2-17 years	72.9	83.3	81.5
18-64 years	56.1	71.7	69.6
65 years and older	59.5	68.1	67.3

Source: U.S. Department of Health and Human Services, *Health United States, 2002*, table 80; *2008*, table 96.

Notes: 'All Races' includes races not shown separately.
'White' excludes White Hispanics.
Data excludes residents of U.S. Territories.
'Poor' persons are defined as below the poverty threshold.
'Non-poor' persons have incomes of 200 percent or greater than the poverty threshold.

Units: Percent of persons with a dental visit in the past year.

Table 2.54: Short Stay Hospitals: Discharges, Days of Care, and Average Length of Stay, 2000–2003

	Hispanic	White	All Races
2000			
Discharges	85.5	92.2	119.8
Days of Care	350.4	354.4	557.8
Average length of stay	4.1	3.8	4.7
2001			
Discharges	100.4	93.2	121.9
Days of Care	403.8	368.6	553.6
Average length of stay	4.0	4.0	4.5
2002			
Discharges	94.9	96.4	122.9
Days of Care	377.4	342.5	541.3
Average length of stay	4.0	3.6	4.4
2003			
Discharges	95.6	93.2	119.9
Days of Care	393.5	378.3	558.9
Average length of stay	4.1	4.1	4.7

Source: U.S. Department of Health and Human Services, Centers for Disease Control and Prevention, National Center for Health Statistics, *Health, United States, 2005*, table 96.

Notes: 'All Races' includes races not shown separately.
Data is age-adjusted.

Units: Number of discharges and days of care per 1,000 population; average length of stay in days.

Table 2.55: Sources of Payment for Health Care, 1987–2005

	Hispanic		White		All Races	
	Under 65	65 and Over	Under 65	65 and Over	Under 65	65 and Over
1987						
Out of Pocket	22.0%	*13.5%	28.2%	23.7%	26.2%	22.0%
Private insurance	36.1	*4.7	50.1	16.7	46.6	15.8
Public coverage	35.8	80.2	15.9	58.0	21.3	60.8
Other	6.0	*1.6	5.8	1.6	6.0	1.5
1997						
Out of Pocket	18.8%	13.6%	21.8%	17.0%	21.1%	16.3%
Private insurance	42.3	5.9	55.8	17.9	53.1	16.5
Public coverage	28.9	77.8	15.3	62.6	18.1	64.8
Other	10.0	*2.7	7.1	2.5	7.7	2.5
2000						
Out of Pocket	20.5%	13.9%	21.7%	18.3%	20.3%	17.5%
Private insurance	45.8	8.4	55.1	15.2	52.5	14.9
Public coverage	27.5	75.6	18.0	64.1	21.3	64.7
Other	6.2	*2.2	5.2	2.4	6.0	2.9
2005						
Out of Pocket	19.1%	17.2%	20.6%	17.7%	19.6%	17.1%
Private insurance	35.9	*13.6	55.7	18.0	52.1	16.5
Public coverage	36.9	67.1	20.4	61.1	24.1	63.4
Other	8.1	*2.2	3.2	3.2	4.2	3.0

Source: U.S. Department of Health and Human Services, *Health United States, 2008*, table 132.

Notes: 'White' excludes Hispanics.
'Public coverage' includes Medicare, Medicaid, the Department of Veterans Affairs, and other federal sources.
* Estimates are considered unreliable and should be treated with caution.

Units: Percent of noninstutionalized population.

Table 2.56: Health Care Expenses by Age Group, 1987 and 2005

	Hispanic	White	All Races
1987			
Under 65 years of age			
Percent with expenses	71.0%	86.9%	83.2%
Mean annual expense	$1,613	$2,029	$2,022
Percent with prescribed medicine expense	41.6%	57.7%	54.0%
Mean annual out-of-pocket expense	$81	$118	$113
65 years old and over			
Percent with expenses	82.5%	94.9%	93.7%
Mean annual expense	$6,109	$6,316	$6,415
Percent with prescribed medicine expense	74.7%	82.3%	81.6%
Mean annual out-of-pocket expense	$465	$359	$353
2005			
Under 65 years of age			
Percent with expenses	69.3%	88.1%	82.9%
Mean annual expense	$2,200	$3,513	$3,239
Percent with prescribed medicine expense	44.2%	65.5%	59.1%
Mean annual out-of-pocket expense	$231	$358	$329
65 years old and over			
Percent with expenses	92.0%	97.3%	96.7%
Mean annual expense	$7,855	$9,178	$9,074
Percent with prescribed medicine expense	85.8%	91.9%	91.1%
Mean annual out-of-pocket expense	$810	$988	$951

Source: U.S. Department of Health and Human Services, *Health, United States, 2008*, table 131.

Notes: 'White' excludes White Hispanics.
Expenses include inpatient hospital services, physician services, prescribed medicines, home health services, dental services, and other medical equipment.
Dollar figures have been updated to 2005 dollars using the Consumer Price Index.

Units: Percent of total people by age; mean annual expenses for people with applicable expenses.

Chapter 3

Education

Chapter Three Highlights

This chapter provides statistics about education for Hispanic persons in the United States, including both the most current data available as well as comparisons of the Hispanic population over time. For almost all tables, corresponding data is provided for the total population of the United States as well as for White persons. This allows for easy comparison between groups. Because 'Hispanic' is not a race or ethnic group, we have included a table with the educational attainment of some of the ethnic groups that comprise the Hispanic designation (table 3.34).

This chapter contains enrollment statistics for students below grade 12 by age (tables 3.01 and 3.06), control of school (public or private) and family status (tables tables 3.02 and 3.03), and for nursery school and Kindergarten students (table 3.03). We have also included tables showing percentages of persons aged 3 to 34 who are enrolled in school (table 3.06), percentage distribution of enrollment in school by state (table 3.07), and percentages of students in gifted and talented programs (table 3.08).

Along with this data on enrollment, we have included enrollment status and enrollment rates of high school graduates and college students (tables 3.21 and 3.23). Also included are statistics on high school dropouts (tables 3.17 and 3.18).

This chapter also provides data on public school teachers, such as highest degree earned and years of teaching experience (tables 3.09 and 3.10).

Also included in this chapter is a variety of data on standardized test results, both for proficiency tests (tables 3.13 and 3.14) and for the SAT test (table 3.15).

Also of note are tables on degrees conferred by field of study for Associate's Degrees (table 3.27), Bachelor's Degrees (table 3.28), Master's Degrees (table 3.29), Doctoral Degrees (table 3.30), and Professional Degrees (table 3.31).

Table 3.01: School Enrollment by Age, 2007

	Enrollment			Enrollment Rate		
	Hispanic	White	All Races	Hispanic	White	All Races
All persons 3 years and over	*13,708*	*58,021*	*75,967*	*32.1%*	*25.3%*	*26.6%*
3 and 4 years old	923	3,406	4,491	48.2	54.1	54.5
5 and 6 years	1,746	5,934	7,792	94.3	94.8	94.7
7 to 9 years	2,357	8,820	11,520	96.3	98.0	98.1
10 to 13 years	3,212	12,194	16,012	99.0	98.7	98.6
14 to 15 years	1,520	6,238	8,137	98.4	98.7	98.7
16 and 17 years	1,320	6,270	8,205	90.6	94.6	94.3
18 and 19 years	870	4,325	5,566	57.2	67.1	66.8
20 and 21 years	468	3,145	3,916	32.3	50.1	48.4
22 to 24 years	415	2,542	3,375	18.8	26.3	27.3
25 to 29 years	348	1,869	2,577	8.3	11.5	12.4
30 to 34 years	179	988	1,379	4.5	6.6	7.2
35 to 44 years	219	1,239	1,617	3.2	3.7	3.8
45 to 54 years	112	806	1069	2.3	2.3	2.4
55 years and over	18	244	311	0.3	0.4	0.4

Source: U.S. Bureau of the Census, Current Population Reports, *School Enrollment: Social and Economic Characteristics of Students, October 2007*, table 1.

Notes: 'All Races' includes races not shown separately.
'White' as shown is equivalent to 'White alone.'
Hispanics may be of any race.

Units: Enrollment in thousands of persons enrolled. Rate as a percent of the civilian non-institutionalized population, by age group.

Table 3.02: School Enrollment by Control of School and Family Status, 2007

	Hispanic	White	All Races
Kindergarten, Elementary, and High School			
All families	*10,984*	*64,359*	*79,095*
Public	5,585	21,808	28,314
Private	290	2,080	2,542
Married couple families	*7,218*	*50,723*	*59,061*
Public	3,640	15,609	18,757
Private	202	1,729	2,030
Unmarried householder	*3,766*	*13,636*	*20,033*
Public	1,945	6,199	9,557
Private	88	351	511

Source: U.S. Bureau of the Census, Current Population Reports, *School Enrollment: Social and Economic Characteristics of Students, October 2007*, table 8.

Notes: 'All Races' includes races not shown separately.
'White' as shown is equivalent to 'White alone.'
Hispanics may be of any race.
'Public' is equivalent to 'Public only' and 'Private' is equivalent to 'Private only.'
Includes civilian noninstitutionalized population only.

Units: Number of families with enrolled children in thousands.

Table 3.03: Nursery School and Kindergarten Enrollment of Children 3 to 6 Years Old, 2007

	Hispanic	White	All Races
Total Children 3–6	*3,765*	*12,552*	*16,466*
Enrolled in Nursery School			
Total	905	3,545	4,628
Public	711	1,880	2,570
Private	194	1,665	2,058
Enrolled in Kindergarten			
Total	954	3,172	4,064
Public	918	2,786	3,589
Private	36	386	475
Enrolled in Elementary School			
Total	810	2,622	3,591
Public	776	2,330	3,198
Private	34	293	393

Source: U.S. Bureau of the Census, Current Population Reports, *School Enrollment: Social and Economic Characteristics of Students, October 2007*, table 3.

Notes: 'All Races' includes races not shown separately.
'White' as shown is equivalent to 'White alone.'
Hispanics may be of any race.
'Public' is equivalent to 'Public only' and 'Private' is equivalent to 'Private only.'

Units: Enrollment in thousands of children enrolled.

Table 3.04: Estimates of the School Age Population, 1980–2008

	Hispanic		White		All Races
	Number	Percent	Number	Percent	Number
1980	4,005	8.5%	35,220	74.6%	47,232
1985	4,609	10.3	32,099	71.7	44,782
1990	NA	NA	NA	NA	45,359
1995	NA	NA	NA	NA	49,838
2000	8,682	16.3	33,016	62.1	53,173
2001	8,921	16.7	32,801	61.6	53,263
2002	9,175	17.2	32,552	61.0	53,325
2003	9,415	17.7	32,206	60.5	53,250
2004	9,646	18.1	31,869	60.0	53,158
2005	9,910	18.7	31,554	59.4	53,132
2006	10,207	19.2	31,284	58.8	53,216
2007	10,503	19.8	30,938	58.2	53,178
2008	10,771	20.3	30,529	57.6	53,009

Source: U.S. Department of Education, Center for Education Statistics, *Digest of Education Statistics, 2008*, table 16.

Notes: The 'school age population' is defined as the population between 5 and 17 years old.
'All Races' includes races not shown separately.
Some data has been revised from previously published figures.

Units: Estimates of the civilian non-institutionalized population, 5–17 years old as of July 1, in thousands of persons. Percent of total 5–17 year-old population.

Table 3.05: Students Who are Foreign Born or Who Have Foreign Born Parents, 2006

	Hispanic	White	All Races
Elementary and High School			
Total	*6,093*	*8,003*	*11,414*
Foreign born students	1,349	1,728	2,513
Students with at least one foreign born parent	4,744	6,275	8,901
College			
Total	*1,073*	*1,817*	*3,089*
Foreign born students	444	742	1,387
Students with at least one foreign born parent	629	1,075	1,702
Graduate School			
Total	*154*	*555*	*980*
Foreign born students	77	288	590
Students with at least one foreign born parent	77	266	390

Source: U.S. Bureau of Census, *Statistical Abstract of the United States, 2009*, table 220.

Notes: 'All Races' includes other races not shown separately

Units: Number of students in thousands.

Table 3.06: Percentage of the Population Enrolled in School, 2007

	Hispanic	White	All Races
Both Sexes			
Total	*32.1%*	*25.3%*	*26.6%*
3–4 years	48.2	54.1	54.5
5–6 years	94.3	94.8	94.7
7–9 years	96.3	98.0	98.1
10–13 years	99.0	98.7	98.6
14–15 years	98.4	98.7	98.7
16–17 years	90.6	94.6	94.3
18–19 years	57.2	67.1	66.8
20–21 years	32.3	50.1	48.4
22–24 years	18.8	26.3	27.3
25–29 years	8.3	11.5	12.4
30–34 years	4.5	6.6	7.2
Male			
Total	*31.1%*	*25.4%*	*26.9%*
3–4 years	50.7	52.9	54.4
5–6 years	94.1	94.1	94.0
7–9 years	96.4	97.9	98.1
10–13 years	99.0	98.6	98.4
14–15 years	97.8	98.3	98.4
16–17 years	91.1	94.5	94.4
18–19 years	55.2	66.4	66.3
20–21 years	24.6	44.6	43.7
22–24 years	14.4	24.2	25.4
25–29 years	6.7	9.6	10.2
30–34 years	3.1	5.7	6.4

(continued on next page)

Table 3.06: Percentage of the Population Enrolled in School, 2007

	Hispanic	White	All Races
Female			
Total	*33.1%*	*25.2%*	*26.3%*
3–4 years	45.6	55.4	54.7
5–6 years	94.5	95.6	95.3
7–9 years	96.2	98.1	98.1
10–13 years	99.0	98.8	98.7
14–15 years	99.1	99.2	99.0
16–17 years	90.0	94.7	94.1
18–19 years	59.2	67.8	67.2
20–21 years	41.0	55.7	53.3
22–24 years	23.7	28.5	29.2
25–29 years	10.3	13.6	14.7
30–34 years	6.1	7.6	7.9

Source: U.S. Bureau of the Census, Current Population Reports, *School Enrollment: Social and Economic Characteristics of Students, October 2007*, table 1.

Notes: 'All Races' includes races not shown separately.
'White' as shown is equivalent to 'White alone.'
Estimates of the civilian non-institutionalized population 3 years old and older as of October 1.

Units: Percent of the total population enrolled in school.

Table 3.07: Percentage Enrollment in Public Elementary and Secondary Schools by State, 1996 and 2006

	Fall 1996		Fall 2006	
	Hispanic	White	Hispanic	White
United States	*14.0%*	*64.2%*	*20.5%*	*56.5%*
Alabama	0.7	61.5	3.2	59.1
Alaska	2.9	63.1	4.4	57.4
Arizona	30.1	56.6	41.0	45.4
Arkansas	1.8	73.5	7.5	67.6
California	39.7	39.5	49.5	30.2
Colorado	18.8	72.0	27.6	61.9
Connecticut	11.9	71.7	16.0	66.0
Delaware	4.3	63.9	9.8	53.9
District of Columbia	7.2	4.0	9.9	5.0
Florida	15.9	56.7	25.0	48.4
Georgia	2.6	57.9	9.5	48.2
Hawaii	4.9	25.0	4.5	19.6
Idaho	8.9	88.0	13.4	82.3
Illinois	12.8	62.8	19.7	55.9
Indiana	2.4	85.4	6.3	79.5
Iowa	2.4	92.2	6.2	85.9
Kansas	6.5	81.9	13.0	73.9
Kentucky	0.5	88.9	2.4	85.8
Louisiana	1.2	50.6	2.4	50.1
Maine	0.4	97.2	1.0	94.6
Maryland	3.5	56.7	8.3	47.8
Massachusetts	9.6	77.9	13.6	72.9
Michigan	2.8	75.8	4.5	71.8
Minnesota	2.2	86.5	5.7	77.2
Mississippi	0.4	47.9	1.7	46.5
Missouri	1.1	81.1	3.4	76.3
Montana	1.5	87.2	2.5	83.9
Nebraska	4.9	86.4	12.2	76.5

(continued on next page)

Hispanic Americans: A Statistical Sourcebook 2009

Table 3.07: Percentage Enrollment in Public Elementary and Secondary Schools by State, 1996 and 2006

	Fall 1996		Fall 2006	
	Hispanic	White	Hispanic	White
Nevada	18.8	65.1	35.4	44.4
New Hampshire	1.3	96.4	2.9	92.9
New Jersey	13.5	62.5	18.8	55.7
New Mexico	47.7	38.8	54.6	30.6
New York	17.6	56.3	20.6	52.1
North Carolina	2.3	63.9	9.6	57.5
North Dakota	1.1	89.1	1.8	86.8
Ohio	1.4	82.0	2.6	78.8
Oklahoma	4.3	68.8	9.5	58.6
Oregon	7.4	84.6	16.7	73.2
Pennsylvania	3.7	80.2	6.8	74.6
Rhode Island	10.7	78.3	18.0	69.5
South Carolina	0.8	56.0	4.6	53.9
South Dakota	0.8	83.7	2.1	84.5
Tennessee	0.9	74.6	4.4	69.1
Texas	37.4	45.6	46.3	35.7
Utah	6.0	89.5	13.2	80.8
Vermont	0.4	97.3	1.0	95.3
Virginia	3.3	67.7	8.3	59.3
Washington	8.3	77.5	14.3	68.9
West Virginia	0.5	95.2	0.8	93.3
Wisconsin	3.5	82.6	7.2	77.3
Wyoming	6.2	89.0	9.4	84.5

Source: U.S. Department of Education, National Center for Education Statistics, *Digest of Education Statistics, 2008*, table 41.

Notes: 'White' excludes persons of Hispanic origin.
Based on students whose ethnicity was reported.

Units: Percent of total enrollment.

Table 3.08: Percentage of Gifted and Talented Students in Public Elementary and Secondary Schools by State, 2006

	Hispanic	White	All Races
United States	*4.2%*	*8.0%*	*6.7%*
Alabama	2.9	7.1	5.5
Alaska	2.5	5.8	4.1
Arizona	3.5	9.1	6.3
Arkansas	5.8	10.7	9.5
California	4.8	11.9	8.3
Colorado	3.8	8.2	6.8
Connecticut	1.8	4.3	3.8
Delaware	3.5	6.8	5.6
District of Columbia	NA	NA	NA
Florida	4.4	6.1	4.7
Georgia	3.1	14.1	9.3
Hawaii	3.9	9.7	6.2
Idaho	1.3	4.7	4.2
Illinois	3.1	7.0	5.8
Indiana	3.9	8.7	7.9
Iowa	3.1	8.8	8.2
Kansas	0.8	3.6	3.0
Kentucky	5.7	15.8	14.6
Louisiana	3.3	4.8	3.4
Maine	2.3	3.3	3.2
Maryland	14.7	21.1	16.1
Massachusetts	0.5	0.6	0.7
Michigan	1.4	3.8	3.4
Minnesota	5.4	8.8	8.8
Mississippi	4.5	9.6	6.1
Missouri	1.3	4.0	3.6
Montana	3.9	5.7	5.2
Nebraska	3.9	13.3	11.4

(continued on next page)

Table 3.08: Percentage of Gifted and Talented Students in Public Elementary and Secondary Schools by State, 2006

	Hispanic	White	All Races
Nevada	0.8	3.0	1.9
New Hampshire	0.9	2.6	2.6
New Jersey	3.5	8.4	7.0
New Mexico	2.4	7.1	4.0
New York	1.5	3.3	2.9
North Carolina	3.1	15.4	10.8
North Dakota	1.4	2.8	2.8
Ohio	3.3	7.8	7.3
Oklahoma	6.8	16.2	13.7
Oregon	2.0	8.0	6.9
Pennsylvania	1.7	5.0	4.5
Rhode Island	1.0	1.5	1.4
South Carolina	4.6	15.9	11.0
South Dakota	0.7	2.9	2.7
Tennessee	0.6	2.0	1.7
Texas	5.5	10.8	7.6
Utah	4.1	4.9	5.0
Vermont	1.3	0.8	0.8
Virginia	7.5	15.6	12.6
Washington	1.7	4.4	3.9
West Virginia	0.9	2.2	2.2
Wisconsin	3.5	7.1	6.4
Wyoming	0.9	2.3	2.2

Source: U.S. Department of Education, National Center for Education Statistics, *Digest of Education Statistics, 2008*, table 54.

Notes: 'All Races' includes races not shown separately.
'White' as shown is equivalent to 'White alone'.

Units: Percentages are of all primary and secondary students.

Table 3.09: Public Elementary and Secondary School Teachers by Selected Characteristics, 1999–2000

	Hispanic	White
Total number of teachers	*169,000*	*2,532,000*
By Highest Degree Earned		
Bachelor's degree	65.8%	51.6%
Master's degree	29.3	44.2
Education specialist	3.0	3.0
Doctorate	1.2	0.6
By Years of Full-Time Teaching Experience		
Less than 3 years	28.4%	17.1%
3–9 years	29.3	23.2
10–20 years	24.6	29.1
Over 20 years	17.7	30.6

Source: U.S. Bureau of Census, *Statistical Abstract of the United States, 2003*, table 249.

Notes: 'All Races' includes races not shown separately. 'White' excludes persons of Hispanic origin.

Units: Number of public elementary and secondary teachers; percent of all public elementary and secondary school teachers.

Table 3.10: Public Elementary and Secondary School Teachers by Selected Characteristics, 2004–2005

	Hispanic	White
Total number of teachers	*124,000*	*2,502,000*
By Highest Degree Earned		
Bachelor's degree	67.9%	49.7%
Master's degree	22.1	43.2
Education specialist	7.6	5.5
Doctorate	0.2	0.6
By Years of Full-Time Teaching Experience		
Less than 3 years	9.8%	5.7%
3–9 years	40.0	31.9
10–20 years	37.8	31.6
Over 20 years	12.4	30.9

Source: U.S. Bureau of Census, *Statistical Abstract of the United States, 2009*, table 243.

Notes: 'White' excludes persons of Hispanic origin.

Units: Number of public elementary and secondary teachers; percent of all public elementary and secondary school teachers.

Table 3.11: Private Elementary and Secondary School Teachers by Selected Characteristics, 1999–2000

	Hispanic	White
Total number of teachers	*21,000*	*402,000*
By Highest Degree Earned		
Bachelor's degree	55.4%	58.3%
Master's degree	26.7	31.8
Education specialist	2.8	1.7
Doctorate	1.5	1.8
By Years of Full-Time Teaching Experience		
Less than 3 years	36.6%	29.1%
3–9 years	26.1	25.0
10–20 years	28.7	27.4
Over 20 years	8.7	18.5

Source: U.S. Bureau of Census, *Statistical Abstract of the United States, 2003*, table 263.

Notes: 'All Races' includes races not shown separately. 'White' excludes persons of Hispanic origin.

Units: Number of public elementary and secondary teachers; percent of all private elementary and secondary school teachers.

Table 3.12: Private Elementary and Secondary School Teachers by Selected Characteristics, 2004–2005

	Hispanic	White
Total number of teachers	*13,000*	*359,000*
By Highest Degree Earned		
Bachelor's degree	78.3%	58.4%
Master's degree	12.6	30.2
Education specialist	NA	2.3
Doctorate	3.3	2.2
By Years of Full-Time Teaching Experience		
Less than 3 years	8.9%	6.4%
3–9 years	32.6	38.2
10–20 years	36.0	28.3
Over 20 years	22.5	27.1

Source: U.S. Bureau of Census, *Statistical Abstract of the United States, 2009*, table 255.

Notes: 'White' excludes persons of Hispanic origin. NA indicates that the data represents or rounds to zero.

Units: Number of private elementary and secondary teachers; percent of all private elementary and secondary school teachers.

Table 3.13: Percent of Students at or Above Selected Reading Proficiency Levels by Age, 2004

	Hispanic	White	All Races
9 year-olds			
Level 150	95%	98%	96%
Level 200	57	78	70
Level 250	9	25	20
13 year-olds			
Level 200	88%	96%	94%
Level 250	43	69	61
Level 300	4	17	13
17 year-olds			
Level 250	64%	86%	80%
Level 300	20	45	38

Source: U.S. Department of Education, National Center for Education Statistics, *Digest of Education Statistics, 2005*, table 111.

Notes: 'All Races' includes races not shown separately. 'White' excludes those identifying as Hispanic. Reading level shown on scale:

150: Able to follow brief written directions and carry out simple discrete reading tasks.
200: Able to understand, combine ideas, and make inferences based on short uncomplicated passages about specific or sequentially related information.
250: Able to search for specific information, interrelate ideas, and make generalizations about literature, science, and social studies materials.
300: Able to find, understand, summarize, and explain relatively complicated literary and informational material.

Units: Percent of students scoring at or above the specified level.

Table 3.14: Percent of Students at or Above Selected Mathematics Proficiency Levels by Age, 2004

	Hispanic	White	All Races
9 year-olds			
Level 150	99.6%	99.7%	99.3%
Level 200	82.6	92.6	88.6
Level 250	26.9	49.0	41.9
13 year-olds			
Level 200	97.3%	99.1%	98.6%
Level 250	68.4	90.5	83.5
Level 300	14.3	36.0	29.0
17 year-olds			
Level 250	92.1%	98.4%	96.7%
Level 300	32.3	69.0	58.6
Level 350	1.3	8.5	6.9

Source: U.S. Department of Education, National Center for Education Statistics, *Digest of Education Statistics, 2005*, table 119.

Notes: 'All Races' includes races not shown separately. 'White' excludes those identifying as hispanic. Mathematics level shown on scale:
- 150: Simple arithmetic facts.
- 200: Beginning skills and understanding.
- 250: Numerical operations and beginning problem-solving.
- 300: Moderately complex procedures and reasoning.
- 350: Multi-step problem-solving and algebra.

Units: Percent of students scoring at or above the specified level.

Table 3.15: SAT Test Scores, 1986–2008

	Mexican	Puerto Rican	Hispanic	White	All Races
1986–1987					
Verbal score	457	436	464	518	499
Math score	455	432	462	513	500
1990–1991					
Verbal score	454	451	458	518	499
Math score	459	439	462	513	500
2000–2001					
Verbal score	451	457	460	529	506
Math score	458	451	465	531	514
2001–2002					
Verbal score	446	455	458	527	504
Math score	457	451	464	533	516
2002–2003					
Verbal score	448	456	457	529	507
Math score	457	453	464	534	519
2003–2004					
Verbal score	451	457	461	528	508
Math score	458	452	465	531	518
2004–2005					
Verbal score	453	460	463	532	508
Math score	463	457	469	536	520

(continued on next page)

Table 3.15: SAT Test Scores, 1986–2008

	Mexican	Puerto Rican	Hispanic	White	All Races
2005–2006					
Critical reading	454	459	458	527	503
Mathematics	465	456	463	536	518
Writing	452	448	450	519	497
2006–2007					
Critical reading	455	459	459	527	502
Mathematics	466	454	463	534	515
Writing	450	447	450	518	494
2007–2008					
Critical reading	454	456	455	528	502
Mathematics	463	453	461	537	515
Writing	447	445	448	518	494

Source: U.S. Department of Education, Center for Education Statistics, *Digest of Education Statistics 2008*, table 141.

Notes: 'All Races' includes races not shown separately.
The SAT test was redesigned for the 2005–2006 school year; data from after 2005–2006 may not be directly comparable with previous years.
The minimum score for a section of the SAT is 200 and the maximum score is 800.
'Other Hispanic' refers to Hispanics not specifying Mexican, Puerto Rican, etc.

Units: Average SAT scores.

Table 3.16: Tenth-Grade Students in Schools
with Specified Physical or Structural Conditions, 2002

	Hispanic	White	All Students
Trash on floor	27.9%	18.1%	21.6%
Trash overflowing	7.4	5.3	6.4
Graffiti	12.3	2.8	5.6
Ceiling in disrepair	8.8	6.6	7.8
Floors/walls not clean	34.3	28.4	30.5
Broken lights	3.6	3.2	3.7
Chipped paint on walls	16.4	6.2	9.6
Broken windows	2.1	0.4	1.0
Doors not on bathroom stalls	23.6	23.3	24.7

Source: U.S. Bureau of Census, *Statistical Abstract of the United States, 2007*, table 231.

Notes: Conditions based on observers' physical inspection of school property. Conditions may be at any location in the school.

Units: Percent of tenth-grade students.

Table 3.17: Labor Force Status of 2008 High School Graduates and 2007–2008 High School Dropouts, October 2008

	Hispanic	White	All Races
2008 high school graduates	458	2,521	3,151
In civilian labor force	246	1,373	1,644
Employed	185	1,114	1,310
Unemployed	61	260	334
Not in labor force	212	1,148	1,507
2007–2008 high school dropouts	111	253	400
In civilian labor force	63	142	194
Employed	35	94	117
Unemployed	27	48	77
Not in labor force	49	111	206

Source: U.S. Department Labor, Bureau of Labor Statistics, *"College Enrollment and Work Activity of 2008 High School Graduates,"* table 1.

Notes: 'All Races' includes races not shown separately.
'White' as shown is equivalent to 'White alone'.

Units: Number in thousands of persons 16 to 24 years.

Table 3.18: Percent of High School Dropouts Among Persons 16 to 24 Years Old, by Sex, 1975–2007

	Hispanic			White			All Races		
	Male	Female	Total	Male	Female	Total	Male	Female	Total
1975	26.7%	31.6%	29.2%	11.0%	11.8%	11.4%	13.3%	14.5%	13.9%
1980	37.2	33.2	35.2	12.3	10.5	11.4	15.1	13.1	14.1
1985	29.9	25.2	27.6	11.1	9.8	10.4	13.4	11.8	12.6
1990	34.3	30.3	32.4	9.3	8.7	9.0	12.3	11.8	12.1
1995	30.0	30.0	30.0	9.0	8.2	8.6	12.2	11.7	12.0
1999	31.0	26.0	28.6	7.7	6.9	7.3	11.9	10.5	11.2
2000	31.8	23.5	27.8	7.0	6.9	6.9	12.0	9.9	10.9
2001	31.6	22.1	27.0	7.9	6.7	7.3	12.2	9.3	10.7
2002	29.6	21.2	25.7	6.7	6.3	6.5	11.8	9.2	10.5
2003	26.7	20.1	23.5	7.1	5.6	6.3	11.3	8.4	9.9
2004	28.5	18.5	23.8	7.1	6.4	6.8	11.6	9.0	10.3
2005	26.4	18.1	22.4	6.6	5.3	6.0	10.8	8.0	9.4
2006	25.7	18.1	22.1	6.4	5.3	5.8	10.3	8.3	9.3
2007	24.7	18.0	21.4	6.0	4.5	5.3	9.8	7.7	8.7

Source: U.S. Department of Education, Center for Education Statistics, *Digest of Education Statistics 2008*, table 109.

Notes: 'All Races' includes other races not shown separately.
'White' excludes persons of Hispanic origin.
'Dropouts' are 16 to 24 year olds who are not enrolled in school and who have not completed a high school program regardless of when they left school.
Based on October enrollment counts.

Units: Percent of total population, persons 16 to 24 years old.

Table 3.19: Attendance Status of College Students 15 Years Old and Over, 2005 and 2006

	Hispanic	White	All Races
2005			
Total enrolled	*1,942*	*13,466*	*17,472*
Undergraduate college, year enrolled			
1st year	533	3,052	4,033
2nd year	515	3,058	3,988
3rd year	361	2,693	3,439
4th year	263	2,130	2,708
Graduate school, year enrolled			
1st year	92	806	1,067
2nd year or higher	178	1,728	2,237
2006			
Total enrolled	*1,969*	*13,274*	*17,232*
Undergraduate college, year enrolled			
1st year	629	3,085	4,077
2nd year	480	3,038	4,048
3rd year	358	2,577	3,257
4th year	230	1,987	2,471
Graduate school, year enrolled			
1st year	97	945	1,234
2nd year or higher	175	1,642	2,144

Source: U.S. Bureau of the Census, Current Population Reports, *School Enrollment, 2004*, table 10; *2005*, table 10; *2006*, table 5.

Notes: 'All Races' includes races not shown separately. 'White' as shown is equivalent to 'White alone.'
College enrollment at the undergraduate level in two-year and four-year institutions including both full-time and part-time students. Figures are based on October enrollment counts.

Units: College enrollment in thousands of students.

Table 3.20: Enrollment in Institutions of Higher Education by Type of Institution, 1980–2007

	Hispanic	White	All Races
1980			
All institutions	*471.7*	*9,883.0*	*12,086.8*
4-year institutions	216.6	6,274.5	7,565.4
2-year institutions	255.1	3,558.5	4,521.4
1990			
All institutions	*782.4*	*10,722.5*	*13,818.6*
4-year institutions	358.2	6,768.1	8,578.6
2-year institutions	424.2	3,954.3	5,240.1
1995			
All institutions	*1093.8*	*10,311.2*	*14,261.8*
4-year institutions	485.5	6,517.2	8,769.3
2-year institutions	608.4	3,794.0	5,492.5
2000			
All institutions	*1461.8*	*10,462.1*	*15,312.3*
4-year institutions	617.9	6,658.0	9,363.9
2-year institutions	843.9	3,804.1	5,948.4
2005			
All institutions	*1,882.0*	*11,495.4*	*17,487.5*
4-year institutions	900.5	7,496.9	10,999.4
2-year institutions	981.5	3,998.6	6,488.1
2007			
All institutions	*2,076.2*	*11,756.2*	*18,248.1*
4-year institutions	1,008.7	7,781.0	11,630.2
2-year institutions	1,067.4	3,975.2	6,617.9

Source: U.S. Department of Education, Center for Education Statistics, *Digest of Education Statistics, 2008*, table 227

Notes: 'All Races' includes other races not shown separately.
'White' excludes persons of Hispanic origin.

Units: Enrollment in thousands of students enrolled.

Table 3.21: Enrollment Rates of 18 to 24 Year Olds in Institutions of Higher Education, 1975–2007

	Hispanic	White	All Races
Enrollment as a Percent of 18–24 Year Olds			
1975	20.4%	27.4%	26.3%
1980	16.1	27.3	25.7
1985	16.9	30.0	27.8
1990	16.2	35.2	32.1
1995	20.7	37.9	34.3
2000	21.7	38.7	35.5
2001	21.7	39.3	36.2
2002	19.9	40.9	36.7
2003	23.5	41.6	37.8
2004	24.7	41.7	38.0
2005	24.8	42.8	38.9
2006	23.6	41.0	37.3
2007	26.6	42.6	38.8
Enrollment as a Percent of High School Graduates			
1975	33.0%	32.3%	32.5%
1980	27.6	32.1	31.8
1985	26.8	34.9	33.7
1990	26.8	39.2	37.7
1995	35.2	44.0	42.3
2000	36.2	44.1	43.2
2001	34.6	45.3	44.2
2002	31.6	46.7	44.7
2003	35.8	47.2	45.7
2004	37.3	47.4	45.8
2005	37.4	48.6	46.8
2006	35.5	46.5	45.0
2007	39.2	47.8	46.1

Source: U.S. Department of Education, National Center for Education Statistics, *Digest of Education Statistics, 2008*, table 204.

Notes: 'All Races' includes other races not shown separately.
'White' excludes those who identify as Hispanic.

Units: Percent as a percent of 18–24 year olds, and high school graduates as shown.

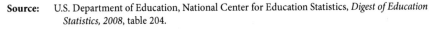

Table 3.22: Enrollment in Institutions of Higher Education by State, Fall, 2007

	Hispanic	White	All Races
United States	*2,076,156*	*11,756,236*	*18,248,128*
Alabama	4,575	173,823	268,183
Alaska	1,251	21,439	30,616
Arizona	95,162	390,606	624,147
Arkansas	3,743	112,516	152,168
California	698,027	1,054,586	2,529,522
Colorado	36,446	232,152	310,637
Connecticut	15,888	127,084	179,005
Delaware	2,112	36,411	52,343
District of Columbia	5,626	53,357	115,153
Florida	177,632	507,172	913,793
Georgia	13,864	262,953	453,711
Hawaii	2,029	16,593	66,601
Idaho	4,107	69,287	78,846
Illinois	99,164	537,737	837,018
Indiana	12,026	310,273	380,477
Iowa	8,925	215,715	256,259
Kansas	9,529	154,967	194,102
Kentucky	3,369	222,845	258,213
Louisiana	5,959	139,707	224,754
Maine	874	61,547	67,173
Maryland	14,022	184,070	327,597
Massachusetts	31,383	329,669	463,366
Michigan	18,759	484,157	643,279
Minnesota	9,063	314,775	392,393
Mississippi	1,489	88,413	155,232
Missouri	11,743	300,035	384,366
Montana	909	40,035	47,371
Nebraska	5,051	108,753	127,378
Nevada	18,856	69,514	116,276

(continued on next page)

Table 3.22: Enrollment in Institutions of Higher Education by State, Fall, 2007

	Hispanic	White	All Races
New Hampshire	1,843	63,112	70,724
New Jersey	56,710	232,585	398,136
New Mexico	55,138	56,621	134,375
New York	138,407	696,109	1,172,811
North Carolina	15,120	334,541	502,330
North Dakota	601	42,386	49,945
Ohio	13,784	503,776	630,497
Oklahoma	8,031	144,178	206,382
Oregon	12,088	162,464	202,928
Pennsylvania	25,163	563,113	725,397
Rhode Island	5,991	64,806	82,900
South Carolina	4,053	145,723	217,755
South Dakota	580	43,424	49,747
Tennessee	5,748	220,327	297,785
Texas	350,776	630,579	1,269,098
Utah	11,179	173,975	203,679
Vermont	990	38,251	42,191
Virginia	20,250	319,728	478,268
Washington	21,743	263,229	352,075
West Virginia	2,673	101,738	116,848
Wisconsin	10,812	291,905	343,747
Wyoming	1,674	31,440	35,246

Source: U.S. Department of Education, Center for Education Statistics, *Digest of Education Statistics, 2008*, table 228.

Notes: 'All Races' includes other races not shown separately.
'White' excludes those who identify as Hispanic.
Degree-granting institutions grant associate's or higher degrees and participate in Title IV federal financial aid programs.
Detail may not sum to totals because of rounding.

Units: Enrollment in number of students enrolled.

Table 3.23: Enrollment Status of High School Graduates by Type of School and Sex, 2007

	Hispanic	White	All Races
Total	*3,490*	*18,809*	*24,006*
Both Sexes:			
Enrolled in 2-year college	329	1,737	2,226
Enrolled in 4-year college	692	5,131	6,494
Enrolled in graduate school	51	661	862
Enrolled in vocational school	45	232	274
Male Students:			
Enrolled in 2-year college	132	770	1,030
Enrolled in 4-year college	296	2,446	3,092
Enrolled in graduate school	51	260	340
Enrolled in vocational school	40	114	140
Female Students:			
Enrolled in 2-year college	198	967	1,196
Enrolled in 4-year college	396	2,684	3,402
Enrolled in graduate school	31	400	522
Enrolled in vocational school	23	118	135

Source: U.S. Bureau of the Census, *Current Population Reports: School Enrollment, 2007*, table 7.

Notes: 'All Races' includes races not shown separately.
'White' as shown is equivalent to 'White alone.'
Numbers are for full-time students only.

Units: Enrollment in thousands of students aged 15–24.

Table 3.24: Enrollment of Persons 14 to 34 Years Old in Institutions of Higher Education, by Sex, 1975–1999

	Enrollment			Percent distribution		
	Hispanic	**White**	**All Races**	**Hispanic**	**White**	**All Races**
1975						
Total	*411*	*8,141*	*9,697*	*4.2%*	*84.0%*	*100%*
Men	219	4,566	5,342	2.3	47.1	55.1
Women	192	3,576	4,355	2.0	36.9	44.9
1980						
Total	*443*	*8,453*	*10,181*	*4.4%*	*83.0%*	*100%*
Men	222	4,225	5,193	2.2	41.5	51.0
Women	221	4,228	5,244	2.2	41.5	49.0
1985						
Total	*579*	*8,781*	*10,863*	*5.3%*	*80.0%*	*100%*
Men	280	4,361	5,345	2.6	40.1	49.2
Women	299	4,420	5,518	2.8	40.7	50.8
1990						
Total	*617*	*8,892*	*11,303*	*5.5%*	*78.7%*	*100%*
Men	297	4,289	NA	2.6	38.0	NA
Women	321	4,594	NA	2.8	40.6	NA
1993						
Total	*867*	*8,592*	*11,409*	*7.6%*	*75.3%*	*100%*
Men	391	4,168	NA	3.4	36.5	NA
Women	475	4,424	NA	4.2	38.8	NA
1999						
Total	*1,081*	*8,853*	*12,506*	*8.6%*	*70.8%*	*100%*
Men	472	4,310	NA	3.8	34.5	NA
Women	609	4,543	NA	4.9	36.3	NA

Source: U.S. Department of Education, Center for Education Statistics, *Digest of Education Statistics, 2000*, table 213.

Notes: 'All Races' includes races not shown separately. 'White' excludes those identifying as Hispanic.
Totals may not add to 100% due to other groups not shown.

Units: Enrollment in thousands of students enrolled; percent of 14–34 year-olds.

Table 3.25: Enrollment Status of Persons 18 to 21 Years Old, 2004, 2005, and 2006

	Hispanic	White	All Races
2004			
Total persons 18–21 yrs	2,718	12,325	15,677
Enrolled in high school	10.3%	8.4%	8.9%
High school graduates			
Total	64.2	80.4	79.4
In college	30.0	48.4	47.6
Not high school graduates	25.5	11.2	11.7
2005			
Total persons 18–21 yrs	2,745	12,510	15,916
Enrolled in high school	10.8%	8.8%	9.4%
High school graduates			
Total	64.5	80.7	80.1
In college	30.1	49.1	48.2
Not high school graduates	24.7	10.5	10.6
2006			
Total persons 18–21 yrs	2,810	12,629	16,176
Enrolled in high school	12.4%	9.4%	10.5%
High school graduates			
Total	64.7	80.1	78.9
In college	29.5	47.0	45.9
Not high school graduates	22.8	10.3	10.5

Source: U.S. Bureau of Census, *Statistical Abstract of the United States, 2007*, table 262; *2008*, table 265; *2009*, table 264.

Notes: 'All Races' includes other races not shown separately

Units: 'Total Persons' in thousands; other data in percent distribution.

Table 3.26: Educational Attainment by Sex, 1960–2006

	Hispanic		White		All Races	
	Male	Female	Male	Female	Male	Female
High School Graduate or Higher						
1960	NA	NA	41.6%	44.7%	39.5%	42.5%
1970	37.9	34.2	54.0	55.0	51.9	52.8
1980	67.3	65.8	69.6	68.1	67.3	65.8
1990	50.3	51.3	79.1	79.0	77.7	77.5
1995	52.9	53.8	83.0	83.0	81.7	81.6
2000	56.6	57.5	84.8	85.0	84.2	84.0
2003	56.3	57.8	84.5	85.7	84.1	85.0
2004	57.3	59.5	85.3	86.3	84.8	85.4
2005	57.9	59.1	85.2	86.2	84.9	85.5
2006	58.5	60.1	85.5	86.7	85.0	85.9
2007	58.2	62.5	85.3	87.1	85.0	86.4
College Graduate or Higher						
1960	NA	NA	10.3%	6.0%	9.7%	5.8%
1970	7.8	4.3	14.4	8.4	13.5	8.1
1980	9.4	6.0	21.3	13.3	20.1	12.8
1990	9.8	8.7	25.3	19.0	24.4	18.4
1995	10.1	8.4	27.2	21.0	26.0	20.2
2000	10.7	10.6	28.5	23.9	27.8	23.6
2003	11.2	11.6	29.4	25.9	28.9	25.7
2004	11.8	12.3	30.0	26.4	29.4	26.1
2005	11.8	12.1	29.4	26.8	28.9	26.5
2006	11.9	12.9	29.7	27.1	29.2	26.9
2007	11.8	13.7	29.9	28.3	29.5	28.0

Source: U.S. Bureau of Census, *Statistical Abstract of the United States, 2009*, table 222.

Notes: Beginning in 2003, 'White' as shown is equivalent to 'White alone.'
'High school graduate' indicates those who have completed 4 years of high school or more.
'College graduate' indicates having completed 4 years of college or more.
Figures are as of April 1 of the respective years.

Units: Percent of total population age 25 and over.

Table 3.27: Associate's Degrees Conferred by Major Field of Study, 2006–2007

	Hispanic	White	All Races
All fields, total	85,410	491,572	728,114
Agriculture and natural resources	172	5,459	5,838
Architecture and related services	115	316	517
Area, ethnic, cultural, and gender studies	33	39	164
Biological and biomedical sciences	342	1,144	2,060
Business	12,413	74,402	116,101
Communications, journalism, and related programs	283	1,889	2,609
Communications technologies	270	2,289	3,095
Computer and information sciences	3,008	18,379	27,712
Construction trades	170	3,342	3,895
Education	1,542	8,479	13,021
Engineering	291	1,338	2,136
Engineering technologies	2,989	21,284	29,199
English language and literature/letters	286	709	1,249
Family and consumer sciences	1,679	4,864	9,124
Foreign languages, literatures, and linguistics	262	784	1,207
Health professions and related clinical sciences	12,294	104,730	145,436
Legal professions and studies	1,324	6,751	10,391
Liberal arts and sciences, general studies, and humanities	33,684	166,142	250,030
Library science	5	69	84
Mathematics and statistics	187	462	827
Mechanics and repair technologies	1,780	11,364	15,432

(continued on next page)

Hispanic Americans: A Statistical Sourcebook 2009

Table 3.27: Associate's Degrees Conferred by Major Field of Study, 2006–2007

	Hispanic	White	All Races
Military technologies	80	539	781
Multi/interdisciplinary studies	2,589	9,248	15,838
Parks, recreation, leisure and fitness studies	116	873	1,251
Philosophy and religious studies	17	329	375
Physical sciences and science technologies	378	2,212	3,404
Precision production	97	1,735	1,973
Psychology	470	1,335	2,213
Public administration and social service professions	616	2,275	4,338
Security and protective services	4,095	18,952	28,208
Social sciences and history	1,446	3,953	7,080
Social sciences	1,366	3,666	6,673
History	80	287	407
Theology and religious vocations	18	469	608
Transportation and materials moving	163	1,276	1,674
Visual and performing arts	2,196	14,141	20,244

Source: U.S. Department of Education, Center for Education Statistics, *Digest of Education Statistics 2008*, table 282.

Notes: 'All Races' includes other races not shown separately.
'White' excludes those identifying as Hispanic.

Units: Earned Associate's degrees conferred in number of degrees.

Table 3.28: Bachelor's Degrees Conferred by Major Field of Study, 2006–2007

	Hispanic	White	All Races
All fields, total	*114,936*	*1,099,850*	*1,524,092*
Agriculture and natural resources	859	20,116	23,133
Architecture and related services	948	6,983	9,717
Area, ethnic, cultural, and gender studies	1,175	4,486	8,194
Biological and biomedical sciences	4,651	50,120	75,151
Business	24,724	223,221	327,531
Communications, journalism, and related programs	5,031	56,929	74,783
Communications technologies	306	2,614	3,637
Computer and information sciences	2,835	27,626	42,170
Construction trades	6	113	129
Education	5,111	89,868	105,641
Engineering	4,092	45,994	67,092
Engineering technologies	854	11,125	14,588
English language and literature/letters	3,669	43,722	55,122
Family and consumer sciences	1,237	16,334	21,400
Foreign languages, literatures, and linguistics	3,366	14,420	20,275
Health professions and related clinical sciences	6,069	75,579	101,810
Legal professions and studies	356	2,290	3,596
Liberal arts and sciences, general studies, and humanities	4,722	29,719	44,255
Library science	1	78	82
Mathematics and statistics	956	10,965	14,954
Mechanics and repair technologies	21	197	263

(continued on next page)

Table 3.28: Bachelor's Degrees Conferred by Major Field of Study, 2006–2007

	Hispanic	White	All Races
Military technologies	6	150	168
Multi/interdisciplinary studies	4,193	23,266	33,792
Parks, recreation, leisure and fitness studies	1,830	21,467	27,430
Philosophy and religious studies	662	9,750	11,969
Physical sciences and science technologies	953	15,909	21,073
Precision production	2	17	23
Psychology	8,334	63,219	90,039
Public administration and social service professions	2,753	13,605	23,147
Security and protective services	4,795	25,215	39,206
Social sciences and history	13,762	117,453	164,183
Social sciences	11,472	88,837	129,737
History	2,290	28,616	34,446
Theology and religious vocations	308	7,323	8,696
Transportation and materials moving	372	4,592	5,657
Visual and performing arts	5,977	65,385	85,186

Source: U.S. Department of Education, Center for Education Statistics, *Digest of Education Statistics 2008*, table 285.

Notes: 'All Races' includes other races not shown separately.
'White' excludes those identifying as Hispanic.

Units: Earned Bachelor's degrees conferred in number of degrees.

Table 3.29: Master's Degrees Conferred
by Major Field of Study, 2006–2007

	Hispanic	White	All Races
All fields, total	*34,822*	*399,267*	*604,607*
Agriculture and natural resources	139	3,469	4,623
Architecture and related services	391	3,902	5,951
Area, ethnic, cultural, and gender studies	163	995	1,699
Biological and biomedical sciences	392	5,525	8,747
Business	7,966	87,416	150,211
Communications, journalism, and related programs	332	4,404	6,773
Communications technologies	17	203	499
Computer and information sciences	479	6,342	16,232
Construction trades	0	0	0
Education	11,857	135,539	176,572
Engineering	1,131	12,415	29,472
Engineering technologies	135	1,395	2,690
English language and literature/letters	395	7,119	8,742
Family and consumer sciences	101	1,489	2,080
Foreign languages, literatures, and linguistics	530	1,960	3,443
Health professions and related clinical sciences	2,875	38,847	54,531
Legal professions and studies	192	1,397	4,486
Liberal arts and sciences, general studies, and humanities	205	2,792	3,634
Library science	351	5,651	6,767
Mathematics and statistics	163	2,342	4,884
Mechanics and repair technologies	0	0	0

(continued on next page)

Table 3.29: Master's Degrees Conferred by Major Field of Study, 2006–2007

	Hispanic	White	All Races
Military technologies	4	178	202
Multi/interdisciplinary studies	260	3,306	4,762
Parks, recreation, leisure and fitness studies	134	3,233	4,110
Philosophy and religious studies	66	1,388	1,716
Physical sciences and science technologies	185	3,549	5,839
Precision production	0	3	5
Psychology	1,523	15,002	21,037
Public administration and social service professions	2,677	19,579	31,131
Security and protective services	349	3,339	4,906
Social sciences and history	952	11,240	17,665
Social sciences	801	8,597	14,521
History	151	2,643	3,144
Theology and religious vocations	213	4,794	6,446
Transportation and materials moving	55	767	985
Visual and performing arts	590	9,687	13,767

Source: U.S. Department of Education, Center for Education Statistics, *Digest of Education Statistics 2008*, table 288.

Notes: 'All Races' includes other races not shown separately.
'White' excludes those identifying as Hispanic.

Units: Earned Master's degrees conferred in number of degrees.

Table 3.30: Doctoral Degrees Conferred by Major Field of Study, 2006–2007

	Hispanic	White	All Races
All fields, total	*2,034*	*34,071*	*60,616*
Agriculture and natural resources	18	634	1,272
Architecture and related services	9	68	178
Area, ethnic, cultural, and gender studies	16	123	233
Biological and biomedical sciences	203	3,463	6,354
Business	66	928	2,029
Communications, journalism, and related programs	5	268	479
Communications technologies	0	1	1
Computer and information sciences	19	496	1,595
Construction trades	0	0	0
Education	383	5,394	8,261
Engineering	147	2,143	8,062
Engineering technologies	3	23	61
English language and literature/letters	41	890	1,178
Family and consumer sciences	10	189	337
Foreign languages, literatures, and linguistics	86	533	1,059
Health professions and related clinical sciences	255	6,530	8,355
Legal professions and studies	2	19	143
Liberal arts and sciences, general studies, and humanities	4	59	77
Library science	2	25	52
Mathematics and statistics	24	508	1,351
Mechanics and repair technologies	0	0	0

(continued on next page)

Table 3.30: Doctoral Degrees Conferred by Major Field of Study, 2006–2007

	Hispanic	White	All Races
Military technologies	0	0	0
Multi/interdisciplinary studies	48	687	1,093
Parks, recreation, leisure and fitness studies	7	134	218
Philosophy and religious studies	24	444	637
Physical sciences and science technologies	107	2,233	4,846
Precision production	0	0	0
Psychology	297	3,853	5,153
Public administration and social service professions	34	409	726
Security and protective services	6	58	85
Social sciences and history	147	2,139	3,844
Social sciences	104	1,547	3,037
History	43	592	807
Theology and religious vocations	30	946	1,573
Transportation and materials moving	0	0	0
Visual and performing arts	41	874	1,364

Source: U.S. Department of Education, Center for Education Statistics, *Digest of Education Statistics 2008*, table 291.

Notes: 'All Races' includes other races not shown separately.
'White' excludes those identifying as Hispanic.

Units: Earned Doctoral degrees conferred in number of degrees.

Table 3.31: First Professional Degrees Conferred by Field of Study, 2006–2007

	Hispanic	White	All Races
All fields, total	*4,700*	*64,546*	*90,064*
Dentistry	199	2,915	4,596
Medicine	736	10,340	15,730
Optometry	52	820	1,311
Osteopathic medicine	117	2,277	2,992
Pharmacy	442	6,735	10,439
Podiatry or podiatric medicine	26	198	331
Veterinary medicine	67	2,228	2,443
Chiropractic medicine	110	2,000	2,525
Naturopathic medicine	12	179	221
Law	2,793	32,552	43,486
Theology	146	4,302	5,990

Source: U.S. Department of Education, National Center for Education Statistics, *Digest of Education Statistics, 2008*, table 294.

Notes: 'All Races' includes other races not shown separately.
'White' excludes those identifying as Hispanic.

Units: Earned first professional degrees conferred, in number of degrees.

Table 3.32: Enrollment in Schools of Medicine, Dentistry, and Related Fields, 1990–1991, 2004–2005, and 2005–2006

	Hispanic	White
1990–1991		
Dentistry	7.9%	70.1%
Allopathic medicine	5.4	73.5
Osteopathic medicine	4.1	83.6
Podiatry	6.7	75.2
Optometry	6.2	77.9
Pharmacy	4.2	80.5
Registered nursing	3.0	82.8
2004–2005		
Dentistry	5.8%	66.1%
Allopathic medicine	6.7	63.3
Osteopathic medicine	3.8	73.5
Podiatry	7.7	60.4
Optometry	5.1	63.2
Pharmacy	3.9	59.7
Registered nursing	NA	NA
2005–2006		
Dentistry	5.7%	62.7%
Allopathic medicine	7.4	63.1
Osteopathic medicine	3.9	71.9
Podiatry	6.9	61.5
Optometry	5.1	63.2
Pharmacy	3.8	89.9
Registered nursing	NA	NA

Source: U.S. Department of Health and Human Services, National Center for Health Statistics, *Health, United States, 2008*, table 114.

Notes: 'All Races' includes other races not shown separately.
'White' excludes those identifying as Hispanic.

Units: Enrollment as a percentage of all students enrolled in schools for each occupation.

Table 3.33: Educational Attainment, Persons 25 Years Old and Older, 2000 and 2007

	Hispanic	White	All Races
2000			
All persons 25 years old and over	*17,150*	*147,067*	*175,230*
Percent of the population:			
Not a high school graduate	43.0%	15.1%	15.8%
High school graduate	27.9	33.4	33.1
With some college, no degree	13.5	17.4	17.6
With associate's degree	5.0	8.0	7.8
With Bachelor's degree	7.3	17.3	17.0
With advanced degree	3.3	8.8	8.6
2007			
All persons 25 years old and over	*24,551*	*159,262*	*194,318*
Percent of the population:			
Not a high school graduate	39.7%	13.8%	14.3%
High school graduate	28.4	31.7	31.6
With some college, no degree	13.0	16.7	16.7
With associate's degree	6.2	8.7	8.6
With Bachelor's degree	9.4	19.1	18.9
With advanced degree	3.3	10.0	9.9

Source: U.S. Bureau of the Census, *Statistical Abstract of the United States, 2001*, table 217; *2009*, table 223.

Notes: 'Advanced degree' indicates Master's, Doctoral, or first professional degree.
'All Races' includes other races not shown separately.
Data as of March.

Units: Percent as a percent of the population 25 years old and older; number in thousands of persons 25 years old and older.

Table 3.34: Educational Attainment of the Hispanic Population by Ethnic Group, 2003 and 2006

	Mexican	Puerto Rican	Cuban	Central American	South American	Other Hispanic	Total Hispanic
2003							
Total population 25 years or older	*13,443*	*2,072*	*1,052*	*1,636*	*1,317*	*1,669*	*21,189*
Percent of population:							
Less than 9th grade	30.7%	13.6%	19.2%	30.7%	10.0%	17.3%	26.1%
9th to 12th grade (no diploma)	18.4	16.7	9.9	18.6	8.0	14.4	16.9
High school graduate	26.3	33.2	34.3	22.4	30.5	28.0	27.4
Some college or associate's degree	16.8	24.1	15.0	15.6	22.9	23.0	18.2
Bachelor's degree	6.0	8.2	14.1	9.8	20.0	12.2	8.3
Advanced degree	1.8	4.1	7.5	3.0	8.7	5.2	3.1
2006							
Total population 25 years or older	*14,621*	*2,052*	*1,094*	*2,133*	*1,654*	*1,946*	*23,499*
Percent of population:							
Less than 9th grade	28.7%	12.4%	14.1%	33.5%	8.1%	15.3%	24.4%
9th to 12th grade (no diploma)	18.3	15.3	11.0	16.0	9.3	11.5	16.3
High school graduate	28.0	31.9	31.3	24.5	28.9	29.6	28.4
Some college or associate's degree	16.6	25.3	19.3	15.8	22.8	25.1	18.5
Bachelor's degree	6.3	11.0	16.3	7.5	20.6	12.7	8.8
Advanced degree	2.2	4.1	8.1	2.7	10.4	5.9	3.6

Source: U.S. Bureau of the Census, Current Population Reports: *The Hispanic Population of the United States, 2003*, table 6.2; *2006*, table 6.2a.

Notes: Includes population 25 years of age and older. 'Other Hispanic' includes Dominicans.

Units: Numbers of persons 25 years old and older in thousands; percent of total persons.

Table 3.35: Undergraduates Receiving Financial Aid: Average Amount Awarded per Student by Type and Source of Aid, 2003–2004

Undergraduates receiving aid	Hispanic	White	All Races
All full-time, full-year enrolled undergraduates	2,426	12,025	19,054
Receiving aid	63.2%	61.5%	63.2%
From grants	53.4	47.8	50.7
From loans	29.9	35.5	35.2
From work-study	6.8	7.3	7.5
Average aid from:			
Any source	$9,006	$9,919	$9,899
Federal source	6,670	7,318	7,304
Non-federal sources	4,838	5,733	5,586
Grants	$5,399	$5,479	$5,565
From federal source	3,431	3,075	3,247
Fom non-federal sources	4,251	4,887	4,828
Loans	$6,990	$7,443	$7,336
From federal source	6,193	6,450	6,426
From non-federal sources	5,500	6,222	6,089
Work-study funds, total	$1,985	$1,917	$1,942

Source: U.S. Department of Education, Center for Education Statistics, *Digest of Education Statistics, 2005*, tables 316 and 317.

Notes: 'All Races' includes races not shown separately.

Units: Number of undergraduates in thousands; percent of total undergraduates receiving financial aid; average financial aid in dollars.

Table 3.36: Average Total Price of Attendance of Undergraduate Education, 2003–2004

	Hispanic	White	All Races
Overall	*$11,454*	*$11,625*	*$11,256*
Public 2-year	6,213	6,161	6,149
Public 4-year:			
Doctorate	10,846	10,698	10,812
Non-doctorate	13,946	13,922	13,809
Public not-for-profit 4-year:			
Doctorate	19,200	19,778	18,700
Non-doctorate	30,444	30,659	30,340
Private for-profit	15,591	15,736	15,657

Source: U.S. Bureau of Census, *Statistical Abstract of the United States, 2007*, table 276.

Notes: Excludes students attending more than one institution.
Price includes tuition, fees, books, suplies, room and board, transportation, and other expenses. Based on the 2003–2004 National Postsecondary Student-Aid Study (NPSAS:04).

Units: Cost of attendance in dollars.

Chapter 4

Government & Elections

Chapter Four Highlights

This chapter provides information about government and elections as they pertain to Hispanic persons in the United States, including both the most current data available as well as comparisons of the Hispanic population over time. For almost all tables, corresponding data is provided for the total population of the United States as well as for White persons. This allows for easy comparison between groups.

The chapter contains data on Hispanic public officials (table 4.01) and members of congress (table 4.20), organizing information by year (table 4.01), by state (table 4.02), and by type of office held (table 4.02).

This chapter also includes a variety of information on the voting-age population (tables 4.03, 4.06, 4.09, 4.12, and 4.15), persons registered to vote (tables 4.03, 4.04, 4.07, 4.10, 4.13, and 4.16), and persons voting (tables 4.03, 4.05, 4.08, 4.11, 4.14, and 4.17). We have also provided data on the reasons given for not registering to vote (table 4.18) and for not voting (table 4.19).

Table 4.01: Hispanic Elected Public Officials by Type of Office Held, Selected Years, 1985–2006

	State Executives & legislators	County & Municipal Officials	Judicial & Law Enforcement	Education & School Boards	Total
1985	129	1,316	517	1,185	3,147
1990	144	1,819	583	1,458	4,004
2000	223	1,846	454	2,682	5,205
2001	217	1,852	447	2,503	5,019
2002	208	1,960	532	1,603	4,303
2003	231	1,958	549	1,694	4,432
2004	253	2,059	638	1,723	4,651
2005	266	2,149	678	1,760	4,853
2006	244	2,151	693	1,835	4,932

Source: U.S. Bureau of the Census, *Statistical Abstract of the United States, 2008*, table 403.

Notes: Data as of September for 1985-2001, and as of January for 2002–2006. Total includes US Representatives not shown separately.

Units: Number of Hispanic elected public officials.

Table 4.02: Hispanic Elected Public Officials
by State and Type of Office Held, 2006

	State Executives & Legislators	County & City Officials	Judicial & Law Enforcement	Education & School Boards	Total
United States	*244*	*2,151*	*693*	*1,835*	*4,932*
Alabama	0	0	0	0	0
Alaska	0	1	0	0	1
Arizona	17	141	47	152	357
Arkansas	0	0	0	0	0
California	30	388	41	600	1,059
Colorado	7	101	7	30	145
Connecticut	6	19	0	4	29
Delaware	1	1	0	0	2
District of Columbia	0	0	0	1	1
Florida	19	70	26	6	121
Georgia	3	2	2	0	7
Hawaii	1	0	0	0	1
Idaho	1	1	0	0	2
Illinois	11	63	6	16	96
Indiana	1	8	3	1	13
Iowa	0	0	0	0	0
Kansas	4	6	0	1	11
Kentucky	0	0	0	0	0
Louisiana	0	1	2	0	3
Maine	0	0	0	0	0
Maryland	4	7	0	2	13
Massachusetts	4	10	0	5	19
Michigan	3	3	3	7	16
Minnesota	1	1	1	0	3
Mississippi	0	0	0	0	0
Missouri	0	1	0	0	1
Montana	0	0	1	0	1
Nebraska	1	1	0	1	3
Nevada	2	5	3	1	11

(continued on next page)

Table 4.02: Hispanic Elected Public Officials by State and Type of Office Held, 2006

	State Executives & Legislators	County & City Officials	Judicial & Law Enforcement	Education & School Boards	Total
United States	244	2,151	693	1,835	4,932
New Hampshire	2	1	0	0	3
New Jersey	5	61	0	43	109
New Mexico	48	337	111	144	649
New York	16	30	15	2	63
North Carolina	2	1	0	0	3
North Dakota	0	1	0	0	1
Ohio	0	3	1	0	4
Oklahoma	0	0	0	1	1
Oregon	3	9	5	0	17
Pennsylvania	1	7	2	2	12
Rhode Island	4	3	0	0	7
South Carolina	1	0	0	0	1
South Dakota	0	0	0	0	0
Tennessee	1	1	0	0	2
Texas	38	851	413	807	2,109
Utah	2	3	0	0	5
Vermont	0	0	0	0	0
Virginia	0	1	0	0	1
Washington	3	4	0	6	13
West Virginia	0	0	0	0	0
Wisconsin	1	5	4	3	13
Wyoming	1	3	0	0	4

Source: U.S. Bureau of the Census, *Statistical Abstract of the United States, 2008*, table 403.

Notes: Data as of September for 1985-2001, and as of January for 2002-2006. Total includes US Representatives not shown separately.

Units: Number of Hispanic elected public officials.

Table 4.03: Voting-Age Population, Registration, and Voting, 1984–2006

	Hispanic	White	All Races
Voting-Age Population			
1984	9.5	146.8	170.0
1986	11.8	149.9	173.9
1988	12.9	152.8	178.1
1990	13.8	155.6	182.1
1992	14.7	157.8	185.7
1994	17.5	160.3	190.3
1996	18.4	162.8	193.7
1998	20.3	165.8	198.2
2000	21.6	168.7	202.6
2002	25.1	174.1	210.4
2004*	27.1	176.6	215.7
2006*	29.0	179.9	220.6
Presidential Election Years			
Percent Reporting Registration			
1984	40.1%	69.6%	68.3%
1988	35.5	67.9	66.6
1992	35.0	70.1	68.2
1996	35.7	67.7	65.9
2000	57.3	70.4	63.9
2004*	34.3	67.9	65.9
Percent Reporting Voting			
1984	32.6%	61.4%	59.9%
1988	28.8	59.1	57.4
1992	28.9	63.6	61.3
1996	26.7	56.0	54.2
2000	45.1	60.5	54.7
2004*	28.0	60.3	58.3

(continued on next page)

Table 4.03: Voting-Age Population, Registration, and Voting, 1984–2006

	Hispanic	White	All Races
Congressional Election Years (Non-Presidential Election Years)			
Percent Reporting Registration			
1982	35.3%	65.6%	64.1%
1986	35.9	65.3	64.3
1990	32.3	63.8	62.2
1994	31.3	64.6	62.5
1998	33.7	63.9	62.1
2002	32.6	63.1	60.9
2006*	32.1	64.0	61.6
Percent Reporting Voting			
1982	25.3%	49.9%	48.5%
1986	24.2	47.0	46.0
1990	21.0	46.7	45.0
1994	20.2	47.3	45.0
1998	20.0	43.3	41.9
2002	18.9	44.1	42.3
2006*	19.3	45.8	43.6

Source: U.S. Bureau of the Census, *Statistical Abstract of the United States, 1989*, table 432; *1999*, table 487; *2008*, table 404.
U.S. Bureau of the Census, Current Population Reports: *Voting and Registration in the Election of November, 1988*, table 8; *1990*, table 2; *1992*, table 2; *1994*, tables 1 and VI; *1996*, table 23; *2000*, table A; *2002*, table 2; *2004*, table 2.

Notes: 'All Races' includes races not shown separately.
* For 2004 and 2006, 'White' is equivalent to 'White Alone.'

Units: Voting-age population in millions of persons; percent reporting registration and percent reporting voting out of the voting-age population.

Table 4.04: Selected Characteristics of Persons Registered to Vote, 1990

	Hispanic	White	All Races
Total 18 years and over	*32.3%*	*63.8%*	*62.2%*
By Age			
18–20 years old	17.2	37.0	35.4
21–24 years old	20.9	43.1	43.3
25–34 years old	27.4	53.2	52.0
35–44 years old	34.8	67.2	65.5
45–54 years old	38.3	71.3	69.8
55–64 years old	45.5	74.9	73.5
65–74 years old	56.6	79.7	78.3
75 years and over	46.0	74.8	73.7
By Sex			
Male	30.0%	63.0%	61.2%
Female	34.5	64.6	63.1
By Years of School Completed			
Elementary			
0–4 years of school	15.3%	26.4%	29.5%
5–7 years of school	15.8	38.7	41.1
8 years of school	28.1	54.3	53.3
High School			
1–3 years high school	24.6%	48.2%	47.9%
4 years high school	36.6	61.2	60.0
College			
1–3 years college	50.6%	70.2%	68.7%
4 years college	51.1	77.1	74.5
5 or more years college	59.3	83.5	81.5

(continued on next page)

Table 4.04: Selected Characteristics of Persons Registered to Vote, 1990

	Hispanic	White	All Races
By Family Income			
Under $5,000	28.2%	53.1%	50.7%
$5,000–$9,999	22.7	47.6	48.3
$10,000–$14,999	23.9	55.4	54.8
$15,000–$19,999	29.0	57.5	56.8
$20,000–$24,999	21.7	59.0	58.0
$25,000–$34,999	37.7	65.0	63.9
$35,000–$49,999	46.5	69.4	68.3
$50,000 and over	51.7	77.8	76.4
Income not reported	29.6	59.7	57.6

Source: U.S. Bureau of the Census, Current Population Reports: *Voting and Registration in the Election of November, 1990*, tables 2, 8 and 13.

Notes: 'All Races' includes races not shown separately.

Units: Percent of voting-age population reporting being registered to vote in election.

Table 4.05: Selected Characteristics of Persons Voting, 1990

	Hispanic	White	All Races
Total 18 years and over	*21.0%*	*46.7%*	*45.0%*
By Age			
18–20 years old	10.1	19.4	18.4
21–24 years old	7.8	21.8	22.0
25–34 years old	16.5	34.9	33.8
35–44 years old	24.2	50.0	48.4
45–54 years old	25.4	54.9	53.2
55–64 years old	33.5	60.4	58.9
65–74 years old	43.8	65.7	64.1
75 years and over	33.4	55.8	54.5
By Sex			
Male	19.4%	46.4%	44.6%
Female	22.6	46.9	45.4
By Years of School Completed			
Elementary			
0–4 years of school	9.4%	14.8%	16.5%
5–7 years of school	11.3	23.7	25.7
8 years of school	15.6	35.7	34.8
High School			
1–3 years high school	13.5%	31.3%	30.9%
4 years high school	22.5	43.6	42.2
College			
1–3 years college	36.0%	51.4%	50.0%
4 years college	38.8	61.6	59.0
5 or more years college	45.8	69.6	67.8

(continued on next page)

Table 4.05: Selected Characteristics of Persons Voting, 1990

	Hispanic	White	All Races
By Family Income			
Under $5,000	14.9%	35.1%	32.2%
$5,000–$9,999	14.6	31.3	30.9
$10,000–$14,999	14.5	38.5	37.7
$15,000–$19,999	16.6	39.9	38.8
$20,000–$24,999	14.9	42.5	41.3
$25,000–$34,999	26.3	47.5	46.4
$35,000–$49,999	29.8	51.8	51.0
$50,000 and over	37.8	60.5	59.2
Income not reported	19.3	45.1	43.3

Source: U.S. Bureau of the Census, Current Population Reports: *Voting and Registration in the Election of November, 1990*, tables 2, 8 and 13.

Notes: 'All Races' includes races not shown separately.

Units: Pecent of voting-age population reporting voting in election.

Table 4.06: Selected Characteristics of the Voting-Age Population, 2000

	Hispanic	White	All Races
Total, 18 years and over	*21,598*	*168,733*	*202,609*
By Sex			
Male	10,653	81,720	97,087
Female	10,945	87,014	105,523
By Age			
18–24 years old	4,169	21,295	26,712
25–44 years old	10,640	66,378	81,780
45–64 years old	4,962	52,038	61,352
65–74 years old	1,110	15,493	17,819
75 years and over	718	13,529	14,945
By Educational Attainment			
Less than 9th grade	5,272	10,626	12,894
9th to 12th grade, no diploma	3,931	15,822	20,108
High school graduate or GED	6,295	55,530	66,339
Some college or associate degree	4,036	45,923	55,308
Bachelor's degree	1,438	27,382	32,254
Advanced degree	627	13,450	15,706
By Employment Status			
In civilian labor force	15,280	115,103	138,378
Unemployed	826	3,544	4,944
By Family Income			
Less than $5,000	532	1,405	2,230
$5,000–$9,999	998	2,732	4,242
$10,000–$14,999	1,073	5,390	7,286
$15,000–$24,999	3,249	11,568	14,600
$25,000–$34,999	2,934	14,578	17,692
$35,000–$49,999	2,518	18,907	22,349
$50,000–$74,999	2,182	24,250	28,144
$75,000 and over	1,695	31,021	35,030
Income not reported	1,304	17,518	20,721

Source: U.S. Bureau of the Census, Current Population Reports: *Voting and Registration in the Election of November, 2000*, tables 2, 6, 7, and 9.

Notes: 'All Races' includes races not shown separately.

Units: Voting-age population (18 years and over) in thousands.

Table 4.07: Selected Characteristics of Persons Registered to Vote, 2000

	Hispanic	White	All Races
Total, 18 years and over	*34.9%*	*65.6%*	*63.9%*
By Sex			
Male	31.7%	64.0%	62.2%
Female	38.1	67.2	65.6
By Age			
18–24 years old	23.2%	46.3%	45.4%
25–44 years old	31.1	61.2	59.6
45–64 years old	45.1	72.7	71.2
65–74 years old	57.2	77.3	76.2
75 years and over	55.9	77.2	76.1
By Educational Attainment			
Less than 9th grade	17.4%	34.8%	36.1%
9th to 12th grade, no diploma	25.4	44.8	45.9
High school graduate or GED	38.0	61.3	60.1
Some college or associate degree	51.1	71.8	70.0
Bachelor's degree	53.5	79.6	76.3
Advanced degree	64.7	83.1	79.4
By Employment Status			
In civilian labor force	34.2%	65.5%	64.0%
Unemployed	22.6	44.9	46.1
By Family Income			
Less than $5,000	25.6%	40.7%	44.0%
$5,000–$9,999	28.2	45.3	48.8
$10,000–$14,999	26.4	47.5	49.8
$15,000–$24,999	26.3	55.1	54.9
$25,000–$34,999	30.0	61.9	61.0
$35,000–$49,999	41.1	68.8	67.1
$50,000–$74,999	49.3	75.9	73.8
$75,000 and over	63.5	80.7	78.4
Income not reported	32.1	55.5	54.2

Source: U.S. Bureau of the Census, Current Population Reports: *Voting and Registration in the Election of November, 2000*, tables 2, 6, 7, and 9.

Notes: 'All Races' includes races not shown separately.

Units: Percent of voting-age population reporting being registered to vote in election.

Table 4.08: Selected Characteristics of Persons Voting, 2000

	Hispanic	White	All Races
Total, 18 years and over	*27.5%*	*56.4%*	*54.7%*
By Sex			
Male	25.1%	54.9%	53.1%
Female	29.8	57.7	56.2
By Age			
18–24 years old	15.4%	33.0%	32.3%
25–44 years old	23.2	51.2	49.8
45–64 years old	38.3	65.6	64.1
65–74 years old	50.9	71.1	69.9
75 years and over	48.7	66.2	64.9
By Educational Attainment			
Less than 9th grade	14.0%	25.8%	26.8%
9th to 12th grade, no diploma	17.4	32.7	33.6
High school graduate or GED	28.7	50.4	49.4
Some college or associate degree	41.1	62.0	60.3
Bachelor's degree	47.0	73.4	70.3
Advanced degree	59.8	79.3	75.5
By Employment Status			
In civilian labor force	26.7%	56.2%	54.8%
Unemployed	15.5	34.6	35.1
By Family Income			
Less than $5,000	16.2%	27.3%	28.2%
$5,000–$9,999	20.8	32.5	34.7
$10,000–$14,999	19.7	35.6	37.7
$15,000–$24,999	19.4	43.3	43.4
$25,000–$34,999	23.6	51.8	51.0
$35,000–$49,999	31.5	58.8	57.5
$50,000–$74,999	39.5	67.1	65.2
$75,000 and over	57.0	73.8	71.5
Income not reported	27.1	49.6	48.2

Source: U.S. Bureau of the Census, Current Population Reports: *Voting and Registration in the Election of November, 2000*, tables 2, 6, 7, and 9.

Notes: 'All Races' includes races not shown separately.

Units: Pecent of voting-age population reporting voting in election.

Hispanic Americans: A Statistical Sourcebook 2009

Table 4.09: Selected Characteristics of the Voting-Age Population, 2002

	Hispanic	White	All Races
Total, 18 years and over	*25,162*	*174,099*	*210,421*
By Sex			
Male	12,855	84,466	100,939
Female	12,307	89,633	109,481
By Age			
18–24 years old	4,825	21,728	27,377
25–44 years old	12,860	66,238	82,228
45–64 years old	5,586	56,204	66,924
65–74 years old	1,131	15,653	17,967
75 years and over	760	14,276	15,925
By Educational Attainment			
Less than 9th grade	5,689	10,195	12,333
9th to 12th grade, no diploma	4,561	16,161	20,908
High school graduate or GED	7,341	57,210	68,866
Some college or associate degree	4,983	47,538	57,343
Bachelor's degree	1,848	28,693	34,095
Advanced degree	740	14,302	16,877
By Employment Status			
In civilian labor force	17,922	118,094	142,635
Unemployed	1,307	5,488	7,735
By Family Income			
Less than $5,000	529	1,280	2,159
$5,000–$9,999	1,042	2,707	4,051
$10,000–$14,999	1,697	4,960	6,696
$15,000–$24,999	3,556	11,696	14,665
$25,000–$34,999	2,988	13,412	16,868
$35,000–$49,999	3,370	18,200	21,945
$50,000–$74,999	2,640	24,932	28,921
$75,000 and over	2,320	35,540	40,309
Income not reported	1,577	18,188	22,278

Source: U.S. Bureau of the Census, Current Population Reports: *Voting and Registration in the Election of November, 2002*, tables 2, 6, 7, and 9.

Notes: 'All Races' includes races not shown separately.

Units: Voting-age population (18 years and over) in thousands.

Table 4.10: Selected Characteristics of Persons Registered to Vote, 2002

	Hispanic	White	All Races
Total, 18 years and over	*32.6%*	*63.1%*	*60.9%*
By Sex			
Male	29.4%	61.3%	58.9%
Female	35.9	64.8	62.8
By Age			
18–24 years old	20.8%	39.2%	38.2%
25–44 years old	28.9	57.4	55.4
45–64 years old	43.6	71.3	69.4
65–74 years old	56.1	77.9	76.1
75 years and over	53.0	76.7	75.5
By Educational Attainment			
Less than 9th grade	17.0%	31.6%	32.4%
9th to 12th grade, no diploma	21.9	41.1	41.6
High school graduate or GED	34.1	58.7	57.1
Some college or associate degree	49.4	68.8	66.7
Bachelor's degree	46.6	76.7	73.3
Advanced degree	54.7	81.3	76.6
by Employment Status			
In civilian labor force	32.6%	62.8%	60.9%
Unemployed	25.6	48.6	48.1
By Family Income			
Less than $5,000	20.4%	39.5%	45.2%
$5,000–$9,999	25.6	40.1	41.5
$10,000–$14,999	31.0	50.3	49.7
$15,000–$24,999	23.7	51.0	51.3
$25,000–$34,999	28.8	58.5	56.2
$35,000–$49,999	32.6	64.1	62.0
$50,000–$74,999	44.9	72.0	69.8
$75,000 and over	56.9	77.8	75.5
Income not reported	29.9	54.4	52.0

Source: U.S. Bureau of the Census, Current Population Reports: *Voting and Registration in the Election of November, 2002*, tables 2, 6, 7, and 9.

Notes: 'All Races' includes races not shown separately.

Units: Percent of voting-age population reporting being registered to vote in election.

Table 4.11: Selected Characteristics of Persons Voting, 2002

	Hispanic	White	All Races
Total, 18 years and over	*18.9%*	*44.1%*	*42.3%*
By Sex			
Male	17.3%	43.5%	41.4%
Female	20.5	44.6	43.0
By Age			
18–24 years old	8.1%	17.4%	17.2%
25–44 years old	15.3	35.3	34.1
45–64 years old	28.7	54.8	53.1
65–74 years old	43.3	65.1	63.1
75 years and over	38.8	60.1	58.6
By Educational Attainment			
Less than 9th grade	10.1%	19.0%	19.4%
9th to 12th grade, no diploma	10.5	23.1	23.3
High school graduate or GED	18.8	38.3	37.1
Some college or associate degree	28.1	47.3	45.8
Bachelor's degree	32.4	59.1	56.2
Advanced degree	42.4	67.7	63.2
By Employment Status			
In civilian labor force	18.3%	42.7%	41.3%
Unemployed	12.4	28.2	27.2
By Family Income			
Less than $5,000	7.6%	19.6%	22.0%
$5,000–$9,999	11.5	19.8	20.7
$10,000–$14,999	17.1	31.1	30.5
$15,000–$24,999	12.5	31.9	32.0
$25,000–$34,999	16.3	40.2	38.3
$35,000–$49,999	18.1	44.2	42.7
$50,000–$74,999	28.2	51.7	50.1
$75,000 and over	36.5	58.3	56.6
Income not reported	20.7	40.5	38.6

Source: U.S. Bureau of the Census, Current Population Reports: *Voting and Registration in the Election of November, 2002*, tables 2, 6, 7, and 9.

Notes: 'All Races' includes races not shown separately.

Units: Pecent of voting-age population reporting voting in election.

Table 4.12: Selected Characteristics of the Voting-Age Population, 2004

	Hispanic	White	All Races
Total, 18 years and over	*27,129*	*176,618*	*215,694*
By Sex			
Male	13,945	85,984	103,812
Female	13,185	90,634	111,882
By Age			
18–24 years old	4,197	21,764	27,808
25–44 years old	13,715	65,317	82,133
45–64 years old	6,347	59,196	71,014
65–74 years old	1,305	15,783	18,363
75 years and over	846	14,557	16,375
By Educational Attainment			
Less than 9th grade	6,298	10,431	12,574
9th to 12th grade, no diploma	4,712	15,793	20,719
High school graduate or GED	7,906	56,254	68,545
Some college or associate degree	5,421	48,154	58,913
Bachelor's degree	2,048	30,678	36,591
Advanced degree	745	15,308	18,352
By Employment Status			
In civilian labor force	19,290	119,726	146,082
Unemployed	1,210	5,030	7,251
By Family Income			
Less than $10,000	1,385	4,088	6,404
$10,000–$14,999	1,808	4,874	6,565
$15,000–$19,999	1,543	4,386	5,859
$20,000–$29,999	3,438	12,339	15,574
$30,000–$39,999	3,190	14,042	17,194
$40,000–$49,999	1,846	11,170	13,281
$50,000–$74,999	3,000	25,568	30,179
$75,000–$99,999	1,266	15,707	18,123
$100,000–$149,999	771	12,894	14,905
$150,000 and over	329	8,003	9,120
Income not reported	2,580	19,886	24,723

Source: U.S. Bureau of the Census, Current Population Reports: *Voting and Registration in the Election of November, 2004*, tables 2, 6, 7, and 9.

Notes: 'All Races' includes races not shown separately. 'White' is equivalent to 'White Alone.'

Units: Voting-age population (18 years and over) in thousands.

Table 4.13: Selected Characteristics of Persons Registered to Vote, 2004

	Hispanic	White	All Races
Total, 18 years and over	*34.3%*	*67.9%*	*65.9%*
By Sex			
Male	31.3%	66.2%	64.0%
Female	37.5	69.5	67.6
By Age			
18–24 years old	27.6%	52.5%	51.5%
25–44 years old	28.8	62.0	60.1
45–64 years old	44.4	74.6	72.7
65–74 years old	55.9	78.4	76.9
75 years and over	53.8	78.4	76.8
By Educational attainment			
Less than 9th grade	15.9%	31.5%	32.5%
9th to 12th grade, no diploma	22.8	44.6	45.7
High school graduate or GED	35.0	62.7	61.5
Some college or associate degree	53.6	75.6	73.7
Bachelor's degree	52.8	80.9	77.0
Advanced degree	64.3	85.5	80.3
By Employment status			
In civilian labor force	34.8%	68.5%	66.5%
Unemployed	29.7	55.2	56.3
By Family income			
Less than $10,000	28.4%	43.8%	49.5%
$10,000–$14,999	19.6	46.2	49.0
$15,000–$19,999	27.1	52.6	53.9
$20,000–$29,999	26.8	58.2	58.1
$30,000–$39,999	31.4	63.9	62.9
$40,000–$49,999	37.9	71.9	69.8
$50,000–$74,999	51.7	77.8	75.6
$75,000–$99,999	57.4	82.3	79.4
$100,000–$149,999	59.6	84.9	82.2
$150,000 and over	60.3	85.2	82.6
Income not reported	27.6	56.1	53.0

Source: U.S. Bureau of the Census, Current Population Reports: *Voting and Registration in the Election of November, 2004*, tables 2, 6, 7, and 9.

Notes: 'All Races' includes races not shown separately. 'White' is equivalent to 'White Alone.'

Units: Percent of voting-age population reporting being registered to vote in election.

Table 4.14: Selected Characteristics of Persons Voting, 2004

	Hispanic	White	All Races
Total, 18 years and over	*28.0%*	*60.3%*	*58.3%*
By Sex			
Male	25.2%	58.6%	56.3%
Female	30.9	62.0	60.1
By Age			
18–24 years old	20.4%	42.6%	41.9%
25–44 years old	23.0	54.0	52.2
45–64 years old	38.5	68.6	66.6
65–74 years old	46.8	72.4	70.8
75 years and over	44.7	68.4	66.7
By Educational Attainment			
Less than 9th grade	11.9%	22.7%	23.6%
9th to 12th grade, no diploma	16.3	33.3	34.6
High school graduate or GED	27.8	53.4	52.4
Some college or associate degree	45.0	68.0	66.1
Bachelor's degree	48.1	76.7	72.6
Advanced degree	60.3	82.7	77.4
By Employment Status			
In civilian labor force	28.5%	61.1%	59.3%
Unemployed	21.9	45.1	46.4
By Family Income			
Less than $10,000	18.8%	31.7%	36.5%
$10,000–$14,999	15.1	36.7	39.1
$15,000–$19,999	21.0	44.0	45.2
$20,000–$29,999	21.8	49.7	49.4
$30,000–$39,999	24.5	55.0	54.3
$40,000–$49,999	29.4	64.4	62.3
$50,000–$74,999	44.4	70.2	68.1
$75,000–$99,999	51.7	76.8	74.1
$100,000–$149,999	55.0	80.4	77.8
$150,000 and over	53.5	81.0	78.3
Income not reported	23.2	50.4	47.6

Source: U.S. Bureau of the Census, Current Population Reports: *Voting and Registration in the Election of November, 2004*, tables 2, 6, 7, and 9.

Notes: 'All Races' includes races not shown separately. 'White' is equivalent to 'White Alone.'

Units: Pecent of voting-age population reporting voting in election.

Table 4.15: Voting-Age Population by Selected Characteristics, 2006

	Hispanic	White	All Races
Total, 18 years and over	*28,945*	*179,873*	*220,603*
By Sex			
Male	14,901	87,860	106,531
Female	14,044	92,013	114,073
By Age			
18–24 years old	4,885	21,668	27,774
25–44 years old	14,538	64,810	82,002
45–64 years old	7,133	62,262	75,006
65–74 years old	1,530	16,112	18,954
75 years and over	860	15,021	16,864
By Educational Attainment			
Less than 9th grade	6,046	9,838	12,085
9th to 12th grade, no diploma	5,008	15,333	20,184
High school graduate or GED	8,719	57,234	69,948
Some college or associate degree	5,845	49,528	60,207
Bachelor's degree	2,390	31,907	38,692
Advanced degree	938	16,034	19,488
By Family Income			
Less than $10,000	1,103	3,069	4,996
$10,000–$14,999	1,552	4,191	6,024
$15,000–$19,999	1,311	3,823	4,977
$20,000–$29,999	3,228	11,488	14,375
$30,000–$39,999	3,353	13,379	16,491
$40,000–$49,999	1,842	10,194	12,271
$50,000–$74,999	3,322	24,923	29,085
$75,000–$99,999	1,624	16,416	19,262
$100,000–$149,999	1,088	14,223	16,341
$150,000 and over	575	10,413	12,096
Income not reported	3,063	21,568	27,238

Source: U.S. Bureau of the Census, Current Population Reports: *Voting and Registration in the Election of November, 2006,* tables 2, 6, and 9.

Notes: 'All Races' includes other races not shown separately. 'White' as shown is equivalent to 'White Alone.'

Units: Voting-age population in thousands of persons.

Table 4.16: Selected Characteristics of Persons Registered to Vote, 2006

	Hispanic	White	All Races
Total, 18 years and over	*53.7%*	*69.5%*	*67.6%*
By Sex			
Male	51.4%	68.2%	66.0%
Female	55.9	70.8	69.0
By Age			
18–24 years old	38.7%	48.0%	46.3%
25–44 years old	52.2	65.2	63.8
45–64 years old	60.7	75.6	73.7
65–74 years old	63.6	80.2	78.4
75 years and over	69.3	78.9	77.6
By Educational Attainment			
Less than 9th grade	47.5%	49.9%	49.8%
9th to 12th grade, no diploma	37.0	47.1	46.6
High school graduate or GED	50.0	63.6	61.9
Some college or associate degree	60.9	72.8	71.3
Bachelor's degree	69.8	80.0	77.9
Advanced degree	71.6	84.4	82.3
By Family Income			
Less than $10,000	40.0%	46.8%	50.7%
$10,000–$14,999	47.7	57.6	57.1
$15,000–$19,999	38.5	58.0	59.7
$20,000–$29,999	50.9	66.5	66.3
$30,000–$39,999	53.9	68.9	67.4
$40,000–$49,999	56.8	73.1	72.1
$50,000–$74,999	64.8	76.9	75.8
$75,000–$99,999	69.3	79.4	77.5
$100,000–$149,999	77.6	84.0	82.3
$150,000 and over	66.0	83.5	82.1
Income not reported	36.1	56.7	53.1

Source: U.S. Bureau of the Census, Current Population Reports: *Voting and Registration in the Election of November, 2006*, tables 2, 6, and 9.

Notes: 'All Races' includes other races not shown separately. 'White' as shown is equivalent to 'White Alone.'

Units: Persons registered to vote as a percent of the voting-age population.

Table 4.17: Selected Characteristics of Persons Voting, 2006

	Hispanic	White	All Races
Total, 18 years and over	*32.3%*	*49.7%*	*47.8%*
By Sex			
Male	31.0%	49.1%	46.9%
Female	33.5	50.3	48.6
By Age			
18–24 years old	16.6%	22.9%	22.1%
25–44 years old	28.2	41.0	39.9
45–64 years old	42.5	59.5	57.6
65–74 years old	46.1	66.2	64.3
75 years and over	48.3	62.1	60.6
By Educational Attainment			
Less than 9th grade	28.8%	28.4%	28.9%
9th to 12th grade, no diploma	20.7	27.6	26.8
High school graduate or GED	26.6	42.2	40.5
Some college or associate degree	36.8	50.9	49.4
Bachelor's degree	49.2	63.3	61.1
Advanced degree	56.5	71.6	69.6
By Family Income			
less than $10,000	17.4%	22.7%	24.3
$10,000–$14,999	26.7	33.0	32.9
$15,000–$19,999	22.7	37.4	36.6
$20,000–$29,999	28.4	45.5	44.1
$30,000–$39,999	27.4	47.1	45.6
$40,000–$49,999	36.0	53.4	52.5
$50,000–$74,999	40.5	55.3	54.4
$75,000–$99,999	46.2	58.9	57.4
$100,000–$149,999	56.5	65.4	63.9
$150,000 and over	47.0	65.9	64.6
Income not reported	21.9	42.0	39.2

Source: U.S. Bureau of the Census, Current Population Reports: *Voting and Registration in the Election of November, 2006*, tables 2, 6, and 9.

Notes: 'All Races' includes other races not shown separately. 'White' as shown is equivalent to 'White Alone.'

Units: Person reporting voting in election as a percent of the voting-age population.

Table 4.18: Reasons for Not Registering, 2006

	Hispanic	White	All Races
Total not registered	5,339	31,646	39,599
Percent Distribution			
Not interested in the election or not involved in politics	39.2%	49.3%	47.6%
Did not meet registration deadlines	13.2	14.0	14.2
Not eligible to vote	12.0	6.0	6.5
Don't know or refused	8.6	5.9	6.1
Permanent illness or disability	3.1	4.8	4.8
Did not know where or how to register	6.9	4.9	5.6
Did not meet residency requirements	5.8	4.7	4.8
My vote would not make a difference	2.5	3.4	3.2
Difficulty with English	3.3	0.8	1.1

Source: U.S. Bureau of the Census, Current Population Reports: *Voting and Registration in the Election of November, 2006*, table E.

Notes: 'All Races' includes other races not shown separately. 'White' as shown is equivalent to 'White Alone.'

Units: Numbers in thousands. Percent distribution of reasons for not registering to vote among voting-age population.

Table 4.19: Reasons for Not Voting, 2006

	Hispanic	White	All Races
Total not voting	3,708	32,748	39,728
Percent Distribution			
Too busy, conflicting schedule	31.1%	27.7%	27.3%
Illness or disability	11.3	12.4	12.4
Other reason	8.7	9.0	9.1
Not interested	11.8	11.7	11.5
Did not like candidates or issues	4.8	7.8	7.3
Out of town	7.4	11.0	10.7
Don't know or refused	6.0	6.6	7.2
Registration problems	2.8	3.8	3.9
Forgot to vote	11.0	5.3	5.7
Inconvenient polling place	3.1	2.4	2.5
Transportation problems	2.0	1.7	2.0
Bad weather conditions	NA	0.5	0.6

Source: U.S. Bureau of the Census, Current Population Reports: *Voting and Registration in the Election of November, 2006,* table F.

Notes: 'All Races' includes other races not shown separately. 'White' as shown is equivalent to 'White Alone.'
NA represents or rounds to zero.

Units: Numbers in thousands. Percent distribution of reasons for not voting.

Table 4.20: Members of Congress, 1981–2007

	Hispanic	White	All Races
House of Representatives			
97th Congress, 1981	6	415	434
98th Congress, 1983	8	411	"
99th Congress, 1985	10	412	435
100th Congress, 1987	11	408	433
101st Congress, 1989	10	406	435
102nd Congress, 1991	11	407	"
103rd Congress, 1993	17	393	"
104th Congress, 1995	17	391	"
106th Congress, 1999	19	NA	"
107th Congress, 2001	19	NA	443
108th Congress, 2003	22	NA	435
109th Congress, 2005	23	NA	"
110th Congress, 2007	23	NA	"
Senate			
97th Congress, 1981	0	97	100
98th Congress, 1983	0	98	"
99th Congress, 1985	0	98	"
100th Congress, 1987	0	98	"
101st Congress, 1989	0	98	"
102nd Congress, 1991	0	98	"
103rd Congress, 1993	0	97	"
104th Congress, 1995	0	97	"
106th Congress, 1999	0	NA	"
107th Congress, 2001	0	NA	"
108th Congress, 2003	0	NA	"
109th Congress, 2005	2	NA	"
110th Congress, 2005	3	NA	"

Source: U.S. Bureau of the Census, *Statistical Abstract of the United States, 2006*, table 395; *2007*, table 395.
U.S. House of Representatives, 'House Press Gallery' (accessed online at http://www.house.gov/daily/hpg.htm).
U.S. Senate, 'Ethnic Diversity in the Senate' (accessed online at http://www.senate.gov/artandhistory/history/common/briefing/minority_senators.htm).

Notes: 'All Races' includes races not shown separately.

Units: Number of members of the House and Senate, respectively.

Chapter 5

Crime, Law
Enforcement & Corrections

Chapter Five Highlights

This chapter provides statistics about crime, law enforcement, and corrections on Hispanic persons in the United States, including both the most current data available as well as comparisons of the Hispanic population over time. For almost all tables, corresponding data is provided for the total population of the United States as well as for White persons. This allows for easy comparison between groups.

This chapter includes data on crime victimization organized in a variety of ways, including by type of crime (tables 5.01–5.04) and by sex (table 5.03).

We have also included statistics on incarceration, including incarceration rates (tables 5.05, 5.08, and 5.10), prisoners under sentence of death (tables 5.12–5.14), and HIV and AIDS rates in prisons and jails (tables 5.15 and 5.16). This chapter also provides data on the incarceration of minors (tables 5.18 and 5.19).

We have also included a table on hate crimes with race or ethnicity as a bias motivation (table 5.20).

Table 5.01: Victimization Rates for Personal Crimes, 2002–2007

	Hispanic Victims	White Victims	Victims of All Races
2002			
Crimes of violence	23.6	22.8	23.1
Rape/sexual assault	0.7*	0.8	1.1
Robbery	3.2	1.9	2.2
Assault	19.7	20.0	19.8
Personal theft	0.4*	0.7	0.7
2004			
Crimes of violence	18.2	21.0	21.4
Rape/sexual assault	0.6*	0.8	0.9
Robbery	2.8	1.8	2.1
Assault	14.9	18.4	18.5
Personal theft	0.7*	0.8	0.9
2005			
Crimes of violence	25.0	20.1	21.2
Rape/sexual assault	1.1*	0.6	0.8
Robbery	4.0	2.2	2.6
Assault	19.9	17.2	17.8
Personal theft	1.0*	0.9	0.9
2006			
Crimes of violence	27.7	23.3	24.7
Rape/sexual assault	*0.9	1.1	1.1
Robbery	4.9	2.8	2.9
Assault	22.0	19.5	20.7
Personal theft	*0.6	0.6	0.7

Source: U.S. Department of Justice, Office of Justice Programs, *Criminal Victimization 2001*, tables 1 and 2; *2002*, tables 3 and 6; *2003*, tables 3 and 6; *2004*; tables 3 and 6; *2005*, tables 5 and 7; *2006*, table 7.

Notes: 'Victims of All Races' includes victims of other races not shown separately.
Personal crimes include completed and attempted rape, robbery, assault, and larceny, but exclude homicide.
'Personal Theft' includes purse-snatching and pocket-picking.
The National Crime Victimization Survey has been redesigned; data based on previous survey procedures (before 2006) are not directly comparable with later data.
*Based on 10 or fewer sample cases.

Units: Rates per 1,000 persons, 12 years old and over.

Table 5.02: Victimization Rates for Personal Crimes by Type of Crime, 2006

	Hispanic Victims	White Victims	Victims of All Races
All personal crimes	*28.4*	*23.9*	*25.4*
Crimes of violence	24.7	23.3	24.7
completed	8.2	7.2	8.2
attempted/threatened	16.5	16.1	16.5
Rape/sexual assault	1.1	1.1	1.1
Rape/attempted rape	0.8	0.8	0.8
- rape	0.5	0.5	0.5
- attempted rape	0.3	0.3	0.3
Sexual assault	0.3	0.3	0.3
Robbery	2.9	2.8	2.9
completed/property taken	2.0	1.8	2.0
- with injury	0.8	0.8	0.8
- without injury	1.1	1.0	1.1
attempted to take property	0.9	0.9	0.9
- with injury	0.2	*0.1	0.2
- without injury	0.8	0.8	0.8
Assault	20.7	19.5	20.7
aggravated	5.4	4.6	5.4
- with injury	1.9	1.4	1.9
- threatened with weapon	3.5	3.2	3.5
simple	15.3	14.9	15.3
- with minor injury	3.6	3.3	3.6
- without injury	11.6	11.6	11.6
Purse-snatching/pocket-picking	0.7	0.6	0.7

Source: U.S. Department of Justice, Office of Justice Programs, *Criminal Victimization 2006*, table 7.

Notes: 'Victims of All Races' includes victims of other races not shown separately.
Personal crimes include completed and attempted rape, robbery, assault, and larceny, but exclude homicide.
'Personal Theft' includes purse-snatching and pocket-picking.
The National Crime Victimization Survey has been redesigned; data based on previous survey procedures (before 2006) are not directly comparable with later data.
*Based on 10 or fewer sample cases.

Units: Rates per 1,000 persons, 12 years old and over.

Table 5.03: Victimization Rates for Personal Crimes by Sex of the Victim, 2006

	Hispanic Victims		White Victims		Victims of All Races	
	Male	Female	Male	Female	Male	Female
Crimes of violence	32.1	23.2	25.7	21.0	26.7	22.7
completed	11.0	8.8	7.4	7.0	8.2	8.1
attempted/threatened	21.1	14.4	18.3	14.0	18.5	14.6
Rape/sexual assault	*0.6	*1.2	0.3	1.8	*0.2	1.8
Robbery	7.9	*1.7	3.9	1.7	3.9	2.0
completed/property taken	5.1	*1.5	2.6	1.1	2.6	1.3
- with injury	*2.0	*0.3	1.2	0.5	1.1	0.6
- without injury	3.1	*1.2	1.4	0.6	1.5	0.7
attempted to take property	2.8	*0.2	1.3	0.5	1.2	0.6
- with injury	*0.0	*0.0	*0.2	*0.1	*0.2	*0.2
- without injury	2.8	*0.2	1.2	0.5	1.0	0.5
Assault	23.6	20.3	21.5	17.6	22.6	18.9
aggravated	7.1	5.4	5.3	4.0	6.3	4.6
- with injury	*2.2	*2.1	1.7	1.2	2.0	1.8
- threatened with weapon	4.9	3.3	3.7	2.7	4.3	2.9
simple	16.5	14.9	16.2	13.6	16.3	14.3
- with minor injury	3.4	4.0	3.1	3.4	3.5	3.8
- without injury	13.1	10.9	13.0	10.2	12.8	10.5
Purse-snatching/pocket-picking	*0.8	*0.4	0.5	0.6	0.7	0.7

Source: U.S. Department of Justice, Office of Justice Programs, *Criminal Victimization 2006*, tables 2, 6, and 8.

Notes: 'All Races' includes other races not shown separately.
The National Crime Victimization Survey has been redesigned; data based on previous survey procedures (before 2006) is not directly comparable with later data.
*Based on 10 or fewer sample cases.

Units: Rates per 1,000 persons, 12 years old and over.

Table 5.04: Household Victimization Rates for Property Crimes by Type of Crime, 2006

	Hispanic Households	White Households	All Households
All property crimes	*211.7*	*156.7*	*160.5*
Household burglary	40.2	28.6	30.2
completed	31.2	23.1	24.2
- forcible entry	12.2	8.0	8.7
- unlawful entry without force	19.1	15.1	15.5
attempted forcible entry	8.9	5.4	6.0
Theft	158.0	120.8	121.9
completed	152.9	116.0	117.0
- less than $50	31.2	32.8	32.4
- $50–$249	60.4	41.0	41.9
- $250 or more	41.2	31.0	31.6
- amount not available	20.0	11.2	11.1
attempted	5.1	4.8	4.8
Motor vehicle theft	13.5	7.3	8.4
completed	10.8	6.0	6.7
attempted	*2.7	1.4	1.7

Source: U.S. Department of Justice, Office of Justice Programs, *Criminal Victimization 2006*, tables 16 and 17.

Notes: Race is given by race of head of household.
'All households' includes households of other races not shown separately.
The National Crime Victimization Survey has been redesigned: comparisons of estimates of crime based on previous survey procedures (before 1993) are not recommended.

Units: Rates per 1,000 households.

Table 5.05: Number of Jail Inmates per 100,000 U.S. Residents, 1990–2008

	Hispanic	White
1990	245	89
1991	247	92
1992	251	93
1993	262	94
1994	274	98
1995	263	104
1996	276	111
1997	293	117
1998	292	125
1999	288	127
2000	280	132
2001	263	138
2002	256	147
2003	269	151
2004	262	160
2005	268	166
2006	283	170
2007	276	170
2008	274	167

Source: U.S. Department of Justice, Bureau of Justice Statistics, *The Annual Survey of Jails and Census of Jail Inmates, 1997, 1998–2006.*
U.S. Department of Justice, Bureau of Justice Statistics, *Jail Inmates at Midyear, 2008.*

Notes: 'White' as shown is equivalent to 'White alone.'

Units: Jail inmates per 100,000 U.S. Residents.

Table 5.06: Jail Population, 1990–2008

	Hispanic	White
1990	58,000	169,400
1991	60,600	175,300
1992	64,500	178,300
1993	69,400	180,700
1994	75,500	191,800
1995	75,700	206,600
1996	80,900	215,700
1997	88,900	230,300
1998	91,800	244,900
1999	93,800	249,900
2000	94,100	260,500
2001	93,000	271,700
2002	98,000	291,800
2003	106,600	301,200
2004	108,300	317,400
2005	111,900	331,000
2006	119,200	336,500
2007	125,500	338,200
2008	128,500	333,300

Source: U.S. Department of Justice, Bureau of Justice Statistics, *The Annual Survey of Jails and Census of Jail Inmates, 1997, 1998-2006.*

U.S. Department of Justice, Bureau of Justice Statistics, *Jail Inmates at Midyear, 2008.*

Notes: 'White' as shown is equivalent to 'White alone.'

Units: Number of persons incarcerated as determined by a one-day count.

Table 5.07: Distribution of Jail Inmates, 1990–2007

	Hispanic	White
1990	14.3%	41.8%
1991	14.2	41.1
1992	14.5	40.1
1993	15.1	39.3
1994	15.4	39.1
1995	14.7	40.1
1996	15.6	41.6
1997	15.7	40.6
1998	15.5	41.3
1999	15.5	41.3
2000	15.1	41.9
2001	14.7	43.0
2002	14.7	43.8
2003	15.4	43.6
2004	15.2	44.4
2005	15.0	44.3
2006	15.6	43.9
2007	16.1	43.3

Source: U.S. Department of Justice, Bureau of Justice Statistics, Sourcebook of Criminal Justice Statistics Online, table 6.17.2007.

Notes: Race totals may not add to total due to other groups not included here.
'White' excludes Hispanic persons.

Units: Percent of local jail inmates.

Table 5.08: Incarceration Rate in State or Federal Prisons and Local Jails, January 2008

	Hispanic		White		All Races	
	Male	Female	Male	Female	Male	Female
Total	1,259	79	481	50	955	69
18–19 years	656	28	238	16	539	24
20–24 years	2,507	134	887	86	1,915	114
25–29 years	2,624	172	1,025	117	2,256	154
30–34 years	2,500	175	1,214	157	2,385	191
35–39 years	2,344	191	1,124	151	2,113	199
40–44 years	2,111	176	1,044	121	1,859	166
45–49 years	1,619	113	658	65	1,196	93
50–54 years	1,164	66	404	31	719	46
55–59 years	787	36	274	17	432	22
60–64 years	526	16	188	10	266	12
65 or older	200	7	68	2	95	3

Source: U.S. Department of Justice, Bureau of Justice Statistics, *Prisoners in 2007*, appendix table 8.

Notes: 'All Races' includes other races not shown separately.
'White' excludes Hispanics and persons who reported two or more races.
Counts are as of January 1, 2008.

Units: Number of inmates per 100,000 residents of each group.

Table 5.09: Prisoners Under Jurisdiction of Federal and State Correctional Authorities, 1995 and 2000–2005

	Hispanic	White	All Races
December 31, 1995			
Total	*174,292*	*455,021*	*1,126,287*
Federal Institutions	27,559	60,261	100,250
State Institutions	146,733	394,760	1,026,037
June 30, 2000			
Total	*203,700*	*453,300*	*1,305,253*
Federal Institutions	33,200	29,800	110,974
State Institutions	151,810	395,637	1,101,202
Private institutions	18,728	27,905	93,077

Source: U.S. Department of Justice, Bureau of Justice Statistics, *Sourcebook of Criminal Justice Statistics, 1999*, table 6.34; *2002*, table 6.24 and 6.28.

Notes: 'All Races' includes races not shown separately. 'White' excludes Hispanic persons.

Units: Number of prisoners under jurisdictional authority.

Table 5.10: Incarceration Rate in State Prisons and Local Jails by State, June 2005

	Hispanic	White	All Races
United States	*742*	*412*	*738*
Alabama	NA	542	890
Alaska	380	500	705
Arizona	1,075	590	808
Arkansas	288	478	673
California	782	460	682
Colorado	1,042	525	728
Connecticut	1,401	211	544
Delaware	683	396	820
District of Columbia	267	56	NA
Florida	382	588	835
Georgia	576	623	1,021
Hawaii	185	453	447
Idaho	1,654	675	784
Illinois	415	223	507
Indiana	579	463	637
Iowa	764	309	412
Kansas	NA	443	582
Kentucky	757	561	720
Louisiana	244	523	1,138
Maine	NA	262	273
Maryland	NA	288	636
Massachusetts	1,229	201	356
Michigan	397	412	663
Minnesota	NA	212	300
Mississippi	611	503	955
Missouri	587	487	715
Montana	846	433	526
Nebraska	739	290	421
Nevada	621	627	756

(continued on next page)

Table 5.10: Incarceration Rate in State Prisons and Local Jails by State, June 2005

	Hispanic	White	All Races
United States	*742*	*412*	*738*
New Hampshire	1,063	289	319
New Jersey	630	190	532
New Mexico	NA	NA	782
New York	778	174	482
North Carolina	NA	320	620
North Dakota	848	267	359
Ohio	613	344	559
Oklahoma	832	740	919
Oregon	573	502	531
Pennsylvania	1,714	305	607
Rhode Island	631	191	313
South Carolina	476	415	830
South Dakota	NA	470	622
Tennessee	561	487	732
Texas	830	667	976
Utah	838	392	466
Vermont	NA	304	317
Virginia	487	396	759
Washington	527	393	465
West Virginia	211	392	443
Wisconsin	NA	415	653
Wyoming	NA	NA	690

Source: U.S. Department of Justice, Bureau of Justice Statistics, *Prison and Jail Inmates at Midyear 2005*, tables 12 and 14.

Notes: 'All Races' includes races not shown separately. 'White' excludes Hispanics and persons who reported two or more races.
Figures are as of June 30, 2005.

Units: Number of inmates per 100,000 residents.

Table 5.11: Chances of Going to State or Federal Prison, 1997 and 2001

	Hispanic	White	All Races
1997			
Incarcerated for the first time, by age			
20	1.5%	0.4%	1.1%
25	3.6	0.9	2.4
30	5.2	1.4	3.3
35	6.3	1.7	4.0
40	7.5	2.0	4.4
45	8.2	2.1	4.7
50	8.8	2.3	4.9
55	9.1	2.4	5.0
65	9.4	2.5	5.1
Lifetime	9.4	2.5	5.1
Incarcerated at some time during the rest of life, by age			
Birth	9.4%	2.5%	5.1%
20	8.7	2.3	4.5
25	6.4	1.7	3.1
30	4.9	1.2	2.1
35	3.8	0.9	1.4
40	2.3	0.6	0.9
45	1.6	0.4	0.6

(continued on next page)

Table 5.11: Chances of Going to State or Federal Prison, 1997 and 2001

	Hispanic			White		
	Male	**Female**	**Total**	**Male**	**Female**	**Total**
2001						
Percent of adult population ever incarcerated, by age						
18-24	4.0%	0.3%	2.2%	1.1%	0.1%	0.6%
25-34	9.0	0.8	5.1	2.8	0.3	1.6
35-44	10.0	1.1	5.8	3.5	0.5	2.0
45-54	9.5	0.9	5.2	3.1	0.3	1.7
55-64	6.6	0.6	3.6	2.5	0.2	1.4
65 and older	4.1	0.3	2.2	2.0	0.2	1.1

Source: U.S. Department of Justice, Bureau of Justice Statistics, *Lifetime Likelihood of Going to State or Federal Prison, March 1997*, tables 1 and 2.
U.S. Department of Justice, Bureau of Justice Statistics, *Prevalence of Imprisonment in the U.S. Population, 1974-2001*, table 7.

Notes: Chances of going to State or Federal Prison for the first time are cumulative percents. These estimates were obtained by sequentially applying age-specific first-incarceration rates and mortality rates for each group to a hypothetical population of 100,000 births. Chances of going to State or Federal Prison at some time are for persons not previously incarcerated. These estimates were obtained by subtracting the cumulative percent first incarcerated for each age from the lifetime likelihood of incarceration.
'White' excludes persons of Hispanic origin.

Units: Percent of total resident population.

Table 5.12: Prisoners Under Sentence of Death by State January 1, 2009

	Hispanic	White	All Races
United States*	375	1,481	3,305
Alabama	3	105	207
Arizona	21	91	129
Arkansas	0	17	42
California	148	252	678
Colorado	1	0	3
Connecticut	1	3	10
Delaware	3	7	20
Florida	36	224	402
Georgia	3	54	109
Idaho	0	18	18
Illinois	2	8	15
Indiana	0	13	17
Kansas	0	6	10
Kentucky	1	29	36
Louisiana	3	27	84
Maryland	0	1	5
Mississippi	0	28	61
Missouri	0	30	52
Montana	0	2	2
Nebraska	4	5	10
Nevada	8	39	79

(continued on next page)

Table 5.12: Prisoners Under Sentence of Death by State January 1, 2009

	Hispanic	White	All Races
New Hampshire	0	0	1
New Mexico	0	2	2
North Carolina	4	65	167
Ohio	3	81	181
Oklahoma	3	45	86
Oregon	2	28	35
Pennsylvania	18	70	226
South Carolina	1	29	63
South Dakota	0	3	3
Tennessee	1	48	92
Texas	104	107	358
Utah	2	6	10
Virginia	1	8	18
Washington	0	5	9
Wyoming	0	1	1

Source: U.S. Department of Justice, Bureau of Justice Statistics, *Sourcebook of Criminal Justice Statistics, Online (2003 and later)*, table 6.80.2009.

Notes: 'All Races' includes other races and ethnic groups not shown separately.
*Includes prisoners under Federal and U.S. Military jurisdiction.

Units: Number prisoners under sentence of death.

Table 5.13: Hispanics under Sentence of Death by Jurisdiction, 2007

	Under sentence of death, 12/31/06	Received under sentence of death	Death sentence removed	Under sentence of death, 12/31/07
United States	*358*	*15*	*11*	*362*
Alabama	1	0	0	1
Arizona	16	1	0	17
California	140	6	2	144
Colorado	1	0	1	0
Connecticut	1	0	0	1
Delaware	2	0	0	2
Florida	31	1	0	32
Georgia	2	0	0	2
Idaho	1	0	0	1
Illinois	2	0	0	2
Indiana	1	0	0	1
Kentucky	1	0	0	1
Louisiana	1	0	0	1
Nebraska	3	0	0	3
Nevada	7	0	0	7
New Mexico	1	0	0	1
North Carolina	4	0	0	4
Ohio	5	0	0	5
Oklahoma	2	1	1	2
Oregon	2	0	0	2
Pennsylvania	21	1	1	21
Tennessee	1	0	0	1
Texas	108	3	6	105
Utah	2	0	0	2

Source: U.S. Department of Justice, Bureau of Justice Statistics, *Sourcebook of Criminal Justice Statistics Online (2003 and later)*, table 6.83.20067

Notes: Estimates for year-end 2006 have been revised. 'Death sentence removed' includes 6 Hispanic men in Texas who were executed in 2007.
Only states with Hispanic prisoners under sentence of death are shown.

Units: Number prisoners under sentence of death.

Table 5.14: Criminal History Profile of Prisoners Under Sentence of Death, 2007

	Hispanic	White	All Races
United States total	*362*	*1,804*	*3,220*
Prior Felony Convictions			
Yes	61.3%	61.8%	65.4%
No	38.7	38.2	34.6
Prior Homicide Convictions			
Yes	6.7%	8.5%	8.4%
No	93.3	91.5	91.6
Legal Status at Time of Capital Offense			
Charges pending	5.2%	9.1%	7.9%
Probation	11.4	8.9	10.6
Parole	20.3	13.3	15.4
Prison escapee	1.8	1.8	1.4
Prison inmate	2.5	4.2	3.6
Other status	0.3	0.4	0.5
None	58.5	62.5	60.6

Source: U.S. Department of Justice, Bureau of Justice Statistics, *Capital Punishment 2007*, tables 4 and 8.

Notes: 'All Races' includes other races not shown separately.
'White' excludes persons of Hispanic origin.
Prisoner counts are as of December 31, 2007

Units: Number of prisoners.

Table 5.15: Inmates Ever Tested for HIV and Results, 1996–1997, 2002, and 2004

	Hispanic	White	All Races
1996			
Local jails			
Number	45,759	110,023	289,991
Percent HIV positive	3.2%	1.4%	2.2%
1997			
State prisons			
Number	123,725	257,919	790,128
Percent HIV positive	2.5%	1.4%	2.2%
Federal prisons			
Number	18,466	21,128	70,902
Percent HIV positive	0.7%	0.3%	0.6%
2002			
State prisons			
Number	55,938	136,069	374,711
Percent HIV positive	2.9%	0.8%	1.3%
2004			
State prisons			
Number	166,500	336,100	967,200
Percent HIV positive	1.8%	1.0%	1.6%
Federal prisons			
Number	24,000	26,800	102,600
Percent HIV positive	0.4%	0.5%	1.0%

Source: U.S. Department of Justice, Bureau of Justice Statistics, *HIV in Prisons and Jails, 1996*, table 8; *200*, table 9; *2004*, table 10.

Notes: 'All Races' includes races not shown separately. 'White' excludes Hispanic persons.

Units: Number of inmates tested who reported results rounded to nearest hundred; percent of inmates testing positive for HIV (Human Immunodeficiency Virus).

Hispanic Americans: A Statistical Sourcebook 2009

Table 5.16: AIDS-related Deaths in State Prisons, 2004–2006

	Hispanic	White	All Races
2004			
Number	11	46	185
Rate	5	11	14
2005			
Number	21	33	176
Rate	9	8	13
2006			
Number	12	29	155
Rate	5	6	11

Source: U.S. Department of Justice, Bureau of Justice Statistics, *HIV in Prisons, 2006*, table 7.

Notes: 'All Races' includes races and ethnic groups not shown separately. 'White' excludes Hispanic persons.

Units: Number of AIDS-related deaths; rate per 100,000 inmates.

Table 5.17: High School Students Who Reported Carrying a Weapon, 2001, 2003, and 2005

	Hispanic	White	All Races
2001			
Anywhere	16.5%	17.9%	17.4%
On school property	6.4	6.1	6.4
2003			
Anywhere	16.5%	16.7%	17.1%
On school property	6.0	5.5	6.1
2005			
Anywhere	19.0%	18.7%	18.5%
On school property	8.2	6.1	6.5

Source: U.S. Census Bureau, *Statistical Abstract of the United States, 2008*, table 237.

Notes: 'All Races' includes races not shown separately. 'White' is equivalent to 'White alone' and excludes Hispanics.
Weapons are such things as guns, knives, and clubs. Responses indicate students who reported carrying a weapon in the previous 30 days.

Units: Percent of students in grades 9 to 12.

Table 5.18: Deaths of Juveniles in State Juvenile Correctional Facilities, 2002–2005

	Hispanic	White	All Races
Total	*6*	*16*	*43*
2002	2	6	13
2003	2	1	10
2004	2	4	11
2005	0	5	9

Source: U.S. Department of Justice, Bureau of Justice Statistics, *Sourcebook of Criminal Justice Statistics Online (2003 and later)*, table 6.0014.2005.

Notes: 'All Races' includes races and ethnic groups not shown separately. 'White' as shown is equivalent to 'White alone' and excludes Hispanics. Breakdowns may not add to totals due to missing data.

Units: Number of juvenile deaths in state juvenile correctional facilities.

Table 5.19: Juveniles in Public and Private Residential Custody Facilities, 2006

	Hispanic	White	All Races
All offenses	*19,027*	*32,495*	*92,854*
Delinquency offenses	18,636	30,133	88,137
Violent offenses	6,279	10,132	31,704
Index offenses	4,592	6,425	21,776
Other	1,687	3,707	9,928
Property offenses	4,863	8,691	23,177
Index offenses	3,801	7,144	18,986
Other	1,062	1,547	4,191
Drug offenses	1,725	2,521	7,996
Public order offenses	2,145	3,423	9,944
Technical violation	3,624	5,366	15,316
Status offenses	391	2,362	4,717

Source: U.S. Department of Justice, Bureau of Justice Statistics, *Sourcebook of Criminal Justice Statistics, 2006*, table 6.10.2006

Notes: 'All Races' includes other races not shown separately.
'White' excludes White Hispanics.
'Status offenses' include running away, underage drinking, truancy, curfew violations, and other offenses that are illegal for juveniles but not for adults. States vary as to what behaviors are considered status offenses.

Units: Number of juveniles by offense type.

Table 5.20: Hate Crimes, Race as Bias Motivation, 2004–2006

	Anti-Hispanic	All Ethnicity/National Origin Motivated	Total Hate Crimes
2004			
Incidents Reported	475	974	7,679
Offenses	611	1,204	9,065
Victims	646	1,257	9,561
Known Offenders	584	1,046	7,175
2005			
Incidents Reported	522	944	7,163
Offenses	660	1,144	8,380
Victims	722	1,228	8,804
Known Offenders	691	1,115	6,804
2006			
Incidents Reported	576	984	7,722
Offenses	770	1,233	9,080
Victims	819	1,305	9,652
Known Offenders	802	1,209	7,330

Source: U.S. Census Bureau, *Statistical Abstract of the United States, 2007*, table 308; *2008*, table 310; *2009*, table 310.

Notes: 'Victim' may refer to a person, business, institution, or society as a whole.
'Known offender' indicates that some attribute of the offender is known, but does not imply that the identity of the suspect is known.

Units: Number of incidents reported.

Table 5.21: Persons Stalked During Their Lifetime, 1996

	Hispanic	White	All Races
Male	3.3%	2.1%	2.2%
Female	7.6	8.2	8.1

Source: U.S. Department of Justice, Bureau of Justice Statistics, *Sourcebook of Criminal Justice Statistics, 1998*, table 3.37.

Notes: 'All Races' includes races/ethnic groups not shown separately.
'Stalking' is defined as a course of conduct directed at a specific person that involves repeated visual or physical proximity, nonconsensual communication, or verbal, written or implied threats that would cause a reasonable person fear.

Units: Percent of persons 12 years old and over.

Chapter 6

Labor, Employment & Unemployment

Chapter Six Highlights

This chapter provides statistics about labor and employment for Hispanic persons in the United States, including both the most current data available as well as comparisons of the Hispanic population over time. For almost all tables, corresponding data is provided for the total population of the United States as well as for White persons. This allows for easy comparison between groups. Because 'Hispanic' is not a race or ethnic group, we have included a variety of tables with statistics on some of the ethnic groups that comprise the Hispanic designation (tables 6.04, 6.05, 6.08, 6.15, and 6.23).

The chapter contains a variety of information on the United States' labor force, including labor force participation (tables 6.01–6.05), full-time and part-time status (tables 6.11 and 6.12), occupation and industry (tables 6.23–6.25), sex (tables 6.03–6.05), age (tables 6.01–6.03), and region of employment (tables 6.11 and 6.12).

The chapter also provides data on unemployment, and includes data organized by age (tables 6.13 and 6.14), sex (tables 6.14, 6.15, and 6.21), region (table 6.20); and reason for unemployment (table 6.18).

We have also included data on tenure of employment (table 6.26), educational attainment of workers (table 6.28), and workers paid at or below minimum wage (table 6.33).

Table 6.01: Civilian Population, Employment, and Unemployment Rate, 1980–2007

	Hispanic	White	All Races
1980			
Civilian Noninstitutional Population	9,598	146,122	167,745
Percent in labor force	64.0%	64.1%	63.8%
Percent of labor force unemployed	10.1	6.3	7.1
1990			
Civilian Noninstitutional Population	15,904	160,425	189,164
Percent in labor force	67.4%	66.9%	66.5%
Percent of labor force unemployed	8.2	4.8	5.6
2000			
Civilian Noninstitutional Population	23,938	176,220	212,577
Percent in labor force	69.7%	67.3%	67.1%
Percent of labor force unemployed	5.7	3.5	4.0
2005			
Civilian Noninstitutional Population	29,133	184,446	226,082
Percent in labor force	68.0%	66.3%	66.0%
Percent of labor force unemployed	6.0	4.4	5.1
2006			
Civilian Noninstitutional Population	30,103	186,264	228,815
Percent in labor force	68.7%	66.5%	66.2%
Percent of labor force unemployed	5.2	4.0	4.6
2007			
Civilian Noninstitutional Population	31,383	188,253	231,867
Percent in labor force	68.8%	66.4%	66.0%
Percent of labor force unemployed	5.6	4.1	4.6

Source: U.S. Bureau of the Census, *Statistical Abstract of the United States, 2009*, tables 567 and 569.

Notes: 'All Races' includes other races not shown separately.
For data after 2003, 'White' is equivalent to 'White alone.'

Units: Civilian noninstitutional population in thousands; percent of civilian population in labor force; percent of labor force unemployed.

Table 6.02: Labor Force Participation of the Civilian Noninstitutional Population 16 Years Old and Over by Age, 1980–2008

	Hispanic	White	All Races
1980			
Civilian Noninstitutional Population			
All persons 16 years old and over	11,915	146,122	167,745
16–19 years old	1,298	13,854	16,543
20 years old and over	10,617	132,268	151,202
65 years old and over	843	22,050	24,350
Civilian Labor Force			
All persons 16 years old and over	7,698	93,600	106,940
16–19 years old	579	8,312	9,378
20 years old and over	7,119	85,286	97,561
65 years old and over	82	2,759	3,054
Labor Force Participation Rate			
All persons 16 years old and over	64.6%	64.1%	63.8%
16–19 years old	44.6	60.0	56.7
20 years old and over	67.1	64.5	64.5
65 years old and over	9.7	12.5	12.5
1990			
Civilian Noninstitutional Population			
All persons 16 years old and over	14,297	160,415	188,049
16–19 years old	1,424	11,095	13,794
20 years old and over	12,873	149,320	174,255
65 years old and over	NA	26,643	29,730
Civilian Labor Force			
All persons 16 years old and over	9,576	107,177	124,787
16–19 years old	672	6,374	7,410
20 years old and over	8,904	100,803	117,377
65 years old and over	NA	3,189	3,535
Labor Force Participation Rate			
All persons 16 years old and over	67.0%	66.8%	66.4%
16–19 years old	47.2	57.5	53.7
20 years old and over	69.2	62.8	62.4
65 years old and over	NA	12.0	11.9

(continued on next page)

Table 6.02: Labor Force Participation of the Civilian Noninstitutional Population 16 Years Old and Over by Age, 1980–2008

	Hispanic	White	All Races
2000			
Civilian Noninstitutional Population			
All persons 16 years old and over	22,393	174,428	209,699
16–19 years old	2,341	12,707	16,042
65 years old and over	1,791	28,947	32,705
Civilian Labor Force			
All persons 16 years old and over	15,368	117,574	140,863
16–19 years old	1,083	7,075	8,369
65 years old and over	218	3,749	4,200
Labor Force Participation Rate			
All persons 16 years old and over	68.6%	67.4%	67.2%
16–19 years old	46.3	55.7	52.2
65 years old and over	12.2	13.0	12.8
2008			
Civilian Noninstitutional Population			
All persons 16 years old and over	32,141	189,540	233,788
16–19 years old	3,042	13,084	17,075
65 years old and over	2,609	32,165	37,161
Civilian Labor Force			
All persons 16 years old and over	22,024	125,635	154,287
16–19 years old	1,121	5,644	6,858
65 years old and over	417	5,463	6,243
Labor Force Participation Rate			
All persons 16 years old and over	68.5%	66.4%	66.0%
16–19 years old	36.9	43.1	40.2
65 years old and over	16.0	17.0	16.8

Source: U.S. Department of Labor, Bureau of Labor Statistics, *Handbook of Labor Statistics, 1989*, tables 3–5.
U.S. Department of Labor, Bureau of Labor Statistics, *Employment and Earnings, 1991*, table 3; *2001*, table 3; *2008*, tables 3 and 4.

Notes: 'All Races' includes races not shown separately.

Units: Civilian noninstitutional population and civilian labor force in thousands of persons, participation rate as a percent (the civilian noninstitutional population divided by the civilian labor force).

Table 6.03: Labor Force Participation of the Civilian Noninstitutional Population 16 Years Old and Over by Sex and Age, 1980–2008

	Hispanic		White		All Races	
	Male	Female	Male	Female	Male	Female
1980						
Civilian Noninstitutional Population						
All persons 16 years old and over	5,885	6,029	69,634	76,489	79,398	88,348
16–19 years old	654	644	6,941	6,914	8,260	8,283
20 years old and over	5,232	5,385	62,694	69,575	71,138	80,065
65 years old and over	354	489	9,027	13,022	9,979	14,372
Civilian Labor Force						
All persons 16 years old and over	4,729	2,970	54,473	39,127	61,453	45,487
16–19 years old	334	245	4,424	3,888	4,999	4,381
20 years old and over	4,395	2,725	50,049	35,239	56,455	41,106
65 years old and over	53	29	1,727	1,032	1,893	1,161
Labor Force Participation Rate						
All persons 16 years old and over	80.3%	49.3%	78.2%	51.2%	77.4%	51.5%
16–19 years old	51.0	38.1	63.7	56.2	60.5	52.9
20 years old and over	84.0	50.6	79.8	50.6	79.4	51.3
65 years old and over	14.9	5.9	19.1	7.9	19.0	8.1
1990						
Civilian Noninstitutional Population						
All persons 16 years old and over	7,087	7,210	77,082	83,332	89,650	98,399
16–19 years old	721	703	5,600	5,495	6,947	6,847
20 years old and over	6,366	6,507	71,482	77,837	82,703	91,552
65 years old and over	NA	NA	11,129	15,514	12,392	17,337
Civilian Labor Force						
All persons 16 years old and over	5,755	3,821	58,298	47,879	68,234	56,554
16–19 years old	401	271	3,329	3,046	3,866	3,544
20 years old and over	5,354	3,550	54,969	44,833	64,368	53,010
65 years old and over	NA	NA	1,865	1,325	2,033	1,502
Labor Force Participation Rate						
All persons 16 years old and over	81.2%	53.0%	76.9%	57.5%	76.1%	57.5%
16–19 years old	55.6	38.5	59.4	55.4	55.7	51.8
20 years old and over	84.1	54.6	78.3	57.6	77.8	57.9
65 years old and over	NA	NA	16.8	8.5	16.4	8.7

(continued on next page)

Table 6.03: Labor Force Participation of the Civilian Noninstitutional Population 16 Years Old and Over by Sex and Age, 1980–2008

	Hispanic		White		All Races	
	Male	Female	Male	Female	Male	Female
2000						
Civilian Noninstitutional Population						
All persons 16 years old and over	11,064	11,329	84,647	89,781	100,731	108,968
16–19 years old	1,205	1,136	6,496	6,211	8,151	7,890
65 years old and over	759	1,032	12,390	16,557	13,925	18,780
Civilian Labor Force						
All persons 16 years old and over	8,919	6,449	63,861	53,714	75,247	65,616
16–19 years old	613	470	3,679	3,396	4,317	4,051
65 years old and over	138	80	2,198	1,550	2,439	1,762
Labor Force Participation Rate						
All persons 16 years old and over	80.6%	56.9%	75.4%	59.8%	74.7%	60.2%
16–19 years old	50.9	41.4	56.6	54.7	53.0	51.3
65 years old and over	18.2	7.7	17.7	9.4	17.5	9.4
2008						
Civilian Noninstitutional Population						
All persons 16 years old and over	16,524	15,616	92,725	96,814	113,113	120,675
16–19 years old	1,553	1,489	6,669	6,414	8,660	8,415
65 years old and over	1,121	1,488	13,972	18,193	16,002	21,160
Civilian Labor Force						
All persons 16 years old and over	13,255	8,769	68,351	57,284	82,520	71,767
16–19 years old	626	495	2,868	2,776	3,472	3,385
65 years old and over	243	174	3,046	2,417	3,436	2,808
Labor Force Participation Rate						
All persons 16 years old and over	80.2%	56.2%	73.7%	59.2%	73.0%	59.5%
16–19 years old	40.3	33.3	43.0	43.3	40.1	40.2
65 years old and over	21.7	11.7	21.8	13.3	21.5	13.3

Source: U.S. Department of Labor, Bureau of Labor Statistics, *Handbook of Labor Statistics, 1989*, tables 3–5.
U.S. Department of Labor, Bureau of Labor Statistics, *Employment and Earnings, 1991*, table 3; *2001*, table 3; *2008*, tables 3 and 4.

Notes: 'All Races' includes races not shown separately.

Units: Civilian noninstitutional population and civilian labor force in thousands of persons; participation rate as a percent (the civilian noninstitutional population divided by the civilian labor force).

Table 6.04: Labor Force Participation of the Hispanic Civilian Noninstitutional Population 16 Years Old and Over by Ethnic Group, 1990 and 2000

	Mexican	Puerto Rican	Cuban	Central/ South American	Other Hispanic	Total Hispanic
1990						
Total population 16 years and over	8,696	1,492	839	2,106	1,079	14,212
In the labor force	5,871	805	554	1,509	709	9,449
Percent of total	67.5%	54.0%	66.0%	71.7%	65.7%	66.5%
Male population 16 years and over	4,493	673	402	991	511	7,069
In the labor force	3,647	466	301	829	385	5,629
Percent of total	81.2%	69.2%	74.9%	83.7%	75.3%	79.6%
Female population 16 years and over	4,203	819	438	1,114	568	7,143
In the labor force	2,224	339	253	680	324	3,821
Percent of total	52.9%	41.4%	57.8%	61.0%	57.0%	53.5%
2000						
Total population 16 years and over	14,144	2,040	1,073	3,472	1,440	22,170
In the labor force	9,720	1,309	658	2,492	984	15,163
Percent of total	68.7%	64.2%	61.3%	71.8%	68.4%	68.4%
Male population 16 years and over	7,197	959	518	1,618	669	10,961
In the labor force	5,903	667	383	1,361	502	8,817
Percent of total	82.0%	69.6%	74.0%	84.1%	75.1%	80.4%
Female population 16 years and over	6,947	1,081	555	1,854	771	11,209
In the labor force	3,816	642	275	1,131	482	6,346
Percent of total	54.9%	59.3%	49.5%	61.0%	62.5%	56.6%

Source: U.S. Bureau of the Census, *The Hispanic Population in the United States: March, 1990*, table 2.

U.S. Bureau of the Census, Current Population Reports, *The Hispanic Population of the United States, 2000*.

Notes: 'Other Hispanic' includes persons from Spain and persons identifying themselves generally as Hispanic, Spanish, Spanish-American, Hispano, Latino, etc.

Units: Total population in thousands of persons 16 years old and over; percent as a percent of total shown (100%).

Table 6.05: Labor Force Participation of the Hispanic Civilian Noninstitutional Population 16 Years Old and Over by Ethnic Group, 2003 and 2007

	Mexican	Puerto Rican	Cuban	Central American	South American	Other Hispanic	Total Hispanic
2003							
Total population 16 years and over	17,563	2,593	1,175	2,166	1,600	2,087	27,184
In the labor force	12,121	1,636	642	1,649	1,155	1,338	18,541
Percent of total	69.0%	63.1%	54.6%	76.1%	72.2%	64.1%	68.2%
Male population 16 years and over	9,183	1,201	594	1,191	813	922	13,903
In the labor force	7,473	848	370	1,015	686	648	11,039
Percent of total	81.4%	70.6%	62.3%	85.2%	84.3%	70.3%	79.4%
Female population 16 years and over	8,381	1,393	581	975	787	1,165	13,281
In the labor force	4,648	788	272	634	469	689	7,502
Percent of total	55.5%	56.6%	46.8%	65.1%	59.7%	59.2%	56.5%
2007							
Total population 16 years and over	18,885	2,591	1,246	2,652	1,992	2,426	28,814
In the labor force	12,870	1,600	762	2,028	1,396	1,607	19,491
Percent of total	68.1%	61.7%	61.1%	76.5%	70.1%	66.2%	67.6%
Male population 16 years and over	9,925	1,222	603	1,479	967	1,114	14,791
In the labor force	8,089	846	427	1,289	773	811	11,760
Percent of total	81.5%	69.2%	70.9%	87.2%	79.9%	72.8%	79.5%
Female population 16 years and over	8,931	1,370	644	1,173	1,025	1,312	14,023
In the labor force	4,781	754	334	739	624	796	7,732
Percent of total	53.4%	55.0%	52.0%	63.0%	60.8%	60.6%	55.1%

Source: U.S. Bureau of the Census, Current Population Reports, *The Hispanic Population of the United States, 2003*, table 9.2; *2006*, table 9.2.

Notes: 'Other Hispanic' includes persons from Spain and persons identifying themselves generally as Hispanic, Spanish, Spanish-American, Hispano, Latino, etc.
'Other Hispanic' includes Dominicans.

Units: Total population in thousands of persons 16 years old and over; percent as a percent of total shown (100%).

Table 6.06: Civilian Labor Force and Civilian Labor Force Participation Rates, Projections for 2014 and 2016

	Hispanic	White	All Races
2014			
Civilian Labor Force			
Total	25.8	129.9	162.1
Men	14.9	70.3	86.2
Women	10.8	59.6	75.9
Labor Force Participation Rate			
Total	69.2%	65.9%	65.6%
Men	78.6	72.7	71.8
Women	59.3	59.3	59.7
2016			
Civilian Labor Force			
Total	26.9	130.7	164.2
Men	15.8	71.3	87.8
Women	11.1	59.4	76.5
Labor Force Participation Rate			
Total	68.6%	65.5%	65.5%
Men	79.0	72.9	72.3
Women	57.8	58.4	59.2

Source: U.S. Bureau of the Census, *Statistical Abstract of the United States, 2007*, table 574; *2009*, table 568.

Notes: 'All Races' includes other races not shown separately.

Units: Civilian labor force population 16 years old and over in millions of persons; labor force participation rate as a percent (the civilian noninstitutional population divided by the civilian labor force).

Table 6.07: Employed Members of the Civilian Labor Force by Sex and Age, 1980–2008

	Hispanic		White		All Races	
	Male	Female	Male	Female	Male	Female
1990						
All employed persons, 16 years old and over	*5,304*	*3,504*	*56,432*	*45,654*	*64,435*	*53,479*
16–19 years old	323	218	2,856	2,662	3,237	3,024
20 years old and over	4,981	3,286	53,576	42,992	61,198	50,455
65 years old and over	NA	NA	1,812	1,288	1,972	1,455
2000						
All employed persons, 16 years old and over	*8,478*	*6,014*	*61,696*	*51,780*	*72,293*	*62,915*
16–19 years old	517	385	3,227	3,043	3,713	3,563
65 years old and over	130	152	2,130	1,512	2,357	1,713
2007						
All employed persons, 16 years old and over	*12,310*	*8,072*	*65,289*	*54,503*	*78,254*	*67,792*
16–19 years old	483	410	2,483	2,507	2,917	2,994
65 years old and over	220	155	2,727	2,193	3,080	2,534
2008						
All employed persons, 16 years old and over	*12,248*	*8,098*	*64,624*	*54,501*	*77,486*	*67,876*
16–19 years old	479	391	2,320	2,377	2,736	2,837
65 years old and over	224	161	2,922	2,325	3,282	2,697

Source: U.S. Department of Labor, Bureau of Labor Statistics, *Handbook of Labor Statistics, 1989*, tables 3–5.
U.S. Department of Labor, Bureau of Labor Statistics, *Employment and Earnings, 1991*, table 3; *2001*, table 3; *2008*, table 3.

Notes: 'All Races' includes races not shown separately.
Data covers members of the civilian labor force.

Units: Employed members of the civilian labor force in thousands of persons, by age group as shown.

Table 6.08: Employment Status for Hispanics by Ethnic Group, 2007 and 2008

	Mexican	Puerto Rican	Cuban	Total Hispanic
2007				
All Sexes				
Civilian noninstitutional population	19,770	2,711	1,421	31,383
Civilian labor force	13,672	1,684	898	21,602
Employed	12,908	1,551	862	20,382
Unemployed	764	133	36	1,220
Unemployment rate	5.6%	7.9%	4.0%	5.6%
Not in labor force	6,098	1,027	523	9,781
Men				
Civilian noninstitutional population	10,415	1,252	712	16,154
Civilian labor force	8,553	865	511	13,005
Employed	8,122	791	490	12,310
Unemployed	431	74	21	695
Unemployment rate	5.0%	8.5%	4.1%	5.3%
Not in labor force	1,862	387	201	3,149
Women				
Civilian noninstitutional population	9,355	1,459	709	15,229
Civilian labor force	5,119	819	387	8,597
Employed	4,786	760	372	8,072
Unemployed	333	60	15	525
Unemployment rate	6.5%	7.3%	3.9%	6.1%
Not in labor force	4,236	640	322	6,632

(continued on next page)

Table 6.08: Employment Status for Hispanics by Ethnic Group, 2007 and 2008

	Mexican	Puerto Rican	Cuban	Total Hispanic
2008				
All Sexes				
Civilian noninstitutional population	20,474	2,854	1,422	32,141
Civilian labor force	14,009	1,822	897	22,024
Employed	12,931	1,634	841	20,346
Unemployed	1078	188	57	1,678
Unemployment rate	7.7%	10.3%	6.3%	7.6%
Not in labor force	6,465	1,032	525	10,116
Men				
Civilian noninstitutional population	10,739	1,369	728	16,524
Civilian labor force	8,762	961	528	13,255
Employed	8,106	849	491	12,248
Unemployed	656	111	37	1007
Unemployment rate	7.5%	11.6%	7.0%	7.6%
Not in labor force	1,978	409	200	3,270
Women				
Civilian noninstitutional population	9,735	1,485	694	15,616
Civilian labor force	5,247	862	369	8,769
Employed	4,825	785	349	8,098
Unemployed	422	77	20	672
Unemployment rate	8.1%	8.9%	5.3%	7.7%
Not in labor force	4,488	623	325	6,847

Source: U.S. Department of Labor, Bureau of Labor Statistics, *Employment and Earnings; 2007*, table 6; *2008*, table 6.

Notes: Total includes Hispanics of Central or South American origin and other Hispanic or Latino origin, not shown separately.
Figures shown for population 16 years old and over.

Units: Numbers in thousands.

Table 6.09: Employment Status for Native-Born and Foreign-Born Workers, 2007

	Hispanic	White	All Races
Native-Born			
Civilian noninstititutional population	14,566	151,596	196,850
Civilian labor force	9,615	100,279	129,130
Participation rate	66.0%	66.1%	65.6%
Employed	8,977	96,411	123,079
Unemployed	638	3,868	6,051
Unemployment rate	6.6%	3.9%	4.7%
Foreign-Born			
Civilian noninstititutional population	16,817	7,292	35,017
Civilian labor force	11,987	4,599	23,994
Participation rate	71.3%	61.4%	68.5%
Employed	11,405	4,428	22,967
Unemployed	582	171	1,027
Unemployment rate	4.9%	3.7%	4.3%

Source: U.S. Bureau of the Census, Statistical Abstract of the United States, 2009, table 570.

Notes: 'All Races' includes other races not shown separately.
'White' excludes people of Hispanic origin, who may be of any race.

Units: Civilian labor force population, employed persons, and unemployed persons in thousands; labor force participation (the civilian noninstitutional population divided by the civilian labor force) and unemployment rate as percents.

Table 6.10: Employment Status of Families, 2005–2008

	Hispanic	White	All Races
2005			
Total families	9,603	62,567	76,443
With employed member(s)	8,312	51,645	62,933
Some usually work full time	7,786	47,883	58,276
With no employed member(s)	1,291	10,922	13,509
With unemployed member(s)	860	3,801	5,318
Some member(s) employed	606	2,782	3,717
Some usually work full time	544	2,477	3,310
2007			
Total families	10,332	63,667	77,894
With employed member(s)	9,048	52,669	64,330
Some usually work full time	8,492	48,879	59,616
With no employed member(s)	1,285	10,997	13,564
With unemployed member(s)	876	3,587	4,914
Some member(s) employed	619	2,653	3,497
Some usually work full time	554	2,350	3,096
2008			
Total families	10,500	63,490	77,943
With employed member(s)	9,135	52,273	64,058
Some usually work full time	8,466	48,271	59,116
With no employed member(s)	1,365	11,217	13,884
With unemployed member(s)	1,159	4,506	6,104
Some member(s) employed	846	3,332	4,319
Some usually work full time	743	2,955	3,830

Source: U.S. Department of Labor, Bureau Labor Statistics, *Employment and Unemployment in Families by Race and Hispanic or Latino Ethnicity, 2005–2006*, annual averages, table 1; *2006–2007* annual averages, table 1; *2007–2008* annual averages, table 1.

Notes: 'All Races' includes other races not shown separately.

Units: Number of families in thousands.

Table 6.11: Full-Time and Part-Time Status of the Labor Force by Region, 2004

	Hispanic	White	Total
Northeast			
Employed Persons			
Full-time workers, total	2,089	17,624	21,185
35 hours of more	1,902	15,402	18,600
At work 1 to 34 hours for economic reasons	134	1,539	1,793
Not at work	54	683	793
Part-time workers, total	374	4,287	4,888
At work for economic reasons	77	399	519
Not at work	18	259	290
Unemployed Persons			
Looking for full-time work	168	878	1,209
Looking for part-time work	23	209	262
Midwest			
Employed Persons			
Full-time workers, total	1,388	22,968	26,084
35 hours of more	1,233	20,081	22,841
At work 1 to 34 hours for economic reasons	113	2,060	2,303
Not at work	41	827	939
Part-time workers, total	224	5,736	6,397
At work for economic reasons	66	595	743
Not at work	12	378	410
Unemployed Persons			
Looking for full-time work	111	1,192	1,607
Looking for part-time work	21	294	365

(continued on next page)

Table 6.11: Full-Time and Part-Time Status of the Labor Force by Region, 2004

	Hispanic	White	Total
South			
Employed Persons			
Full-time workers, total	5,626	32,419	41,424
35 hours of more	4,980	28,529	36,477
At work 1 to 34 hours for economic reasons	507	2,847	3,622
Not at work	139	1,043	1,325
Part-time workers, total	889	6,150	7,610
At work for economic reasons	219	697	1,012
Not at work	35	386	456
Unemployed Persons			
Looking for full-time work	352	1,424	2,291
Looking for part-time work	46	294	427
West			
Employed Persons			
Full-time workers, total	6,189	21,175	25,826
35 hours of more	5,455	18,452	22,579
At work 1 to 34 hours for economic reasons	551	1,971	2,336
Not at work	183	752	911
Part-time workers, total	1,132	4,903	5,838
At work for economic reasons	267	680	839
Not at work	57	309	356
Unemployed Persons			
Looking for full-time work	533	1,278	1,653
Looking for part-time work	86	278	334

Source: U.S. Department of Labor, Bureau of Labor Statistics, *Geographic Profile of Employment and Unemployment, 2004*, table 3.

Notes: 'Total' includes other races and ethnic groups not shown separately.
The full-time labor force includes persons working part time for economic reasons (slack work, material shortages, repairs to plant or equipment, start or termination of a job during the week, and inability to find full-time work).
* Data not shown due to not meeting Bureau of Labor Statistics' publication standards for reliability.

Units: Members of the civilian labor force in thousands of persons, by status, as shown.

Table 6.12: Full-Time and Part-Time Status of Employed Persons in Nonagricultural Industries, 2005–2008

	Hispanic	White	All Races
2005			
All employed persons in nonagricultural industries	*17,688*	*110,298*	*134,115*
Full-time	14,004	83,589	102,397
Part-time	3,684	26,709	31,717
Part time for economic reasons	886	3,322	4,271
2006			
All employed persons in nonagricultural industries	*18,638*	*112,020*	*136,571*
Full-time	14,871	85,219	104,710
Part-time	3,767	26,801	31,861
Part time for economic reasons	869	3,194	4,071
2007			
All employed persons in nonagricultural industries	*19,366*	*113,128*	*138,321*
Full-time	15,425	86,328	106,419
Part-time	3,941	26,800	31,902
Part time for economic reasons	974	3,407	4,317
2008			
All employed persons in nonagricultural industries	*19,347*	*112,550*	*137,739*
Full-time	15,000	84,986	104,903
Part-time	4,346	27,564	32,836
Part time for economic reasons	1,418	4,604	5,773

Source: U.S. Department of Labor, Bureau of Labor Statistics, *Employment and Earnings*, *2005*, table 22; *2006*, table 22; *2007*, table 22; *2008*, table 22.

Notes: 'All Races' includes races not shown separately.
'Economic reasons' for persons who are employed part-time are: slack work, material shortages, repairs to plant or equipment, start or termination of a job during the week, and inability to find full-time work.
Employed workers are 16 years old and over.
Full-time employment is defined as 35 hours or more a week.

Units: Employed members of the civilian labor force in thousands of persons, by status, as shown.

Table 6.13: Unemployment Rates for the Civilian Labor Force by Age, 2000–2008

	Hispanic	White	All Races
2000			
All workers 16 years and older	*5.7%*	*3.5%*	*4.0%*
16–19 years old	16.7	11.4	13.1
20–24 years old	7.5	5.8	7.1
25–54 years old	4.4	2.7	3.1
55–64 years old	4.5	2.4	2.5
65 years old and over	5.7	2.8	3.1
2006			
All workers 16 years and older	*5.2%*	*4.0%*	*4.6%*
16–19 years old	15.9	13.2	15.4
20–24 years old	7.2	6.9	8.2
25–54 years old	4.3	3.3	4.7
55–64 years old	3.3	2.8	3.0
65 years old and over	3.9	2.8	2.9
2007			
All workers 16 years and older	*5.6%*	*4.1%*	*4.6%*
16–19 years old	18.1	13.9	15.7
20–24 years old	7.8	7.0	8.2
25–54 years old	4.6	3.3	3.7
55–64 years old	4.5	2.9	3.1
65 years old and over	4.9	3.2	3.3
2008			
All workers 16 years and older	*7.6%*	*5.2%*	*5.8%*
16–19 years old	22.4	16.8	18.7
20–24 years old	11.5	9.0	10.2
25–54 years old	6.2	4.3	4.8
55–64 years old	5.6	3.4	3.7
65 years old and over	7.8	4.0	4.2

Source: U.S. Department of Labor, Bureau of Labor Statistics, *Handbook of Labor Statistics, 1989*, table 28.
U.S. Department of Labor, Bureau of Labor Statistics, *Employment and Earnings, 1991*, table 3; *2001*, table 3; *2006*, table 3; *2007*, table 3; *2008*, table 3.

Notes: 'All Races' includes races not shown separately.
Data covers members of the civilian labor force.

Units: Unemployment rate as percent of labor force.

Table 6.14: Unemployment Rates for the Civilian Labor Force by Sex and Age, 2000–2008

	Hispanic		White		All Races	
	Male	Female	Male	Female	Male	Female
2000						
All workers 16 years and older	*4.9%*	*6.7%*	*3.4%*	*3.6%*	*3.9%*	*4.1%*
16-19 years old	15.7	18.1	12.3	10.4	14.0	12.1
20-24 years old	6.5	8.9	5.9	5.8	7.3	7.0
25-54 years old	3.7	5.3	2.5	2.9	2.9	3.3
55-64 years old	4.1	5.1	2.4	2.4	2.4	2.5
65 years old and over	6.3	4.8	3.1	2.4	3.4	2.8
2006						
All workers 16 years and older	*4.8%*	*5.9%*	*4.0%*	*4.0%*	*4.6%*	*4.6%*
16-19 years old	17.3	14.1	14.6	11.7	16.9	13.8
20-24 years old	6.7	8.1	7.3	6.3	8.7	7.6
25-54 years old	3.8	5.1	3.2	3.4	3.6	3.9
55-64 years old	3.5	3.1	2.8	2.8	3.0	2.9
65 years old and over	3.7	4.2	2.7	3.0	2.8	3.0
2007						
All workers 16 years and older	*5.3%*	*6.1%*	*4.2%*	*4.0%*	*4.7%*	*4.5%*
16-19 years old	19.7	16.1	15.7	12.1	17.6	13.8
20-24 years old	7.4	8.5	7.6	6.2	8.9	7.3
25-54 years old	4.2	5.1	3.3	3.4	3.7	3.8
55-64 years old	3.9	5.2	3.0	2.8	3.2	3.0
65 years old and over	5.5	4.0	3.3	3.1	3.4	3.1
2008						
All workers 16 years and older	*7.6%*	*7.6%*	*5.5%*	*4.0%*	*6.1%*	*5.4%*
16-19 years old	23.4	21.1	19.1	14.4	21.2	16.2
20-24 years old	11.8	11.1	10.2	7.5	11.4	8.8
25-54 years old	6.2	6.4	4.5	4.2	5.0	4.6
55-64 years old	5.1	4.4	3.4	3.5	3.8	3.7
65 years old and over	7.8	7.7	4.1	3.8	4.5	3.9

Source: U.S. Department of Labor, Bureau of Labor Statistics, *Employment and Earnings, 1991*, table 3; *2001*, table 3; *2006*, tables 3 and 4; *2007*, tables 3 and 4; *2008*, tables 3 and 4.

Notes: 'All Races' includes races not shown separately.
Data covers members of the civilian labor force.

Units: Unemployment rate as percent of labor force.

Table 6.15: Unemployment Rates for the Hispanic Civilian Labor Force by Sex and Ethnic Group, 1990–2006

	Mexican	Puerto Rican	Cuban	Central/South American	Other Hispanic	Total Hispanic
1990						
Both sexes	9.0%	8.6%	5.8%	6.6%	6.2%	8.2%
Men	8.6	8.2	6.3	6.9	6.2	8.0
Women	9.8	9.1	5.1	6.3	5.9	8.5
2000						
Both sexes	7.0%	8.1%	5.8%	5.1%	7.8%	6.8%
Men	6.1	8.0	6.7	4.5	8.8	6.2
Women	8.5	8.3	4.6	5.9	6.7	7.7

	Mexican	Puerto Rican	Cuban	Central American	South American	Other Hispanic	Total Hispanic
2003							
Both sexes	8.7%	9.2%	7.3%	8.7%	5.9%	8.9%	8.5%
Men	8.2	9.7	9.8	8.8	3.7	9.2	8.2
Women	9.5	8.6	3.9	8.4	9.0	8.6	9.0
2006							
Both sexes	5.5%	8.3%	4.2%	6.1%	4.5%	6.7%	6.4%
Men	4.9	8.4	5.4	5.9	5.0	7.0	6.2
Women	6.5	8.2	2.7	6.5	3.9	6.4	6.7

Source: U.S. Bureau of the Census, *The Hispanic Population in the United States, March, 1990*, table 2; 1992, table 2.
U.S. Bureau of the Census, Current Population Reports: *The Hispanic Population of the United States, 2000*, table 9.2; *2003*, table 9.2; *2006*, table 9.2.

Notes: 'Other Hispanic origin' includes persons from Spain and persons identifying themselves generally as Hispanic, Spanish, Spanish-American, Hispano, Latino, etc. For 2003 and 2006, 'other Hispanic' also includes Dominicans.

Units: Unemployment rates based on persons in the civilian labor force.

Table 6.16: Civilian Labor Force and Unemployment Rate by State, 2006

	Civilian Labor Force			Unemployment Rate		
	Hispanic	White	All Races	Hispanic	White	All Races
United States	*20,694*	*123,834*	*151,428*	*5.2%*	*4.0%*	*4.6%*
Alabama	53	1,640	2,210	1.1	3.0	4.1
Alaska	13	273	349	10.3	5.3	6.9
Arizona	848	2,670	2,969	4.9	4.0	4.2
Arkansas	76	1,137	1,374	4.7	4.4	5.3
California	5,822	13,833	17,751	5.6	4.7	4.8
Colorado	428	2,389	2,610	6.9	4.0	4.2
Connecticut	186	1,592	1,858	8.2	3.8	4.3
Delaware	29	337	448	4.0	3.0	3.5
District of Columbia	30	144	291	4.2	2.3	5.8
Florida	1,954	7,413	9,054	3.4	2.8	3.2
Georgia	379	3,177	4,694	4.8	3.3	4.6
Hawaii	40	147	657	4.4	2.6	2.7
Idaho	63	724	759	4.5	3.3	3.5
Illinois	734	5,358	6,584	5.5	3.7	4.5
Indiana	138	2,947	3,253	5.3	4.5	5.0
Iowa	69	1,619	1,701	4.8	3.2	3.6
Kansas	90	1,338	1,480	5.6	3.7	4.4
Kentucky	34	1,870	2,042	4.4	5.3	5.6
Louisiana	53	1,370	1,960	5.7	2.7	4.6
Maine	NA	695	715	NA	4.5	4.6
Maryland	242	1,990	3,001	3.5	2.9	3.9
Massachusetts	215	2,976	3,368	10.9	4.7	5.1
Michigan	178	4,232	5,086	5.5	6.2	7.0
Minnesota	115	2,667	2,933	4.7	3.6	4.0
Mississippi	43	841	1,296	4.5	4.0	6.4
Missouri	79	2,634	3,069	7.3	3.9	4.8
Montana	10	475	505	5.1	3.2	3.6
Nebraska	69	906	982	4.5	2.7	3.1

(continued on next page)

Table 6.16: Civilian Labor Force and Unemployment Rate by State, 2006

	Civilian Labor Force			Unemployment Rate		
	Hispanic	White	All Races	Hispanic	White	All Races
United States	*20,694*	*123,834*	*151,428*	*5.2%*	*4.0%*	*4.6%*
Nevada	300	1,052	1,296	4.9	3.8	4.1
New Hampshire	13	710	741	3.6	3.3	3.4
New Jersey	722	3,473	4,490	6.4	4.2	4.8
New Mexico	354	814	944	5.3	4.3	4.4
New York	1,379	7,187	9,464	5.7	3.9	4.4
North Carolina	362	3,344	4,426	3.1	3.5	4.7
North Dakota	NA	338	368	NA	2.6	3.3
Ohio	155	5,163	5,975	7.2	4.5	5.4
Oklahoma	91	1,380	1,733	6.2	3.3	3.9
Oregon	148	1,719	1,897	6.3	5.1	5.4
Pennsylvania	213	5,606	6,308	8.8	4.3	4.7
Rhode Island	56	519	577	8.5	4.9	5.2
South Carolina	82	1,492	2,124	5.5	5.0	6.5
South Dakota	9	408	434	6.7	2.4	3.1
Tennessee	127	2,483	3,028	3.5	4.3	5.2
Texas	3,909	9,509	11,465	4.6	4.1	4.8
Utah	148	1,231	1,309	3.5	2.8	2.9
Vermont	NA	352	365	NA	3.6	3.6
Virginia	275	2,973	3,971	2.7	2.5	3.1
Washington	216	2,802	3,335	7.2	4.9	5.0
West Virginia	NA	782	815	NA	5.1	5.1
Wisconsin	113	2,830	3,079	7.8	4.3	4.8
Wyoming	17	275	287	8.2	3.1	3.4

Source: U.S. Department of Labor, Bureau of Labor Statistics, *Geographic Profile of Employment and Unemployment*, 2006 Annual Averages.

Notes: 'All Races' includes races not shown separately.
Data covers members of the civilian labor force.

Units: Civilian labor force in thousands; percent unemployed in civilian labor force.

Table 6.17: Civilian Labor Force and Unemployment Rate by State, 2008

	Civilian Labor Force			Unemployment Rate		
	Hispanic	White	All Races	Hispanic	White	All Races
United States	*17,314*	*123,834*	*151,428*	*8.9%*	*4.0%*	*4.6%*
Alabama	516	1,640	2,210	7.5	3.0	4.1
Alaska	11	273	349	10.7	5.3	6.9
Arizona	113	2,670	2,969	6.1	4.0	4.2
Arkansas	194	1,137	1,374	10.3	4.4	5.3
California	1,058	13,833	17,751	9.4	4.7	4.8
Colorado	85	2,389	2,610	6.6	4.0	4.2
Connecticut	182	1,592	1,858	8.1	3.8	4.3
Delaware	91	337	448	5.5	3.0	3.5
District of Columbia	131	144	291	10.0	2.3	5.8
Florida	1,310	7,413	9,054	5.9	2.8	3.2
Georgia	1,342	3,177	4,694	7.9	3.3	4.6
Hawaii	NA	147	657	NA	2.6	2.7
Idaho	NA	724	759	NA	3.3	3.5
Illinois	846	5,358	6,584	10.0	3.7	4.5
Indiana	258	2,947	3,253	10.9	4.5	5.0
Iowa	34	1,619	1,701	16.5	3.2	3.6
Kansas	67	1,338	1,480	12.4	3.7	4.4
Kentucky	132	1,870	2,042	10.8	5.3	5.6
Louisiana	539	1,370	1,960	9.1	2.7	4.6
Maine	NA	695	715	NA	4.5	4.6
Maryland	825	1,990	3,001	6.3	2.9	3.9
Massachusetts	192	2,976	3,368	9.0	4.7	5.1
Michigan	610	4,232	5,086	12.8	6.2	7.0
Minnesota	107	2,667	2,933	10.7	3.6	4.0
Mississippi	424	841	1,296	11.3	4.0	6.4
Missouri	339	2,634	3,069	12.2	3.9	4.8
Montana	NA	475	505	NA	3.2	3.6
Nebraska	34	906	982	9.2	2.7	3.1

(continued on next page)

Table 6.17: Civilian Labor Force and Unemployment Rate by State, 2008

	Civilian Labor Force			Unemployment Rate		
	Hispanic	White	All Races	Hispanic	White	All Races
Nevada	92	1,052	1,296	6.8	3.8	4.1
New Hampshire	NA	710	741	NA	3.3	3.4
New Jersey	599	3,473	4,490	9.7	4.2	4.8
New Mexico	24	814	944	5.5	4.3	4.4
New York	1,451	7,187	9,464	7.8	3.9	4.4
North Carolina	902	3,344	4,426	9.0	3.5	4.7
North Dakota	NA	338	368	NA	2.6	3.3
Ohio	649	5,163	5,975	12.3	4.5	5.4
Oklahoma	113	1,380	1,733	8.2	3.3	3.9
Oregon	28	1,719	1,897	16.1	5.1	5.4
Pennsylvania	558	5,606	6,308	8.2	4.3	4.7
Rhode Island	33	519	577	7.2	4.9	5.2
South Carolina	592	1,492	2,124	10.2	5.0	6.5
South Dakota	NA	408	434	NA	2.4	3.1
Tennessee	460	2,483	3,028	10.0	4.3	5.2
Texas	1,286	9,509	11,465	10.7	4.1	4.8
Utah	NA	1,231	1,309	NA	2.8	2.9
Vermont	NA	352	365	NA	3.6	3.6
Virginia	761	2,973	3,971	5.7	2.5	3.1
Washington	110	2,802	3,335	7.8	4.9	5.0
West Virginia	23	782	815	6.7	5.1	5.1
Wisconsin	145	2,830	3,079	11.9	4.3	4.8
Wyoming	NA	275	287	NA	3.1	3.4

Source: U.S. Department of Labor, Bureau of Labor Statistics, *Geographic Profile of Employment and Unemployment*, 2008 Annual Averages.

Notes: 'All Races' includes races not shown separately.
Data covers members of the civilian labor force.

Units: Civilian labor force in thousands; percent unemployed in civilian labor force.

Table 6.18: Unemployment by Reason for Unemployment, 2000–2008

	Hispanic	White	All Races
2000			
Total unemployed	*876*	*4,099*	*5,655*
Job losers	390	1,866	2,492
Job leavers	98	593	775
Re-entrants to the labor force	289	1,356	1,957
New entrants to the labor force	NA	284	431
2006			
Total unemployed	*1,081*	*5,002*	*7,001*
Job losers	522	2,479	3,321
Job leavers	107	608	827
Re-entrants to the labor force	331	1,514	2,237
New entrants to the labor force	121	401	616
2007			
Total unemployed	*1,220*	*5,143*	*7,078*
Job losers	635	2,667	3,515
Job leavers	111	595	793
Re-entrants to the labor force	346	1,474	2,142
New entrants to the labor force	127	407	627
2008			
Total unemployed	*1,678*	*6,509*	*8,924*
Job losers	936	3,576	4,789
Job leavers	144	677	896
Re-entrants to the labor force	433	1,767	2,472
New entrants to the labor force	164	519	766

Source: U.S. Department of Labor, Bureau of Labor Statistics, *Employment and Earnings, 2001*, table 28, *2007*, tables 27 and 28; *2008*, tables 27 and 28.

Notes: 'All Races' includes races not shown separately.
Data covers members of the civilian labor force.

Units: Unemployed members of the civilian labor force in thousands of persons, by reason for unemployment as shown.

Table 6.19: Unemployment Rate by Marital Status, 2005–2008

	Hispanic		White		All Races	
	Male	Female	Male	Female	Male	Female
2005						
Total	*5.4%*	*6.9%*	*4.4%*	*4.4%*	*5.1%*	*5.1%*
Married, spouse present	3.6	5.4	2.5	3.0	2.8	3.3
Widowed, divorced, or separated	4.5	6.2	5.0	4.9	5.6	5.4
Single (never married)	8.7	9.8	8.2	6.8	9.5	8.3
2006						
Total	*4.8%*	*5.9%*	*4.0%*	*4.0%*	*4.6%*	*4.6%*
Married, spouse present	3.0	4.5	2.2	2.7	2.4	2.9
Widowed, divorced, or separated	4.2	5.5	4.7	4.7	5.2	4.9
Single (never married)	7.8	8.2	7.5	6.4	8.6	7.7
2007						
Total	*5.3%*	*6.1%*	*4.2%*	*4.0%*	*4.7%*	*4.5%*
Married, spouse present	3.5	4.7	2.4	2.6	2.5	2.8
Widowed, divorced, or separated	5.1	6.0	4.9	4.9	5.3	5.0
Single (never married)	8.3	8.3	7.8	6.3	8.8	7.2
2008						
Total	*7.6%*	*7.7%*	*5.5%*	*4.9%*	*6.1%*	*5.4%*
Married, spouse present	5.2	6.3	3.1	3.5	3.4	3.6
Widowed, divorced, or separated	7.4	6.9	6.5	5.6	7.1	5.9
Single (never married)	11.5	10.1	9.9	7.3	11.0	8.5

Source: U.S. Department of Labor, Bureau of Labor Statistics, *Employment and Earnings, 2006*, table 24; *2007*, table 24; *2008*, table 24.

Notes: 'All Races' includes races not shown separately. All persons 16 years old and over.

Units: Percent unemployed by marital status.

Table 6.20: Duration of Unemployment by Region of Residence, 2000 and 2003

	Hispanic	White	All Races
2000			
Northeast			
Less than 5 weeks	34.6%	42.0%	40.1%
5–14 weeks	30.7	31.9	32.1
15 weeks and over	34.6	26.1	27.9
27 weeks and over	22.8	13.0	14.3
52 weeks and over	15.7	7.4	8.5
Midwest			
Less than 5 weeks	50.7%	50.1%	47.4%
5–14 weeks	31.3	31.1	32.0
15 weeks and over	16.4	18.8	20.6
27 weeks and over	9.0	8.4	9.8
52 weeks and over	NA	NA	4.5
South			
Less than 5 weeks	46.3%	49.1%	45.2%
5–14 weeks	32.2	31.6	32.4
15 weeks and over	21.6	19.4	22.5
27 weeks and over	10.6	8.8	10.8
52 weeks and over	5.9	4.8	5.9
West			
Less than 5 weeks	47.1%	47.1%	46.0%
5–14 weeks	31.9	31.3	31.2
15 weeks and over	21.1	21.6	22.9
27 weeks and over	11.2	10.5	11.5
52 weeks and over	5.4	5.1	5.7

(continued on next page)

Table 6.20: Duration of Unemployment by Region of Residence, 2000 and 2003

	Hispanic	White	All Races
2003			
Northeast			
Less than 5 weeks	28.6%	29.1%	27.5%
5–14 weeks	32.5	29.3	29.2
15–26 weeks	16.9	17.9	17.9
27–51 weeks	10.4	11.8	11.9
52 weeks and over	12.1	11.9	13.4
Median duration	10.8	11.1	11.8
Midwest			
Less than 5 weeks	39.3%	33.2%	31.9%
5–14 weeks	31.4	30.6	30.5
15–26 weeks	13.6	15.4	15.7
27–51 weeks	7.1	10.5	10.5
52 weeks and over	8.6	10.3	11.4
Median duration	7.6	9.4	9.9
South			
Less than 5 weeks	39.1%	36.2%	32.8%
5–14 weeks	31.1	29.8	29.6
15–26 weeks	16.6	15.6	16.7
27–51 weeks	5.7	8.6	9.5
52 weeks and over	7.6	9.7	11.4
Median duration	8.1	8.8	9.8
West			
Less than 5 weeks	38.6%	35.4%	33.4%
5–14 weeks	29.9	29.8	29.7
15 weeks and over	15.1	15.6	15.6
27 weeks and over	8.3	9.2	9.7
52 weeks and over	8.2	10.2	11.6
Median duration	8.2	9.0	9.6

Source: U.S. Department of Labor, Bureau of Labor Statistics, *Geographic Profile of Employment and Unemployment, 2000*, table 11; *2003*, table 13.

Notes: 'All Races' includes races not shown separately.

Units: Percent of total unemployment in each region; median duration in weeks.

Table 6.21: Duration of Unemployment by Sex, 2006–2008

	Hispanic		White		All Races	
	Male	Female	Male	Female	Male	Female
2006						
By Duration						
Total	601	480	2,730	2,271	3,753	3,247
Less than 5 weeks	265	198	1,073	919	1,391	1,222
5-14 weeks	177	149	825	710	1,112	1,009
15-26 weeks	76	66	372	308	549	482
27 weeks and over	83	67	461	335	700	534
Average duration	14.8	14.0	16.3	14.7	17.5	16.1
Median duration	6.6	7.2	7.7	7.2	8.5	8.1
2007						
By Duration						
Total	695	525	2,869	2,274	3,882	3,196
Less than 5 weeks	285	210	1,070	877	1,370	1,172
5-14 weeks	222	158	913	721	1,228	1,004
15-26 weeks	93	76	413	335	578	483
27 weeks and over	94	80	474	341	706	537
Average duration	14.6	15.5	16.3	15.1	17.3	16.2
Median duration	7.2	7.5	8.0	7.8	8.7	8.4
2008						
By Duration						
Total	1007	672	3,727	2,782	5,033	3,891
Less than 5 weeks	387	230	1,321	960	1,674	1,258
5-14 weeks	305	219	1140	904	1,536	1,269
15-26 weeks	148	98	587	424	813	615
27 weeks and over	167	124	679	494	1011	750
Average duration	15.3	16.9	16.8	16.6	18.0	17.7
Median duration	8.1	8.7	8.8	8.7	9.5	9.3

Source: U.S. Department of Labor, Bureau of Labor Statistics, *Employment and Earnings*, *2006*, table 31; *2007*, table 31; *2008*, table 31.

Notes: 'All Races' includes races not shown separately.

Units: Thousands of unemployed persons, average (mean) and median duration of unemployment in weeks.

Table 6.22: Unemployed Jobseekers by Active Job Search Methods Used, 2007 and 2008

	Hispanic	White	All Races
2007			
Total unemployed	1,220	5,143	7,078
Total jobseekers	1,035	4,337	6,102
Methods Used as a Percent of Total Jobseekers			
Employer directly	56.8%	57.5%	57.4%
Sent out resumes or filled out applications	42.7	51.1	50.7
Placed or answered ads	12.9	16.5	16.0
Friends or relatives	30.2	21.8	21.7
Public employment agency	16.5	16.5	17.7
Private employment agency	6.8	7.3	7.6
Other	11.8	13.3	12.9
Average number of methods used	1.78	1.85	1.84
2008			
Total unemployed	1,678	6,509	8,924
Total jobseekers	1,421	5,540	7,749
Methods Used as a Percent of Total Jobseekers			
Employer directly	56.9%	57.3%	56.9%
Sent out resumes or filled out applications	45.7	53.0	52.3
Placed or answered ads	13.1	17.1	17.1
Friends or relatives	30.5	23.4	23.8
Public employment agency	18.0	17.4	18.9
Private employment agency	7.6	7.8	8.0
Other	11.2	14.6	14.1
Average number of methods used	1.84	1.91	1.92

Source: U.S. Department of Labor, Bureau of Labor Statistics, *Employment and Earnings, 2005*, table 33; *2007*, table 33; *2008*, table 33.

Notes: 'All Races' includes races not shown separately.
'Jobseekers' does not include persons on temporary layoff.
Percents will add to more than 100% because people used multiple job search methods.

Units: Persons in thousands of persons; percent of jobseekers using specified search methods.

Table 6.23: Occupations of Employed Hispanic Persons by Sex and Ethnic Group, 2003 and 2006

	Mexican	Puerto Rican	Cuban	Central American	South American	Other Hispanic	Total Hispanic
2003							
Total employed	11,067	1,486	595	1,506	1,087	1,219	16,960
Male	6,860	766	333	926	660	589	10,133
Female	4,207	720	261	581	427	630	6,827
By Occupation:							
Male							
Management/professional	758	148	89	79	155	139	1,370
Percent	11.1%	19.4%	26.7%	8.6%	23.5%	23.6%	13.5%
Sales and office	837	154	78	111	122	138	1,441
Percent	12.2%	20.2%	23.4%	12.0%	18.5%	23.5%	14.2%
Service occupations	1,463	142	35	197	143	110	2,089
Percent	21.3%	18.5%	10.4%	21.3%	21.7%	18.7%	20.6%
Construction/maintenance	1,706	150	76	293	110	83	2,418
Percent	24.9%	19.6%	22.9%	31.7%	16.7%	14.1%	23.9%
Farming, fishing & forestry	247	1	0	4	4	1	258
Percent	3.6%	0.2%	0.0%	0.5%	0.6%	0.2%	2.5%
Production & transport	1,848	170	55	241	126	117	2,557
Percent	26.9%	22.2%	16.6%	26.0%	19.1%	19.9%	25.2%
Female							
Management/professional	773	177	85	91	108	182	1,416
Percent	18.4%	24.5%	32.4%	15.6%	25.2%	29.0%	20.7%
Sales and office	1,431	315	92	152	135	198	2,322
Percent	34.0%	43.7%	35.2%	26.2%	31.6%	31.4%	34.0%
Service occupations	1,303	164	53	239	135	186	2,081
Percent	31.0%	22.8%	20.5%	41.2%	31.6%	29.6%	30.5%
Construction/maintenance	40	4	3	6	2	4	59
Percent	1.0%	0.5%	1.1%	1.1%	0.6%	0.6%	0.9%
Farming, fishing & forestry	62	2	0	5	0	3	72
Percent	1.5%	0.2%	0.0%	0.9%	0.0%	0.5%	1.0%
Production & transport	599	59	28	88	47	56	877
Percent	14.2%	8.2%	10.9%	15.1%	11.0%	8.9%	12.8%

(continued on next page)

Table 6.23: Occupations of Employed Hispanic Persons by Sex and Ethnic Group, 2003 and 2006

	Mexican	Puerto Rican	Cuban	Central American	South American	Other Hispanic	Total Hispanic
2006							
Total employed	*12,160*	*1,467*	*729*	*1,903*	*1,333*	*1,499*	*19,091*
Male	7,689	775	404	1,212	734	754	11,569
Female	4,470	692	325	691	599	744	7,522
By Occupation:							
Male							
Management/professional	804	153	100	121	160	150	1,488
Percent	10.5%	19.8%	24.9%	9.9%	21.8%	19.9%	12.9%
Sales and office	974	126	90	134	147	175	1,648
Percent	12.7%	16.3%	22.4%	11.1%	20.1%	23.3%	14.2%
Service occupations	1,637	169	41	262	113	132	2,354
Percent	21.3%	21.9%	10.1%	21.6%	15.4%	17.5%	20.3%
Construction/maintenance	2,328	147	87	438	156	161	3,316
Percent	30.3%	19.0%	21.5%	36.1%	21.2%	21.3%	28.7%
Farming, fishing & forestry	259	2	1	11	6	2	280
Percent	3.4%	0.2%	0.3%	0.9%	0.8%	0.2%	2.4%
Production & transport	1,688	177	84	247	152	135	2,482
Percent	22.0%	22.8%	20.8%	20.3%	20.7%	17.9%	21.5%
Female							
Management/professional	944	199	100	107	162	170	1,682
Percent	21.1%	28.7%	30.7%	15.5%	27.1%	22.9%	22.4%
Sales and office	1,463	257	118	168	169	275	2,450
Percent	32.7%	37.2%	36.3%	24.3%	28.2%	37.0%	32.6%
Service occupations	1,351	190	78	293	187	213	2,312
Percent	30.2%	27.5%	23.8%	42.3%	31.3%	28.6%	30.7%
Construction/maintenance	50	3	3	17	7	8	87
Percent	1.1%	0.5%	0.8%	2.5%	1.1%	1.0%	1.2%
Farming, fishing & forestry	56	0	0	5	0	1	63
Percent	1.3%	0.0%	0.0%	0.8%	0.0%	0.2%	0.8%
Production & transport	606	43	27	101	74	78	928
Percent	13.6%	6.2%	8.3%	14.6%	12.4%	10.4%	12.3%

Source: U.S. Bureau of the Census, Current Population Reports: *The Hispanic Population of the United States, 2003*, table 10.2; *2006*, tables 10.2a, 10.2b, and 10.2c.

Notes: 'Other Hispanic' includes Dominicans.

Units: Number of employed persons ages 16 and over in thousands; percent as a percent of total employed for ethnic group.

Table 6.24: Employed Hispanic Persons as Percent of the Civilian Labor Force by Selected Occupation, 2008

	Hispanic	All Races
All occupations	*14.0%*	*145,362*
Management occupations	*7.3*	*15,852*
Chief executive	4.8	1,655
General and operations managers	6.2	985
Computer and information systems managers	5.3	475
Financial managers	8.6	1,168
Education administrators	7.6	829
Medical and health services managers	7.3	561
Business and financial operations occupations	*7.9*	*6,207*
Accountants and auditors	7.6	1,762
Insurance underwriters	7.1	82
Wholesale and retail buyers, except farm products	12.2	191
Computer and mathematical occupations	*5.1*	*3,676*
Computer scientists and systems analysts	5.3	837
Computer programmers	4.0	534
Computer software engineers	3.7	1034
Database administrators	3.8	93
Operations research analysts	8.3	75
Architecture and engineering occupations	*6.7*	*2,931*
Architects, except naval	8.2	233
Aerospace engineers	5.0	137
Chemical engineers	NA	64
Civil engineers	9.2	346
Engineering technicians, except drafters	10.3	416
Life, physical, and social science occupations	*4.7*	*1,307*
Medical scientists	2.7	132
Environmental scientists and geoscientists	4.1	85
Psychologists	6.6	176
Legal occupations	*6.6*	*1,671*
Lawyers	3.8	1,014
Judges, magistrate, and other judicial workers	3.2	54
Education, training and library occupations	*7.5*	*8,605*
Librarians	3.7	197
Arts, design, entertainment, sports and media occupations	*8.3*	*2,820*
Writers and authors	3.3	186

(continued on next page)

Table 6.24: Employed Hispanic Persons as Percent of the Civilian Labor Force by Selected Occupation, 2008

	Hispanic	All Races
Healthcare practitioner and technical occupations	*5.9*	*7,399*
Dentists	5.2	152
Physicians and surgeons	5.8	877
Registered nurses	4.7	2,778
Healthcare support occupations	*13.6*	*3,212*
Protective service occupations	*10.9*	*3,047*
Fire fighters	9.4	293
Police and sheriff's patrol officers	11.6	674
Food preparation and serving related occupations	*21.0*	*7,824*
Building and grounds cleaning and maintenance	*33.4*	*5,445*
Personal care and service occupations	*14.2*	*4,923*
Sales and related occupations	*11.7*	*16,295*
Cashiers	16.6	3,031
Retail salespersons	12.3	3,416
Real estate brokers and sales agents	8.6	962
Office and administrative occupations	*12.8*	*19,249*
Farming, fishing and forestry occupations	*39.3*	*988*
Construction and extraction occupations	*29.6*	*8,667*
Carpenters	25.7	1,562
Construction laborers	44.1	1,651
Electricians	16.2	874
Installation, maintenance and repair	*14.5*	*5,152*
Production occupations	*21.1*	*8,973*
Electrical and electronic assemblers	19.4	203
Machinists	12.1	409
Printing machine operators	20.5	213
Transportation and material moving	*19.7*	*8,827*
Aircraft pilots and flight engineers	2.5	141
Industrial truck and tractor operators	26.7	568
Refuse and recyclable material collectors	31.1	98

Source: U.S. Department of Labor, Bureau of Labor Statistics, *Employment and Earnings, 2008*, table 11.

Notes: Only selected subcategories of occupational groups displayed.
NA indicates no data or data that does not meet publication criteria.

Units: Employed Hispanic persons as a percent of all employed persons, by occupation.
Employed persons in thousands.

Table 6.25: Employed Hispanic Persons as Percent of the Civilian Labor Force by Industry Group, 2008

	Hispanic	All Races
All industries	*14.0%*	*145,362*
Agriculture, forestry, fishing, and hunting	20.4	2,168
Mining	15.5	819
Construction	24.6	10,974
Manufacturing	14.6	15,904
Durable goods	12.3	10,273
Nondurable goods	18.9	5,631
Wholesale and retail trade	13.8	20,585
Wholesale trade	14.5	4,052
Retail trade	13.6	16,533
Transportation and warehousing	15.8	6,501
Utilities	10.6	1,225
Information	9.1	3,481
Finance and insurance	9.8	7,279
Real estate and rental and leasing	12.6	2,949
Legal services	7.8	1,642
Architectural, engineering and related services	7.8	1,615
Scientific research and development services	7.2	543
Management, administrative and waste services	23.8	6,178
Educational services	8.8	13,169
Hospitals	7.9	6,241
Health services, except hospitals	10.7	8,865
Social assistance	13.9	3,127
Arts, entertainment, and recreation	10.7	2,972
Accommodation and food services	20.8	9,795
Services	17.1	7,005
Public administration	9.3	6,763

Source: U.S. Department of Labor, Bureau of Labor Statistics, *Employment and Earnings, 2008*, table 18.

Notes: Only selected subcategories of industry groups are displayed.

Units: Employed Hispanic persons as a percent of all employed persons, by industry group; total employed persons are 16 years and older and in thousands.

Table 6.26: Tenure of Workers with Current Employer by Sex, 2006

	Hispanic		White		All Races	
	Male	Female	Male	Female	Male	Female
Number of workers	10,550	7,191	54,241	48,659	65,212	60,456
Tenure:						
Under 1 year	29.7	30.6	23.4%	24.6%	23.9%	24.9%
1–2 years	6.0	7.3	6.7	7.2	6.8	7.2
2 years	7.7	6.8	5.1	5.0	5.3	5.0
3–4 years	20.5	19.7	16.6	17.0	16.7	17.2
5–9 years	20.5	20.1	20.7	21.1	20.7	21.2
10–14 years	7.4	7.0	9.9	9.4	9.6	9.3
15–19 years	4.7	4.4	6.9	6.9	6.6	6.8
20+ years	3.5	4.1	10.8	8.7	10.3	8.4

Source: U.S. Bureau of the Census, *Statistical Abstract of the United States, 2008*, table 593.

Notes: 'All Races' includes races not shown separately. Data is for employed wage and salary workers 16 years old and over, and excludes self-employed workers.

Units: Unemployment rates (percent of the civilian labor force that is unemployed) as a percent of the total civilian labor force; number of unemployed in thousands.

Table 6.27: Labor Force Status of the Civilian Noninstitutional Population 16–24 Years of Age by School Enrollment, 2008

	Hispanic	White	All Races
All persons enrolled in school	NA	NA	21,348
Civilian labor force	NA	NA	8,974
Employed	NA	NA	7,907
Unemployed	NA	NA	1,067
Below college level	1,804	7,274	9,677
Civilian labor force	365	2,153	2,661
Employed	238	1,729	2,099
Unemployed	127	424	562
At college level	1,385	9,283	11,671
Civilian labor force	775	5,289	6,313
Employed	682	4,900	5,809
Unemployed	93	389	505
All persons not enrolled in school	3,531	12,485	16,220
Civilian labor force	2,684	10,244	12,957
Employed	2,279	8,971	11,113
Unemployed	405	1,273	1,845

Source: U.S. Department of Labor, Bureau of Labor Statistics, *College Enrollment and Work Activity of 2008 High School Graduates*, table 2.

Notes: 'All Races' includes races not shown separately. Data are as of October of the year indicated.

Units: Civilian noninstitutional population, civilian labor force, employed and unemployed, in thousands of persons.

Table 6.28: Educational Attainment of Persons 16 Years and Over by Labor Force Status and Sex, 2000 and 2006

	Hispanic		White		All Races	
	Male	Female	Male	Female	Male	Female
2000						
High school graduate						
Employed	2,446	1,739	19,043	16,232	22,377	19,681
Unemployed	140	110	828	641	1,136	951
Not in labor force	415	1,106	5,968	12,740	7,173	14,757
Bachelor's degree						
Employed	551	510	11,312	9,846	13,028	11,786
Unemployed	19	20	186	188	250	225
Not in labor force	66	161	1,961	3,444	2,248	4,032
2006						
High school graduate						
Employed	3,505	2,229	19,377	14,875	23,898	18,565
Unemployed	200	146	1,046	645	1,497	1,009
Not in labor force	614	1,554	7,175	13,459	8,938	15,983
Bachelor's degree						
Employed	863	844	12,135	11,128	14,322	13,684
Unemployed	30	24	330	267	430	350
Not in labor force	153	275	2,601	4,482	3,037	5,344

Source: U.S. Bureau of the Census, Current Population Reports: *Educational Attainment in the United States: 2000*, table 5a; *2006*, table 5a.

Notes: 'All Races' includes other races not shown separately.
For 2006 data, 'White' is equivalent to 'White Alone' and refers to people who reported 'White' and did not report any other race category.

Units: Number of persons 16 years old and over in thousands.

Table 6.29: Unemployment Rates of the Civilian Labor Force by Educational Attainment, 2000–2007

	Hispanic	White	All Races
2000			
Number of unemployed	569	2,644	3,589
All levels of education	4.4%	2.6%	3.0%
Less than 4 years of high school	6.2	5.6	6.3
4 years of high school only	3.9	2.9	3.4
1–3 years of college	3.2	2.4	2.7
4 or more years of college	2.2	1.6	1.7
2005			
Number of unemployed	773	3,627	5,070
All levels of education	4.8%	3.5%	4.0%
Less than 4 years of high school	6.2	6.5	7.6
4 years of high school only	4.5	4.0	4.7
1–3 years of college	4.1	3.4	3.9
4 or more years of college	2.9	2.1	2.3
2006			
Number of unemployed	716	3,376	4,648
All levels of education	4.2%	3.2%	3.6%
Less than 4 years of high school	5.5	5.9	6.8
4 years of high school only	4.1	3.7	4.3
1–3 years of college	3.6	3.2	3.6
4 or more years of college	2.2	2.0	2.0
2007			
Number of unemployed	810	3,487	4,735
All levels of education	4.6%	3.3%	3.6%
Less than 4 years of high school	6.0	6.5	6.3
4 years of high school only	4.4	3.9	3.4
1–3 years of college	4.1	3.2	2.7
4 or more years of college	2.3	1.9	1.7

Source: U.S. Bureau of the Census, *Statistical Abstract of the United States, 2007*, table 614; *2008*, table 609; *2009*, table 607.

Notes: 'All Races' includes races not shown separately.
Data is for persons 25 years old and over.

Units: Unemployment rates (percent of the civilian labor force that is unemployed) as a percent of the total civilian labor force; number of unemployed in thousands.

Hispanic Americans: A Statistical Sourcebook 2009

Table 6.30: Self-Employed Workers, 1994–2008

	Hispanic	White	All Races
1994	533	8,179	9,003
1995	507	8,105	8,902
1996	561	8,106	8,971
1997	598	8,153	9,056
1998	590	8,030	8,962
1999	651	7,846	8,790
2000	616	7,692	8,674
2001	659	7,639	8,594
2002	845	7,914	8,923
2003	935	8,160	9,344
2004	1,008	8,252	9,467
2005	1,019	8,247	9,509
2006	1,130	8,342	9,685
2007	1,213	8,268	9,557
2008	1,203	7,972	9,219

Source: U.S. Department of Labor, Bureau of Labor Statistics, *Employment and Earnings, 1994*, table 41; *1999*, table 12; *2000*, table 12; *2001*, table 12; *2002*, table 12; *2004*, table 12; *2005*, table 12; *2006*, tables 12 and 13; *2007*, tables 12 and 13; *2008*, tables 12 and 13.

Notes: 'All Races' includes races not shown separately.
Data shown for non-agricultural workers only.

Units: Self-employed workers in thousands of persons.

Table 6.31: Work at Home, 2001 and 2004

	Hispanic	White	All Races
2001			
Worked at home	191	3,138	3,436
Less than 8 hours per week	15.9%	24.4%	24.5%
8 hours or more	51.8	48.0	47.6
35 hours or more	27.6	15.0	15.7
Mean hours worked per week	23.2	17.7	18.0
2004			
Worked at home	240	2,999	3,349
Less than 8 hours per week	12.6%	20.9%	21.1%
8 hours or more	54.7	50.8	49.5
35 hours or more	16.9	15.3	14.8
Mean hours worked per week	21.1	19.0	18.6

Source: U.S. Department of Labor, Bureau of Labor Statistics, *Work at Home in 2001*, table 3; *2004*, table 3.

Notes: Data refers to employed persons (excluding self-employed) in nonagricultural industries who reported that they usually work at home at least once per week as part of their primary job.
'All Races' includes races not shown separately.

Units: Numbers of workers in thousands; percent of total working at home.

Table 6.32: Union Membership by Sex, 2007 and 2008

	Hispanic	White	All Races
2007			
Men			
Total employed	11,163	55,771	67,468
Members of unions	1,108	7,134	8,767
Percent of total	9.9%	12.8%	13.0%
Represented by unions	1,208	7,708	9,494
Percent of total	10.8%	13.8%	14.1%
Women			
Total employed	7,615	49,743	62,299
Members of unions	728	5,352	6,903
Percent of total	9.6%	10.8%	11.1%
Represented by unions	818	6,007	7,749
Percent of total	10.7%	12.1%	12.4%
2008			
Men			
Total employed	10,998	55,197	66,846
Members of unions	1,204	7,309	8,938
Percent of total	11.0%	13.2%	13.4%
Represented by unions	1,317	7,961	9,724
Percent of total	12.0%	14.4%	14.5%
Women			
Total employed	7,574	49,855	62,532
Members of unions	756	5,555	7,160
Percent of total	10.0%	11.1%	11.4%
Represented by unions	852	6,261	8,036
Percent of total	11.2%	12.6%	12.9%

Source: U.S. Department of Labor, Bureau of Labor Statistics, *Employment and Earnings,*
2007, table 40; *2008*, table 40.

Notes: 'All Races' includes races not shown separately.
'Members of unions' includes members of a labor union or an employee association
similar to a union.
'Represented by unions' includes members of a labor union or an employee association similar to a union as well as workers who report no union affiliation but
whose jobs are covered by a union or an employee association contract.

Units: Total employed, members of unions and represented by unions in thousands of
persons 16 years old and older; percent as shown.

Table 6.33: Workers Paid Hourly Rates With Earnings at or Below the Minimum Wage, 2001, 2007, and 2008

	Hispanic	White	All Races
2001			
Number of workers			
All workers paid hourly rates	10,030	59,152	72,486
At or below $5.15 per hour	302	1,861	2,238
At $5.15 per hour	114	502	636
Below $5.15 per hour	187	1,359	1,602
Percent of workers paid hourly rates			
All at or below $5.15 per hour	3.0%	3.1%	3.1%
Median hourly earnings	$8.98	$10.25	$10.17
2007			
Number of workers			
All workers paid hourly rates	13,168	61,061	75,873
At or below $5.85 per hour	246	1,420	1,729
At $5.85 per hour	41	204	267
Below $5.85 per hour	205	1,216	1,462
Percent of workers paid hourly rates			
All at or below $5.85 per hour	1.9%	2.3%	2.3%
2008			
Number of workers			
All workers paid hourly rates	13,070	60,464	75,305
At or below $6.55 per hour	285	1,783	2,226
At $6.55 per hour	39	215	286
Below $6.55 per hour	324	1,568	1,940
Percent of workers paid hourly rates			
All at or below $6.55 per hour	2.5%	2.9%	3.0%

Source: U.S. Bureau of the Census, *Statistical Abstract of the United States, 2003*, table 617. U.S. Department of Labor, Bureau of Labor Statistics, *Employment and Earnings, 2007*, table 44; *2008*, table 44.

Notes: 'All Races' includes races not shown separately. Workers 16 years and over.

Units: Number of workers in thousands, percent of total workers paid hourly, median hourly earnings in dollars per hour.

Hispanic Americans: A Statistical Sourcebook 2009

Chapter 7

Earnings, Income, Poverty & Wealth

Chapter Seven Highlights

This chapter provides information about earnings, income, poverty, and wealth of Hispanic persons in the United States, including both the most current data available as well as comparisons of the Hispanic population over time. For almost all tables, corresponding data is provided for the total population of the United States as well as for White persons. This allows for easy comparison between groups. Because 'Hispanic' is not a race or ethnic group, we have included a variety of tables with statistics on some of the ethnic groups that comprise the Hispanic designation (tables 7.05, 7.13, 7.20, and 7.27).

The chapter includes data on the income of households (tables 7.01–7.06) and families (tables 7.06–7.13) organized in a variety of ways, including by age, by state, and by ethnic group.

We have also included data on individual persons by selected characteristics for the years 1985, 1990, 2006, and 2007 (tables 7.14–7.17). The chapter also contains data on per capita income by state (table 7.23) and per capita income for the years 1990 to 2006 (table 7.22).

The chapter features data on poverty levels of families (tables 7.26–7.28), individual persons (table 7.25), children (table 7.29), and persons over 65 (table 7.30).

Also of note are statistics on social assistance and welfare (table 7.31) and child support payments (table 7.32).

Table 7.01: Money Income of Households, 1980–2007

	Hispanic	White	All Races
Median Income			
1980	$32,704	$44,762	$42,429
1985	32,095	45,772	43,402
1990	34,341	48,029	46,049
1995	30,882	48,317	46,034
2000	39,935	52,876	50,557
2001	39,310	52,136	49,455
2002	38,152	51,963	48,878
2003	37,200	51,443	48,835
2004	37,619	51,216	48,665
2005	38,200	51,569	49,202
2006	38,853	52,111	49,568
2007	38,679	52,115	50,233
Mean Income			
1980	$39,947	$52,498	$50,462
1985	40,103	55,606	53,413
1990	43,018	59,842	57,521
1995	42,150	63,128	60,708
2000	52,951	71,344	68,792
2001	51,979	70,869	68,171
2002	51,734	69,343	66,677
2003	50,131	69,431	66,590
2004	50,359	69,055	66,373
2005	50,065	70,057	67,277
2006	52,010	71,067	68,459
2007	50,828	70,331	67,609

Source: U.S. Bureau of the Census, Current Population Reports, *Income, Poverty, and Health Insurance in the United States: 2007*, table A1.

Notes: 'All Races' includes other races not shown separately.
Data after 2002 uses a changed race classification: 'White' or 'White alone' refers to people who reported White and not any other race category

Units: Median and mean money income in 2007 CPI-U-RS adjusted dollars.

Table 7.02: Money Income of Households by Selected Household Characteristics, 2001 and 2006

	Hispanic	White	All Races
2001			
Number of households	*10,499*	*90,682*	*109,297*
Percent of households with current dollar incomes:			
Under $5,000	3.9%	2.4%	3.1%
$5,000–$9,999	6.7	5.2	5.9
$10,000–$14,999	8.3	6.7	6.9
$15,000–$24,999	17.5	13.0	13.3
$25,000–$34,999	15.4	12.2	12.4
$35,000–$49,999	17.3	15.5	15.4
$50,000–$74,999	16.5	18.8	18.4
$75,000–$99,999	7.5	11.4	10.8
$100,000 and over	7.0	14.8	13.8
Median income	$33,565	$44,517	$42,228
Mean income	$44,383	$60,512	$58,208
Median income:			
By type of residence			
Inside metropolitan area	$34,256	$47,759	$45,219
Outside metropolitan area	28,527	34,971	33,601
By type of household			
Family households	$36,018	$55,051	$52,275
Married couple families	40,942	61,137	60,471
Non-family households	22,141	26,114	25,631
Male householder living alone	20,720	29,049	28,283
Female householder living alone	12,677	18,199	17,868

(continued on next page)

Table 7.02: Money Income of Households by Selected Household Characteristics, 2001 and 2006

	Hispanic	White	All Races
2001 (continued)			
Median income:			
By age of householder			
15–24 years old	$29,530	$30,860	$28,196
25–34 years old	34,447	47,412	45,080
35–44 years old	36,585	56,642	53,320
45–54 years old	41,652	61,643	58,045
55–64 years old	35,734	47,907	45,864
65 years old and over	16,870	23,769	23,118
By size of household			
One person	$16,511	$22,079	$21,761
Two persons	30,045	47,109	45,245
Three persons	34,199	58,007	54,481
Four persons	38,077	65,815	62,595
Five persons	39,832	62,931	59,898
Six persons	42,004	59,573	57,548
Seven or more persons	47,080	57,488	54,560
By number of earners			
No earners	$9,952	$16,765	$15,452
One earner	24,368	35,830	34,104
Two earners or more	48,865	69,522	68,106
By work experience of the householder			
All civilian householders	$33,565	$44,517	$42,228
Worked	39,526	55,618	53,002
Worked year-round full-time	42,570	60,783	58,608
Did not work	16,780	22,192	20,887

(continued on next page)

Table 7.02: Money Income of Households by Selected Household Characteristics, 2001 and 2006

	Hispanic	White	All Races
2006			
Number of households	*12,973*	*94,705*	*116,011*
Percent of households with current dollar incomes:			
Under $5,000	3.5%	2.5%	3.1%
$5,000–$9,999	5.7	3.7	4.4
10,000–$14,999	7.1	5.6	5.9
$15,000–$24,999	15.5	11.5	11.8
$25,000–$34,999	14.0	11.3	11.5
$35,000–$49,999	17.5	14.6	14.6
$50,000–$74,999	17.3	18.8	18.2
$75,000–$99,999	8.9	11.8	11.3
$100,000 and over	10.5	20.2	19.1
Median income	$37,781	$50,673	$48,201
Mean income	$50,575	$69,107	$66,570
Median income:			
By type of residence			
Inside metropolitan area	$38,616	$52,694	$50,616
Outside metropolitan area	30,365	40,311	38,293
By type of household			
Family households	$41,336	$62,277	$59,894
Married couple families	46,561	70,353	69,716
Non-family households	25,504	30,260	29,083
Male householder living alone	24,888	32,431	31,268
Female householder living alone	14,180	21,723	21,346
By age of householder			
15–24 years old	$30,213	$32,504	$30,937
25–34 years old	40,095	51,579	49,164
35–44 years old	42,515	63,663	60,405
45–54 years old	46,458	68,869	64,874
55–64 years old	35,561	57,126	54,592
65 years old and over	19,925	28,580	27,798

(continued on next page)

Table 7.02: Money Income of Households by Selected Household Characteristics, 2001 and 2006

	Hispanic	White	All Races
2006 (continued)			
Median income:			
By size of household			
One person	$20,199	$26,365	$25,504
Two persons	35,942	53,796	51,536
Three persons	40,473	65,196	61,436
Four persons	43,829	75,915	72,870
Five persons	45,746	69,810	66,823
Six persons	47,849	65,680	61,859
Seven or more persons	51,826	62,182	60,864
By number of earners			
No earners	$10,462	$19,705	$17,865
One earner	28,490	41,110	39,309
Two earners or more	57,041	80,310	78,994
By work experience of the householder			
All civilian householders	$37,781	$50,673	$48,201
Worked	44,696	62,863	60,613
Worked year-round full-time	47,987	68,997	66,210
Did not work	19,955	26,581	24,840

Source: U.S. Bureau of the Census, Current Population Reports: *Historical Income Tables,* tables 1 and H-17.
U.S. Bureau of the Census, Current Population Reports, *Annual Social and Economic Supplement, 2006,* household income table HINC-01.

Notes: 'All Races' includes races not shown separately. 'White' as shown here is equivalent to 'White Alone.'
Number of households as of March of the following year.
'Occupation of the householder' represents the longest job held by the householder.

Units: Number of households in thousands; mean and median income in current dollars.

Table 7.03: Money Income of Households by Selected Household Characteristics, 2007

	Hispanic	White	All Races
Number of households	*13,339*	*95,112*	*116,783*
Median income	$38,679	$52,115	$50,233
Mean income	$50,828	$70,331	$67,609
Median income by:			
Type of residence			
Inside metropolitan area	$39,439	$54,779	$51,831
Outside metropolitan area	31,595	42,499	40,615
Type of household			
Family households	$41,971	$65,628	$62,359
Married couple families	48,572	73,640	72,785
Non-family households	27,076	31,034	30,176
Male householder living alone	25,291	32,833	31,606
Female householder living alone	15,068	21,866	21,546
Age of householder			
15-24 years old	$31,628	$35,124	$31,790
25-34 years old	38,223	53,458	51,016
35-44 years old	43,480	65,745	62,124
45-54 years old	47,534	70,185	65,476
55-64 years old	40,541	60,859	57,386
65 years old and over	21,860	29,171	28,305
Size of household			
One person	$20,170	$26,366	$25,703
Two persons	37,429	57,030	54,841
Three persons	42,171	68,200	64,403
Four persons	46,596	77,697	75,263
Five persons	45,253	73,925	70,977
Six persons	47,338	65,569	64,827
Seven or more persons	51,023	67,741	63,823

(continued on next page)

Table 7.03: Money Income of Households by Selected Household Characteristics, 2007

	Hispanic	White	All Races
Number of earners			
No earners	$11,034	$19,314	$17,492
One earner	29,648	42,245	40,710
Two earners or more	60,274	83,409	82,044
Work experience of the householder			
All civilian householders	$38,679	$52,115	$50,233
Worked	45,878	65,438	62,209
Worked year-round full-time	51,166	71,837	69,257
Did not work	20,581	26,468	24,805

Source: U.S. Bureau of the Census, *Current Population Reports: Income 2001*, tables 1 and H-17.
U.S. Bureau of the Census, *Current Population Reports, Annual Social and Economic Supplement, 2008*, Household Income table HINC-01.

Notes: 'All Races' includes other races not shown separately.
'White' as shown here is equivalent to 'White Alone.'
Number of households as of March of the following year.
'Occupation of the householder' represents the longest job held by the householder.

Units: Number of households in thousands, mean and median income in current dollars.

Table 7.04: Median Household Income by State, 2007

	Hispanic	White	All Races
United States	*$39,852*	*$53,000*	*$50,007*
Alabama	35,453	46,095	40,052
Alaska	54,857	67,919	61,766
Arizona	38,175	50,958	48,609
Arkansas	31,494	40,863	37,555
California	45,068	61,842	58,361
Colorado	36,819	56,471	54,262
Connecticut	39,513	70,314	65,496
Delaware	41,366	59,144	55,303
District of Columbia	44,699	88,925	52,187
Florida	41,137	46,224	46,602
Georgia	39,003	55,568	48,540
Hawaii	55,036	63,870	62,543
Idaho	33,096	45,601	44,901
Illinois	45,808	58,156	53,745
Indiana	36,719	49,224	47,034
Iowa	35,936	47,078	46,399
Kansas	35,351	48,381	46,669
Kentucky	36,823	41,263	40,138
Louisiana	39,215	47,980	40,160
Maine	33,706	45,670	45,211
Maryland	60,728	73,597	66,873
Massachusetts	31,075	64,818	61,785
Michigan	38,187	51,608	48,642
Minnesota	39,081	57,314	55,616
Mississippi	36,881	44,659	35,632
Missouri	39,359	46,896	44,545
Montana	33,809	43,461	42,425
Nebraska	36,374	48,319	46,954

(continued on next page)

Table 7.04: Median Household Income by State, 2007

	Hispanic	White	All Races
Nevada	45,323	55,966	53,753
New Hampshire	55,611	61,500	61,459
New Jersey	46,408	72,244	66,509
New Mexico	34,481	43,829	41,042
New York	37,019	58,907	52,944
North Carolina	34,711	49,333	43,867
North Dakota	34,479	44,569	43,442
Ohio	35,733	49,271	46,296
Oklahoma	31,652	43,055	40,371
Oregon	35,447	48,288	47,385
Pennsylvania	31,391	50,545	47,913
Rhode Island	31,620	57,279	54,060
South Carolina	35,527	49,745	42,405
South Dakota	33,642	45,164	43,586
Tennessee	34,935	44,642	41,821
Texas	34,306	50,497	46,248
Utah	39,621	54,323	53,324
Vermont	46,567	49,624	49,382
Virginia	56,284	63,147	58,378
Washington	36,998	55,520	53,940
West Virginia	30,779	36,495	36,088
Wisconsin	36,165	52,231	50,309
Wyoming	44,840	50,845	50,009

Source: U.S. Bureau of the Census, *American Community Survey, 2007*, table B19013.

Notes: For civilian, noninstitutional population only: use caution when comparing this data to other Census data.
Estimates are only given where the specified population is larger than 65,000.

Units: Income in current (2007) dollars.

Table 7.05: Money Income of Households by Ethnic Group, 2002, 2003, and 2005

	Mexican	Puerto Rican	Cuban	Central American	South American	Other Hispanic	All Hispanic
2002							
All households	*7,126*	*1,256*	*551*	*813*	*649*	*944*	*11,339*
Percent with incomes of:							
$1 to $2,499 or loss	2.3%	4.5%	2.9%	2.4%	2.9%	3.8%	2.7%
$2,500 to $4,999	1.5	2.8	1.1	1.1	0.8	1.6	1.5
$5,000 to $9,999	6.0	9.2	11.0	4.9	5.0	9.1	6.7
$10,000 to $14,999	8.2	8.4	11.8	8.3	4.5	7.3	8.1
$15,000 to $19,999	8.9	8.3	7.0	8.5	7.6	6.9	8.5
$20,000 to $24,999	9.6	6.5	9.1	7.5	7.3	7.9	8.8
$25,000 to $34,999	16.7	15.2	11.3	16.2	12.0	13.6	15.7
$35,000 to $49.999	16.4	15.2	14.6	18.6	16.7	16.5	16.4
$50,000 to $74,999	17.2	15.4	13.5	15.5	21.1	16.6	16.9
$75,000 and over	13.3	14.5	17.8	17.0	22.1	16.6	14.7
2003							
All households	*7,227*	*1,279*	*600*	*909*	*693*	*985*	*11,692*
Percent with incomes of:							
$1 to $2,499 or loss	3.1%	3.5%	2.6%	3.5%	2.8%	2.7%	3.1%
$2,500 to $4,999	1.2	3.0	1.4	1.3	1.2	1.8	1.4
$5,000 to $9,999	6.0	8.7	9.9	4.3	3.5	6.9	6.3
$10,000 to $14,999	8.2	9.3	7.4	7.5	5.3	8.1	8.1
$15,000 to $19,999	9.7	7.6	8.4	8.1	6.3	7.7	8.9
$20,000 to $24,999	9.3	7.4	6.2	8.7	7.9	7.8	8.7
$25,000 to $34,999	16.7	13.2	14.1	18.3	12.8	13.7	15.8
$35,000 to $49.999	17.3	13.9	12.0	19.6	19.0	14.1	16.7
$50,000 to $74,999	15.9	16.3	17.7	12.9	16.2	17.0	15.9
$75,000 and over	12.7	17.2	20.4	15.9	25.1	20.1	15.2

(continued on next page)

Table 7.05: Money Income of Households by Ethnic Group, 2002, 2003, and 2005

	Mexican	Puerto Rican	Cuban	Central American	South American	Other Hispanic	All Hispanic
2005							
All households	*7,702*	*1,239*	*587*	*1,026*	*806*	*1,159*	*12,519*
Percent with incomes of:							
Under $5,000	3.7%	5.8%	3.9%	4.5%	2.7%	3.8%	3.9%
$5,000 to $9,999	5.4	11.5	6.5	3.8	4.2	8.0	6.1
$10,000 to $14,999	8.1	7.5	6.3	5.4	4.2	7.3	7.4
$15,000 to $19,999	8.9	6.7	7.2	5.3	6.8	8.5	8.1
$20,000 to $24,999	8.8	7.2	6.5	6.8	6.6	7.6	8.1
$25,000 to $34,999	15.1	14.2	16.4	17.0	15.8	12.0	15.0
$35,000 to $49.999	17.7	13.7	13.1	19.4	17.3	16.9	17.1
$50,000 to $74,999	17.1	16.1	16.2	19.8	18.8	16.3	17.2
$75,000 to $100,000	7.5	8.6	11.8	7.9	10.7	9.1	8.2
$100,000 and over	7.6	8.8	12.2	10.2	13.0	10.6	8.8

Source: U.S. Bureau of the Census, Current Population Reports: *The Hispanic Population of the United States, 2003*, table 12.2; *2004*, table 12.2; *2006*, table 12.2.

Notes: 'Other Hispanic' includes persons from Spain and persons identifying themselves generally as Hispanic, Spanish, Spanish-American, Hispano, Latino, etc. After 2003, 'Other Hispanic' includes Dominicans. Income includes wages and salaries, net income from self-employment, and income other than earnings.

Units: Number of households in thousands; percent of total.

Table 7.06: Income of Households from Specified Sources, 1992

	Hispanic	White	All Races
All households	*6,626*	*82,083*	*96,391*
One or more members received:			
Social Security	16.8%	28.5%	27.7%
AFDC or other non-SSI cash assistance	12.1	3.7	5.2
Supplemental Security Income	6.9	3.2	4.1
Food stamps	18.7	6.6	8.8
Housing assistance	7.9	3.3	4.6
Free or reduced-price school lunches	21.8	5.5	7.4
Employer subsidized health insurance	43.5	54.3	52.9
Medicare	16.5	26.6	25.9
Medicaid	28.5	10.1	12.8
Mean household income from:			
Social Security	$7,306	$8,980	$8,708
AFDC or other non-SSI cash assistance	4,513	3,444	3,489
Supplemental Security Income	4,336	3,651	3,666
Food stamps	1,713	1,430	1,564
Housing assistance	2,297	1,957	2,022
Free or reduced-price school lunches	605	547	553
Employer subsidized health insurance	3,231	3,163	3,139
Medicare	3,116	3,652	3,511
Medicaid	1,558	1,696	1,595

Source: U.S. Bureau of the Census, Current Population Reports: *Measuring the Effect of Benefits and Taxes on Income and Poverty: 1992* (Series P60-186RD), table 7.

Notes: 'All Races' includes races not shown separately.

Units: Number of households in thousands; percent of all households; mean income in dollars.

Table 7.07: Money Income of Families, 1980–2007

	Hispanic	White	All Races
Median Income			
1980	$29,943	$44,569	$42,776
1985	29,855	45,742	43,518
1990	30,772	48,480	46,429
1995	28,341	49,191	46,843
2000	35,403	54,509	52,148
2001	34,490	54,067	51,407
2002	34,185	54,633	51,680
2003	34,272	55,768	52,680
2004	35,401	56,700	54,061
2005	37,867	59,317	56,194
2006	40,000	61,280	58,407
2007	40,566	64,427	61,355
Mean Income			
1980	$35,842	$50,744	$48,781
1985	36,327	53,937	51,692
1990	38,494	58,484	56,015
1995	37,665	61,821	59,234
2000	47,092	70,386	67,609
2001	45,229	69,856	66,863
2002	46,213	69,803	66,970
2003	46,002	71,770	68,563
2004	47,821	73,395	70,402
2005	48,847	76,546	73,304
2006	52,634	80,271	77,315
2007	52,972	82,043	78,845

Source: U.S. Bureau of the Census, *Current Population Reports: Historical Income Tables for Families, 1967-2003*, table F-23.
U.S. Bureau of the Census, *Current Population Reports: Income 2003*; table FINC-01; *2004*, table FINC-01; *2005*, table FINC-01; *2006*, table FINC-01; *2007*, table FINC-01; *2008*, table FINC-01.

Notes: 'All Races' includes other races not shown separately. Data from 2002 forward use a changed race classification: 'White' or 'White alone' refers to people who reported White and not any other race category.

Units: Median and mean money income in 2001 CPI-U-RS adjusted dollars, as shown except for 2002-2007, which are in current dollars or that year.

Table 7.08: Money Income of Families by Selected Family Characteristics, 1985

	Hispanic	White	All Races
Number of families	*4,206*	*54,991*	*63,558*
Percent of families with incomes:			
Under $2,500	2.9%	1.6%	1.9%
$2,500–$4,499	5.4	2.1	2.9
$5,000–$7,499	8.5	3.6	4.2
$7,500–$9,999	8.5	3.9	4.3
$10,000–$12,499	8.1	4.8	5.2
$12,500–$14,999	6.8	4.9	5.0
$15,000–$19,999	12.1	10.3	10.5
$20,000–$24,999	11.3	10.4	10.3
$25,000–$34,999	16.0	19.2	18.6
$35,000–$49,999	12.5	19.7	18.8
$50,000 and over	8.1	19.6	18.3
Median income	$19,027	$29,152	$27,735
Mean income	$23,152	$34,375	$32,944
Median family income:			
By type of family			
Married-couple families	$22,269	$31,602	$31,100
Wife in paid labor force	28,132	36,992	36,431
Wife not in paid labor force	17,116	25,307	24,556
Male householder, no wife present	19,773	24,190	22,622
Female householder, no husband present	8,792	15,825	13,660

(continued on next page)

Table 7.08: Money Income of Families by Selected Family Characteristics, 1985

	Hispanic	White	All Races
Median income (continued)			
By type of income			
Wages and salaries	$22,566	$31,277	$30,258
Non-farm self-employment	14,628	14,565	14,420
Farm self-employment	NA	4,593	4,557
Property income	1,483	3,486	3,327
Interest income	1,017	2,440	2,328
Transfer payments and all other income	5,347	7,776	7,469
Social Security or railroad retirement	6,014	7,684	7,488
Public assistance and suplemental income	4,458	3,416	3,498

Source: U.S. Bureau of the Census, Current Population Reports, *Money Income of Households Families and Persons in the United States, March 1985* (Series P-60, #156), tables 9, 10, 13, 14, 17, and 25.

Notes: 'All Races' includes races not shown separately.
Number of families as of March of the following year. 'Occupation of the householder' represents the longest job held by the householder. 'Property income' includes interest, dividends, net rental income, income from trusts and estates, and net royalty income.

Units: Number of families and families with income in thousands; percent of total families; mean and median income in current dollars.

Table 7.09: Money Income of Families by
Selected Family Characteristics, 1990

	Hispanic	White	All Races
Number of families	*4,981*	*58,803*	*66,322*
Percent of families with current dollar incomes of:			
Under $5,000	6.3%	2.5%	3.6%
$5,000–$9,999	12.3	4.7	5.8
$10,000–$14,999	12.6	7.0	7.5
$15,000–$24,999	21.7	16.0	16.4
$25,000–$34,999	16.6	16.5	16.2
$35,000–$49,999	15.7	20.8	20.0
$50,000–$74,999	10.0	19.3	18.2
$75,000–$99,999	2.9	7.3	6.9
$100,000 and over	1.9	5.9	5.4
Mean income	$29,311	$44,532	$42,652
Median income	$23,341	$36,915	$35,353
Median income:			
By type of residence			
Nonfarm	$23,402	$36,974	$35,376
Farm	NA	34,476	34,171
Inside metropolitan area	23,898	40,086	37,893
Outside metropolitan area	19,061	29,693	28,272
By type of family			
Married-couple families	$27,996	$40,331	$39,895
Wife in paid labor force	34,778	47,247	46,777
Wife not in paid labor force	21,168	30,781	30,265
Male householder, no wife present	21,744	30,570	29,046
Female householder, no husband present	11,914	19,528	16,932

(continued on next page)

Table 7.09: Money Income of Families by Selected Family Characteristics, 1990

	Hispanic	White	All Races
Median income (continued)			
By age of householder			
15–24 years old	$13,009	$18,234	$16,219
25–34 years old	20,439	33,457	31,497
35–44 years old	27,350	42,632	41,061
45–54 years old	29,908	49,249	47,165
55–64 years old	30,839	40,416	39,035
65 years old and over	17,962	25,864	25,049
By size of family			
Two persons	$19,230	$31,734	$30,428
Three persons	22,778	38,858	36,644
Four persons	25,808	43,352	41,451
Five persons	25,727	41,037	39,452
Six persons	24,786	40,387	38,379
Seven or more persons	30,549	39,845	35,363
By number of earners			
No earners	$8,858	$17,369	$15,047
One earner	16,795	27,670	25,878
Two earners or more	33,704	46,261	45,462

Source: U.S. Bureau of the Census, Current Population Reports: *Money Income of Households, Families, and Persons in the United States: March 1990* (Series P-60, #174), tables 13 and 14.

Notes: 'All Races' includes races not shown separately.
Number of families as of March of the following year.

Units: Number of families and families with income in thousands; percent of total families; mean and median income in current dollars.

Table 7.10: Money Income of Families by Selected Family Characteristics, 2006

	Hispanic	White	All Races
Number of families	*10,155*	*64,120*	*78,454*
With current dollar incomes of:			
Under $5,000	342	1,252	1,948
$5,000–$9,999	384	1,215	1,884
$10,000–$14,999	651	1,891	2,714
$15,000–$24,999	1,566	5,526	7,216
$25,000–$34,999	1,486	6,486	8,208
$35,000–$49,999	1,823	9,277	11,351
$50,000–$74,999	1,672	11,832	14,126
$75,000–$99,999	946	9,083	10,601
$100,000 and over	1,150	16,389	19,000
Median income	$40,000	$61,280	$58,407
Mean income	$52,634	$80,271	$77,315
Median income:			
By type of family			
Married couple families	$46,135	$70,182	$69,404
Wife in paid labor force	58,799	83,807	82,788
Wife not in paid labor force	32,319	46,134	45,757
Male householder, no wife present	40,217	44,308	41,844
Female householder, no husband present	24,111	30,973	28,829
By age of householder			
15–24 years old	$30,811	$34,025	$31,471
25–34 years old	36,848	52,733	50,122
35–44 years old	42,422	68,949	65,282
45–54 years old	50,054	79,588	75,692
55–64 years old	40,248	70,903	68,747
65 years old and over	29,385	40,252	39,649

(continued on next page)

Table 7.10: Money Income of Families by Selected Family Characteristics, 2006

	Hispanic	White	All Races
Median income (continued)			
By size of family			
Two persons	$32,409	$52,032	$50,107
Three persons	37,174	64,094	60,415
Four persons	42,438	76,342	73,415
Five persons	43,784	70,333	67,158
Six persons	46,287	65,723	62,032
Seven or more persons	49,958	60,622	58,428
By number of earners			
No earners	$11,785	$27,099	$24,564
One earner	27,472	42,635	40,717
Two earners or more	56,511	82,552	81,413

Source: U.S. Bureau of the Census, Current Population Reports, *Annual Social and Economic Supplement 2007*, income table FINC-01.

Notes: 'All Races' includes races not shown separately. 'White' as shown here is equivalent to 'White Alone.'
Number of families as of March of the following year.

Units: Number of families and families with income in thousands; mean and median income in current dollars.

Table 7.11: Money Income of Families by Selected Family Characteristics, 2007

	Hispanic	White	All Races
Number of families	*10,397*	*63,595*	*77,908*
Median income	$40,566	$64,427	$61,355
Mean income	$52,972	$82,043	$78,845
Median income by:			
Type of family			
Married couple families	$48,244	$73,449	$72,589
Wife in paid labor force	62,129	87,194	86,435
Wife not in paid labor force	32,000	47,772	47,329
Male householder, no wife present	38,786	46,000	44,358
Female householder, no husband present	24,489	32,850	30,296
Age of householder			
15–24 years old	$28,991	$34,756	$31,283
25–34 years old	36,481	55,984	52,291
35–44 years old	42,146	71,308	67,849
45–54 years old	52,941	81,389	77,440
55–64 years old	49,608	75,091	72,286
65 years old and over	31,544	42,594	41,851

(continued on next page)

Table 7.11: Money Income of Families by Selected Family Characteristics, 2007

	Hispanic	White	All Races
Size of family			
Two persons	$34,557	$55,475	$52,774
Three persons	39,740	67,721	63,186
Four persons	44,773	78,048	75,945
Five persons	43,200	74,515	71,228
Six persons	47,055	66,058	65,228
Seven or more persons	48,048	65,845	61,789
Number of earners			
No earners	$11,734	$27,093	$24,875
One earner	28,975	44,961	41,603
Two earners or more	60,016	85,957	84,713

Source: U.S. Bureau of the Census, Current Population Reports, *Annual Social and Economic Supplement 2008*, Income table FINC-01.

Notes: 'All Races' includes other races not shown separately.
'All Races' includes other races not shown separately.
'White' as shown here is equivalent to 'White Alone.'
Number of families as of March of the following year.

Units: Number of families in thousands of families, mean and median income in current dollars.

Table 7.12: Median Family Income by State, 2007

	Hispanic	White	All Races
United States	*$41,165*	*$64,832*	*$60,374*
Alabama	33,735	57,115	50,210
Alaska	54,802	80,243	72,008
Arizona	39,198	61,252	57,004
Arkansas	31,852	50,070	46,340
California	45,134	72,967	66,420
Colorado	38,870	70,705	67,069
Connecticut	41,523	87,009	80,906
Delaware	40,190	72,180	66,828
District of Columbia	44,368	155,348	60,970
Florida	43,804	59,633	55,534
Georgia	38,035	66,720	57,724
Hawaii	56,662	75,267	71,784
Idaho	33,543	54,053	53,186
Illinois	47,056	71,800	65,504
Indiana	37,991	60,043	57,602
Iowa	36,367	59,430	58,513
Kansas	36,743	61,095	58,791
Kentucky	37,858	51,248	49,832
Louisiana	43,245	59,596	49,649
Maine	36,648	56,123	55,346
Maryland	57,996	89,228	80,669
Massachusetts	33,296	81,860	77,409
Michigan	40,698	63,696	60,269
Minnesota	39,687	71,257	68,849
Mississippi	37,550	55,002	44,169
Missouri	43,423	57,693	55,014
Montana	34,730	53,888	52,357
Nebraska	36,789	60,354	58,523
Nevada	45,003	65,575	62,222

(continued on next page)

Table 7.12: Median Family Income by State, 2007

	Hispanic	White	All Races
New Hampshire	59,420	73,526	73,246
New Jersey	48,298	88,579	80,780
New Mexico	38,026	53,374	48,798
New York	39,716	72,707	64,107
North Carolina	33,806	60,719	53,770
North Dakota	39,697	58,617	57,299
Ohio	40,748	61,099	57,999
Oklahoma	33,378	53,656	50,119
Oregon	34,638	59,314	57,716
Pennsylvania	33,164	63,098	60,243
Rhode Island	33,170	74,183	68,740
South Carolina	33,881	60,831	51,954
South Dakota	39,797	56,678	54,306
Tennessee	35,455	54,651	51,438
Texas	35,941	60,181	54,165
Utah	39,879	61,865	60,564
Vermont	65,321	61,301	61,143
Virginia	55,898	75,945	69,609
Washington	36,839	68,161	65,428
West Virginia	40,423	46,129	45,705
Wisconsin	38,765	65,153	62,607
Wyoming	51,491	61,390	60,344

Source: U.S. Bureau of the Census, *American Community Survey, 2007*, table B19113.

Notes: For civilian, noninstitutional population only: use caution when comparing this data to other Census data.
Estimates are only given where the specified population is larger than 65,000.

Units: Income in current (2007) dollars.

Table 7.13: Money Income of Families
by Ethnic Group, 2002, 2003, and 2005

	Mexican	Puerto Rican	Cuban	Central American	South American	Other Hispanic	Total Hispanic
2002							
Total families	*5,832*	*964*	*415*	*676*	*522*	*681*	*9,090*
Percent with incomes of:							
$1 to $2,499 or loss	1.8%	4.1%	2.1%	2.3%	2.1%	2.2%	2.1%
$2,500 to $4,999	1.4	2.3	0.4	0.8	0.5	1.1	1.3
$5,000 to $9,999	4.2	5.4	5.4	2.6	2.4	6.2	4.3
$10,000 to $14,999	7.1	8.5	8.6	7.7	4.1	6.8	7.2
$15,000 to $19,999	8.8	7.8	8	8.5	8.1	6.6	8.4
$20,000 to $24,999	9.7	7.3	9.9	8	6.5	7.7	9
$25,000 to $34,999	17.2	15.1	11.9	16.4	12.6	15.1	16.2
$35,000 to $49.999	17	15.2	15.9	18.8	16.7	17.6	16.9
$50,000 to $74,999	18.4	16.8	15.3	16.9	23	17.8	18.2
$75,000 and over	14.4	17.6	22.4	18	24	18.8	16.3
2003							
Total families	*5,856*	*985*	*437*	*739*	*531*	*725*	*9,272*
Percent with incomes of:							
$1 to $2,499 or loss	2.4%	2.7%	1.9%	2.7%	2.0%	2.4%	2.4%
$2,500 to $4,999	1.0	2.5	1.0	0.8	0.3	1.3	1.1
$5,000 to $9,999	4.4	5.6	2.4	2.1	2.4	3.7	4.1
$10,000 to $14,999	7.2	8.4	6.0	6.2	5.3	7.7	7.1
$15,000 to $19,999	9.6	7.6	7.1	7.4	5.8	8.0	8.8
$20,000 to $24,999	9.4	7.4	6.9	8.3	6.3	7.9	8.7
$25,000 to $34,999	16.9	13.8	15.5	19.3	11.8	14.4	16.2
$35,000 to $49.999	18.2	13.6	13.8	21.7	19.7	14.5	17.6
$50,000 to $74,999	17.0	18.5	20.7	13.4	19.6	17.6	17.3
$75,000 and over	13.8	19.9	24.8	18.0	26.8	22.6	16.7

(continued on next page)

Table 7.13: Money Income of Families
by Ethnic Group, 2002, 2003, and 2005

	Mexican	Puerto Rican	Cuban	Central American	South American	Other Hispanic	Total Hispanic
2005							
Total families	6,244	901	429	819	630	845	9,868
Percent with incomes of:							
$1 to $2,499 or loss	4.1%	5.7%	2.4%	3.8%	2.4%	3.1%	3.9%
$2,500 to $4,999	4.1	8.3	3.2	3.1	2.7	4.2	4.3
$5,000 to $9,999	7.1	6.7	4.7	4.5	3.4	6.4	6.5
$10,000 to $14,999	8.9	7.1	6.2	5.6	6.1	8.5	8.2
$15,000 to $19,999	8.8	6.9	6.2	6.9	7.3	8.2	8.2
$20,000 to $24,999	15.1	14.3	15.9	18.4	15.5	13.5	15.2
$25,000 to $34,999	18.0	13.7	14.5	19.4	17.2	16.1	17.4
$35,000 to $49.999	17.8	17.7	18.3	21.5	19.7	17.8	18.2
$50,000 to $74,999	7.9	10.1	13.8	8.7	11.3	10.2	8.9
$75,000 and over	8.2	9.5	14.8	8.1	14.4	12.1	9.3

Source: US Bureau of the Census, Current Population Reports, *The Hispanic Population of the United States, 2003*, table 12.2; *2004*, table 12.2; *2006*, 13.2.

Notes: 'Other Hispanic' includes persons from Spain and persons identifying themselves generally as Hispanic, Spanish, Spanish-American, Hispano, Latino, etc. 'Other Hispanic' includes Dominicans. Income includes wages and salaries, net income from self-employment, and income other than earnings.

Units: Numbers of families in thousands; percent of total families.

Table 7.14: Money Income of Persons 15 Years Old and Older by Selected Characteristics, 1985

	Hispanic		White		All Races	
	Male	Female	Male	Female	Male	Female
Number of persons	*6,232*	*6,366*	*76,617*	*82,345*	*88,474*	*96,354*
Percent with current dollar incomes:						
Under $2,000	444	957	5,180	14,024	6,304	15,848
$2,000–$2,999	199	370	1,808	4,420	2,297	5,425
$3,000–$3,999	264	371	2,190	4,856	2,671	5,958
$4,000–$4,999	203	390	2,095	4,635	2,642	5,693
$5,000–$5,999	368	328	2,169	4,201	2,595	4,848
$6,000–$6,999	301	311	2,278	3,992	2,708	4,648
$7,000–$8,499	416	406	3,402	5,006	4,132	5,855
$8,500–$9,999	325	228	2,896	3,779	3,353	4,288
$10,000–$12,499	599	422	5,895	6,579	6,859	7,576
$12,500–$14,999	392	241	4,527	4,672	5,245	5,339
$15,000–$17,499	431	241	4,940	4,359	5,739	5,012
$17,500–$19,999	281	175	3,869	2,980	4,423	3,432
$20,000–$24,999	468	206	7,521	4,839	8,410	5,513
$25,000–$29,999	349	98	6,374	2,759	7,018	3,194
$30,000–$34,999	221	59	5,324	1,437	5,767	1,633
$35,000–$49,999	267	29	7,730	1,450	8,211	1,585
$50,000–$74,999	71	8	3,421	484	3,588	509
$75,000 and over	224	4	1,603	169	1,669	177
Median income	$11,434	$6,020	$17,111	$7,357	$16,311	$7,217
Mean income	$14,490	$8,178	$21,523	$10,317	$20,652	$10,173
Mean income:						
By occupation						
Managerial, professional specialty	$27,148	$17,471	$34,711	$17,763	$34,201	$17,857
Technical, sales, administrative	17,692	10,461	24,050	10,988	23,293	11,076
Service occupations	11,712	5,879	13,161	5,935	12,549	6,104
Farming, forestry, fishing	7,451	NA	8,241	3,865	8,024	3,762
Precision production, craft, repair	16,015	11,217	20,593	12,998	20,277	12,595
Operators, fabricators, laborers	13,289	9,649	16,378	9,528	15,971	9,548

(continued on next page)

Table 7.14: Money Income of Persons 15 Years Old and Older by Selected Characteristics, 1985

	Hispanic		White		All Races	
	Male	**Female**	**Male**	**Female**	**Male**	**Female**
By work experience						
Worked at full-time jobs	$16,297	$11,616	$24,531	$14,556	$23,767	$14,364
Worked 50–52 weeks	19,666	14,576	28,140	17,249	27,414	17,028
By type of income						
Wages and salaries	$14,689	$9,557	$21,848	$11,295	$21,056	$11,239
Non-farm self-employment	14,026	7,818	16,083	5,885	15,834	5,867
Farm self-employment	NA	NA	4,234	1,654	4,184	1,695
Property income	877	866	1,866	2,021	1,794	1,937
Interest income	541	605	1,305	1,454	1,254	1,395
Transfer payments and all other income	4,313	3,686	6,812	4,428	6,572	4,318
Social security or railroad retirement	4,793	3,733	5,803	4,330	5,701	4,261
Public assistance and supplemental income	3,010	3,696	2,526	2,881	2,560	2,919

Source: U.S. Bureau of the Census, Current Population Reports: *Money Income of House-holds in the United States: March 1985* (Series P-60, #156), tables 31, 35, 37, 40, and 41.

Notes: 'All Races' includes races not shown separately.
Number of persons as of March of the following year.
Data is based on persons living in households. Persons with incomes under $2,000 includes those with a loss. Occupation represents the longest job held by the person during the year. Educational attainment covers persons 25 years old and older; income covers persons 15 years old and older. 'Property income' includes interest, dividends, net rental income, income from trusts and estates, and net royalty income.

Units: Number of persons in thousands; median and mean income in current dollars.

Table 7.15: Money Income of Persons 15 Years Old and Older by Selected Characteristics, 1990

	Hispanic		White		All Races	
	Male	Female	Male	Female	Male	Female
Number of persons	*7,502*	*7,559*	*79,555*	*85,012*	*92,240*	*100,680*
With current dollar incomes:						
Under $5,000	1,053	2,059	8,539	22,062	10,820	26,337
$5,000–$9,999	1,353	1,502	9,249	16,358	11,312	19,563
$10,000–$14,999	1,298	901	9,529	11,652	11,253	13,566
$15,000–$24,999	1,572	892	16,679	15,162	19,166	17,516
$25,000–$34,999	776	346	12,707	7,547	14,185	8,707
$35,000–$49,999	459	149	10,531	3,895	11,604	4,457
$50,000–$74,999	184	43	5,973	1,382	6,433	1,535
$75,000 and over	72	12	3,274	509	3,446	565
Median income	$13,470	$7,532	$21,170	$10,317	$20,293	$10,070
Mean income	$17,452	$10,587	$27,142	$14,138	$26,041	$13,913
Mean income:						
By work experience						
Worked at full-time jobs	$19,414	$14,750	$30,498	$19,269	$29,524	$19,010
Worked 50–52 weeks	22,859	17,760	34,300	22,198	33,334	21,977
By educational attainment						
Less than 8 years of school	$13,448	$8,269	$15,057	$8,598	$14,914	$8,602
High school graduates	20,400	13,212	25,520	13,955	24,727	13,999
1–3 years of college	25,468	17,852	31,235	17,148	30,340	17,188
4 or more years of college	32,398	20,061	45,709	25,230	44,864	25,388

(continued on next page)

Hispanic Americans: A Statistical Sourcebook 2009

Table 7.15: Money Income of Persons 15 Years Old and Older by Selected Characteristics, 1990

	Hispanic		White		All Races	
	Male	Female	Male	Female	Male	Female
Median income (continued)						
By age						
15–24 years old	$9,257	$6,444	$8,915	$7,161	$8,693	$6,998
25–34 years old	17,895	11,262	25,442	15,317	24,365	14,955
35–44 years old	22,419	14,015	35,723	17,724	34,468	17,667
45–54 years old	22,624	13,393	38,632	17,845	37,182	17,831
55–64 years old	21,618	10,117	33,396	14,159	31,899	13,834
65 years old and over	12,280	6,496	20,918	11,864	20,011	11,441
By marital status						
Single	$12,286	$10,149	$16,902	$14,504	$16,112	$13,656
Married	20,462	10,711	32,362	13,828	31,488	13,858
Spouse present	21,316	10,896	32,627	13,805	31,888	13,883
Spouse absent	13,428	9,700	25,396	14,255	23,158	13,508
Widowed	11,504	9,337	18,528	13,822	17,440	13,190
Divorced	22,070	14,471	26,830	19,448	25,787	19,058

Source: U.S. Bureau of the Census, Current Population Reports: *Money Income of Households, Families, and Persons in the United States: March 1990* (Series P-60, #174), tables 24–26, 28–29, and 31.

Notes: 'All Races' includes races not shown separately.
Number of persons as of March of the following year.
Data is based on persons living in households. Persons with incomes under $2,000 includes those with a loss. Occupation represents the longest job held by the person during the year. Educational attainment covers persons 25 years old and older; income covers persons 15 years old and older. 'Property income' includes interest, dividends, net rental income, income from trusts and estates, and net royalty income.

Units: Number of persons in thousands; median and mean income in current dollars.

Table 7.16: Money Income of Persons 15 Years Old and Older by Selected Characteristics, 2006

	Hispanic		White		All Races	
	Male	Female	Male	Female	Male	Female
Total persons	*16,444*	*15,449*	*94,029*	*97,550*	*114,576*	*121,443*
Total with income	14,358	11,090	86,674	84,955	103,909	104,502
Persons with incomes:						
$1–$2,499 or loss	461	939	3,344	7,140	4,214	8,610
$2,500–$4,999	367	689	1,948	3,952	2,529	4,939
$5,000–$7,499	598	997	2,628	5,952	3,584	7,444
$7,500–$9,999	652	874	2,647	5,561	3,432	7,071
$10,000–$12,499	1,049	1,173	4,047	6,421	5,096	7,903
$12,500–$14,999	624	610	2,894	4,561	3,594	5,554
$15,000–$17,499	1,204	864	4,098	5,218	5,033	6,399
$17,500–$19,999	719	491	3,070	3,521	3,671	4,338
$20,000–$22,499	1,278	696	4,412	4,636	5,413	5,781
$22,500–$24,999	597	390	2,635	2,801	3,166	3,445
$25,000–$27,499	910	588	3,837	3,905	4,696	4,827
$27,500–$29,999	352	234	2,229	2,227	2,596	2,767
$30,000–$32,499	1,008	432	4,463	3,597	5,440	4,596
$32,500–$34,999	281	182	2,022	1,735	2,341	2,035
$35,000–$37,499	603	287	3,388	2,815	4,096	3,516
$37,500–$39,999	203	112	1,686	1,458	1,974	1,764
$40,000–$42,499	631	264	3,723	2,529	4,399	3,186
$42,500–$44,999	146	94	1,316	1,159	1,531	1,372
$45,000–$47,499	357	174	2,566	1,603	3,012	1,950
$47,500–$49,999	161	69	1,345	1,015	1,559	1,212
$50,000–$52,499	390	157	3,459	1,832	4,047	2,221
$52,500–$54,999	72	52	1,044	766	1,195	924
$55,000–$57,499	137	88	1,608	1,029	1,855	1,233
$57,500–$59,999	79	41	858	616	981	703

(continued on next page)

Table 7.16: Money Income of Persons 15 Years Old and Older by Selected Characteristics, 2006

	Hispanic		White		All Races	
	Male	Female	Male	Female	Male	Female
$60,000–$62,499	238	94	2,222	1,250	2,630	1,513
$62,500–$64,999	62	24	782	450	880	510
$65,000–$67,499	112	43	1,380	701	1,595	915
$67,500–$69,999	43	18	739	325	807	397
$70,000–$72,499	128	70	1,437	721	1,667	899
$72,500–$74,999	30	26	528	363	600	425
$75,000–$77,499	125	35	1,192	470	1,407	602
$77,500–$79,999	30	11	506	276	579	336
$80,000–$82,499	98	36	1,069	474	1,230	579
$82,500–$84,999	26	15	461	170	521	188
$85,000–$87,499	24	20	645	288	768	353
$87,500–$89,999	15	14	310	127	345	166
$90,000–$92,499	52	17	760	230	894	284
$92,500–$94,999	18	7	329	126	393	155
$95,000–$97,499	23	17	445	203	511	229
$97,500–$99,999	29	10	299	127	330	146
$100,000 and over	423	136	8,304	2,605	9,295	3,091
Median income	$23,452	$15,758	$33,843	$20,082	$32,265	$20,014
Mean income	$31,432	$21,676	$48,315	$28,612	$46,677	$28,416

Source: U.S. Bureau of the Census, Current Population Reports, *Annual Social and Economic Supplement 2007*, person income table PINC-01.

Notes: 'All Races' includes races and ethnic groups not shown separately. 'White' as shown here is equivalent to 'White Alone.'
Number of persons as of March of the following year.

Units: Number of persons with income in thousands of persons; mean and median income in current dollars.

Table 7.17: Money Income of Persons 15 Years Old and Older by Selected Characteristics, 2007

	Hispanic		White		All Races	
	Male	Female	Male	Female	Male	Female
Total persons	*16,837*	*15,853*	*94,769*	*98,197*	*115,678*	*122,470*
Total with income	14,609	11,265	87,223	85,230	104,789	105,230
Persons with incomes:						
$1–$2,499 or loss	442	807	3,269	6,374	4,156	7,764
$2,500–$4,999	377	685	1,976	3,655	2,544	4,734
$5,000–$7,499	619	987	2,651	5,683	3,610	7,098
$7,500–$9,999	697	918	2,779	5,768	3,679	7,335
$10,000–$12,499	1,027	1,063	3,744	6,222	4,781	7,675
$12,500–$14,999	649	602	3,016	4,535	3,659	5,462
$15,000–$17,499	1,190	814	4,136	4,875	5,027	6,094
$17,500–$19,999	682	488	2,892	3,562	3,486	4,385
$20,000–$22,499	1,176	751	4,251	4,537	5,157	5,605
$22,500–$24,999	570	400	2,561	2,799	3,049	3,494
$25,000–$27,499	1,044	529	3,842	3,906	4,748	4,816
$27,500–$29,999	378	293	2,151	2,248	2,529	2,795
$30,000–$32,499	1,012	529	4,407	3,802	5,394	4,733
$32,500–$34,999	237	183	1,736	1,777	2,068	2,154
$35,000–$37,499	657	408	3,534	2,915	4,254	3,663
$37,500–$39,999	237	164	1,842	1,576	2,161	1,907
$40,000–$42,499	566	294	3,579	2,752	4,281	3,362
$42,500–$44,999	157	107	1,349	1,214	1,565	1,453
$45,000–$47,499	333	179	2,612	1,912	3,082	2,369
$47,500–$49,999	153	95	1,295	1,147	1,492	1,389
$50,000–$52,499	415	191	3,069	2,021	3,677	2,522
$52,500–$54,999	116	46	1,179	752	1,327	910
$55,000–$57,499	212	89	1,856	1,097	2,178	1,290
$57,500–$59,999	66	33	979	640	1,109	739

(continued on next page)

Table 7.17: Money Income of Persons 15 Years Old and Older by Selected Characteristics, 2007

	Hispanic		White		All Races	
	Male	Female	Male	Female	Male	Female
$60,000–$62,499	288	99	2,253	1,232	2,712	1,548
$62,500–$64,999	69	36	760	496	843	585
$65,000–$67,499	126	46	1,321	778	1,532	985
$67,500–$69,999	30	21	651	399	727	471
$70,000–$72,499	137	59	1,537	733	1,818	924
$72,500–$74,999	42	30	661	326	757	382
$75,000–$77,499	120	39	1,261	560	1,471	664
$77,500–$79,999	31	16	557	285	631	347
$80,000–$82,499	89	25	1,211	450	1,383	568
$82,500–$84,999	30	16	436	215	500	254
$85,000–$87,499	59	16	694	291	809	356
$87,500–$89,999	23	9	336	157	374	193
$90,000–$92,499	45	29	771	324	908	418
$92,500–$94,999	28	5	331	162	371	181
$95,000–$97,499	36	8	496	191	549	223
$97,500–$99,999	18	9	397	115	445	136
$100,000 and over	425	148	8,844	2,743	9,949	3,246
Median income	$24,451	$16,748	$35,141	$21,069	$33,196	$20,922
Mean income	$31,693	$22,649	$48,975	$29,441	$47,137	$29,249

Source: U.S. Bureau of the Census, Current Population Reports, *Annual Social and Economic Supplement 2008*, Person income table PINC-01.

Notes: 'All Races' includes other races and ethnic groups not shown separately. 'White' as shown here is equivalent to 'White Alone.' Number of persons as of March of the following year.

Units: Number of persons with income in thousands of persons, mean and median income in current dollars.

Table 7.18: Median Weekly Earnings of Families by Type of Family and Number of Earners, 1990 and 1993

	Hispanic	White	All Races
1990			
All families with earners	$496	$681	$653
Married couple families	555	745	732
With one earner	322	473	455
With two or more earners	716	892	880
Families maintained by women	326	382	363
Families maintained by men	468	539	514
1993			
All families with earners	*$505*	*$739*	*$707*
Married couple families	566	816	804
With one earner	334	492	481
With two or more earners	744	984	973
Families maintained by women	353	415	393
Families maintained by men	432	547	523

Source: U.S. Department of Labor, Bureau of Labor Statistics, *Employment and Earnings, January, 1991*, table 52; *1994*, table 52.

Notes: 'All Races' includes races not shown separately.
Data excludes families in which there is no wage or salary earner, or in which the husband, wife, or other person maintaining the family is either self-employed or in the armed forces.

Units: Median weekly earnings in dollars.

Table 7.19: Median Weekly Earnings of Full-Time and Part-Time Wage and Salary Workers by Sex and Age, 2006–2008

	Hispanic		White		All Races	
	Male	Female	Male	Female	Male	Female
2006						
Full-Time Wage and Salary Workers						
All full-time wage and salary workers	$591	$519	$761	$609	$743	$600
16–24 years old	NA	NA	NA	NA	418	395
25 years old and over	NA	NA	NA	NA	797	627
Part-Time Wage and Salary Workers						
All part-time wage and salary workers	$190	$191	$193	$216	$192	$213
16–24 years old	NA	NA	NA	NA	153	148
25 years old and over	NA	NA	NA	NA	255	253
2007						
Full-Time Wage and Salary Workers						
All full-time wage and salary workers	$630	$533	$788	$626	$766	$614
16–24 years old	NA	NA	NA	NA	443	409
25 years old and over	NA	NA	NA	NA	823	646
Part-Time Wage and Salary Workers						
All part-time wage and salary workers	$205	$200	$203	$220	$203	$218
16–24 years old	NA	NA	NA	NA	162	155
25 years old and over	NA	NA	NA	NA	264	259
2008						
Full-Time Wage and Salary Workers						
All full-time wage and salary workers	$559	$501	$825	$654	$798	$638
16–24 years old	NA	NA	NA	NA	461	420
25 years old and over	NA	NA	NA	NA	857	370
Part-Time Wage and Salary Workers						
All part-time wage and salary workers	$232	$211	$209	$225	$209	$223
16–24 years old	NA	NA	NA	NA	164	161
25 years old and over	NA	NA	NA	NA	276	261

Source: U.S. Department of Labor, Bureau of Labor Statistics, *Employment and Earnings, 2008*, tables 37 and 38.

Notes: 'All Races' includes other races not shown separately.

Units: Median weekly earning in dollars.

Table 7.20: Earnings of Full-Time Workers by Sex and Ethnic Group, 2003 and 2005

	Mexican	Puerto Rican	Cuban	Central American	South American	Other Hispanic	Total Hispanic
2003							
All workers	*8,275*	*1,105*	*573*	*1,164*	*861*	*942*	*12,921*
Males	5,601	614	344	748	536	492	8,335
Percent with incomes of:							
$1 to $2,499 or loss	1.0%	0.9%	0.3%	0.7%	0.6%	1.9%	1.0%
$2,500 to $4,999	0.5	NA	NA	0.2	0.4	0.1	0.4
$5,000 to $9,999	2.5	1.7	3.9	3.4	1.2	1.5	2.4
$10,000 to $14,999	13.0	6.8	3.7	14.3	7.7	9.0	11.7
$15,000 to $19,999	17.4	11.3	14.0	20.0	10.1	7.4	16.0
$20,000 to $24,999	15.8	13.0	15.7	17.3	12.8	9.3	15.2
$25,000 to $34,999	21.2	21.7	17.0	16.8	25.9	21.3	21.0
$35,000 to $49.999	15.7	21.2	16.4	14.8	18.3	20.3	16.5
$50,000 to $74,999	9.4	15.5	16.7	8.0	11.2	17.6	10.7
$75,000 and over	3.3	8.0	12.2	4.5	11.8	11.7	5.2
Females	2,674	491	229	416	325	450	4,586
Percent with incomes of:							
$1 to $2,499 or loss	0.9%	0.3%	1.1%	2.6%	1.7%	1.0%	1.3%
$2,500 to $4,999	0.9	NA	0.6	1.7	0.3	0.8	0.8
$5,000 to $9,999	4.8	3.4	5.7	3.7	4.0	4.5	3.9
$10,000 to $14,999	18.8	9.9	12.6	18.0	14.5	12.1	11.5
$15,000 to $19,999	19.2	13.6	16.5	26.8	9.9	14.8	17.8
$20,000 to $24,999	15.6	15.2	8.9	14.8	18.0	16.3	11.9
$25,000 to $34,999	17.9	28.8	18.8	17.0	23.0	20.6	22.1
$35,000 to $49.999	14.1	16.9	16.3	8.3	14.1	16.0	14.4
$50,000 to $74,999	6.0	9.8	10.3	4.2	8.5	10.8	10.7
$75,000 and over	1.7	2.2	9.1	2.8	5.9	3.1	5.6

(continued on next page)

Table 7.20: Earnings of Full-Time Workers by Sex and Ethnic Group, 2003 and 2005

	Mexican	Puerto Rican	Cuban	Central American	South American	Other Hispanic	Total Hispanic
2005							
All workers	*9,016*	*1,149*	*597*	*1,407*	*1,019*	*1,141*	*14,329*
Males	6,136	663	360	943	621	603	9,327
Percent with incomes of:							
Under $5,000	1.1%	1.1%	0.6%	2.1%	0.3%	0.6%	1.1%
$5,000 to $9,999	3.3	2.1	0.1	1.8	1.9	1.6	2.7
$10,000 to $14,999	10.0	3.8	5.2	8.4	5.9	4.9	8.6
$15,000 to $19,999	16.7	11.0	12.1	16.3	10.8	8.9	15.2
$20,000 to $24,999	16.8	11.9	12.6	19.4	16.7	11.4	16.2
$25,000 to $34,999	21.1	21.4	22.9	25.7	20.5	22.5	21.7
$35,000 to $49.999	16.4	22.0	17.7	13.9	18.2	20.8	17.0
$50,000 to $74,999	9.4	16.9	14.9	7.2	14.3	16.9	10.7
$75,000 to $99,999	2.8	5.0	5.5	2.6	5.0	4.2	3.2
$100,000 and over	2.5	4.7	8.4	2.5	6.3	8.2	3.5
Females	2,879	486	238	464	398	538	5,003
Percent with incomes of:							
Under $5,000	1.1%	0.8%	1.1%	1.1%	2.0%	2.3%	1.3%
$5,000 to $9,999	4.5	2.0	5.3	2.8	4.0	3.1	4.0
$10,000 to $14,999	16.4	9.7	10.8	19.0	9.5	11.0	14.6
$15,000 to $19,999	18.0	10.5	11.5	18.4	14.3	15.4	16.4
$20,000 to $24,999	15.6	12.9	17.4	20.1	12.2	13.6	15.4
$25,000 to $34,999	19.9	25.0	18.7	18.0	20.8	24.4	20.7
$35,000 to $49.999	14.9	24.2	18.6	10.0	16.5	16.2	15.8
$50,000 to $74,999	6.5	9.3	13.8	6.8	12.8	9.9	8.0
$75,000 to $99,999	1.8	3.2	1.3	3.1	3.2	2.5	2.2
$100,000 and over	1.3	2.4	1.4	0.8	4.9	1.5	1.7

Source: U.S. Bureau of the Census, Current Population Reports, *The Hispanic Population of the United States, 2004*, table 11.2; *2006*, table 11.2.

Notes: 'Other Hispanic' includes Dominicans. Represents full-time, year-round workers, 15 years old and older.
Income is wages or salaries and net income from farm and nonfarm self-employment.

Units: Numbers of workers in thousands; percent of total workers.

Table 7.21: Median Income of Year-Round, Full-Time Workers by Sex, 1980–2007

| | Hispanic | | White | | All Races | |
	Male	Female	Male	Female	Male	Female
1980	$23,113	$16,500	$32,658	$19,224	$31,729	$19,088
1985	22,233	17,037	32,678	20,596	31,548	20,372
1990	20,542	16,823	31,002	21,521	29,711	21,278
1995	20,553	17,855	33,515	24,264	32,199	23,777
2000	25,041	21,026	40,350	29,659	39,020	28,823
2001	25,271	21,973	40,790	30,849	40,136	30,420
2002	26,137	22,355	41,375	31,400	40,507	30,970
2003	26,414	23,062	42,142	32,192	41,503	31,653
2004	26,921	24,255	42,601	32,683	41,667	32,101
2005	26,966	25,022	43,696	34,100	42,188	33,256
2006	29,571	25,694	45,933	35,525	44,958	34,989
2007	30,454	27,154	47,235	36,728	46,224	36,167

Source: U.S. Bureau of the Census, Current Population Reports: *Money Income of Households, Families, and Persons in the United States: March 1992* (Series P-60, #184), table B-17; *1996* (Series P-60, #197), table 7.
U.S. Bureau of the Census, *Current Population Reports: Income 2001*, table 7.
U.S. Bureau of the Census, Current Population Reports, *Annual Social and Economic Supplement, 2002*, Person income table PINC-01; *2003*, table PINC-01; *2004*, table PINC-01; *2005*, table PINC-01; *2006*, table PINC-01; *2007*, PINC-01; *2008*, PINC-01.

Notes: 'All Races' includes other races not shown separately.
Data covers the earnings of wage and salary workers who usually worked 35 or more hours per week for 50 to 52 weeks during the year.
Data prior to 1989 is for civilian workers only.
For 2002 and later, 'White' as shown here is equivalent to 'White alone.'

Units: Median money earnings in dollars.

Table 7.22: Per Capita Money Income, 1990–2006

	Hispanic	White	All Races
Current Dollars			
1990	$8,424	$15,265	$14,387
1995	9,300	18,304	17,227
2000	12,651	23,582	22,346
2001	13,003	24,127	22,851
2002	13,487	24,142	22,794
2003	13,492	24,626	23,276
2004	14,105	25,223	23,857
2005	14,483	26,496	25,036
2006	15,421	27,821	26,352
Constant Dollars			
1990	$12,598	$22,828	$21,515
1995	12,217	24,045	22,631
2000	14,812	27,610	26,163
2001	14,808	27,477	26,024
2002	15,115	27,057	25,546
2003	14,791	26,997	25,517
2004	15,056	26,923	25,465
2005	14,958	27,365	25,857
2006	15,421	27,821	26,352

Source: U.S. Bureau of the Census, *Statistical Abstract of the United States, 2008*, table 682.

Notes: 'All Races' includes other races not shown separately.
For 2002 and later, 'White' as shown here is equivalent to 'White alone.'
Constant dollars based on 2006.

Units: Income in current and constant (2006) dollars.

Table 7.23: Per Capita Income by State, 2007

	Hispanic	White	All Races
United States	*$15,190*	*$28,953*	*$26,178*
Alabama	12,697	25,327	22,011
Alaska	18,251	33,087	27,988
Arizona	13,759	27,387	24,587
Arkansas	10,616	22,365	20,309
California	15,206	32,771	28,049
Colorado	14,826	30,718	28,642
Connecticut	17,784	38,707	35,295
Delaware	14,478	30,736	27,879
District of Columbia	25,579	66,241	38,009
Florida	18,789	29,057	26,125
Georgia	13,856	29,061	24,558
Hawaii	18,143	37,150	27,814
Idaho	11,907	22,523	21,844
Illinois	15,178	31,338	27,511
Indiana	13,958	24,855	23,620
Iowa	12,753	24,787	24,078
Kansas	13,330	26,043	24,579
Kentucky	14,238	22,323	21,618
Louisiana	17,737	25,588	21,176
Maine	14,992	24,849	24,344
Maryland	21,021	38,014	32,933
Massachusetts	15,553	34,448	32,113
Michigan	15,347	26,878	24,966
Minnesota	14,616	30,185	28,536
Mississippi	14,741	23,496	18,820
Missouri	14,877	25,163	23,667
Montana	13,630	23,268	22,152
Nebraska	12,629	25,069	23,900

(continued on next page)

Table 7.23: Per Capita Income by State, 2007

	Hispanic	White	All Races
Nevada	15,474	29,544	26,980
New Hampshire	19,734	30,084	29,672
New Jersey	18,644	37,335	33,219
New Mexico	15,513	24,541	21,586
New York	16,624	34,239	29,230
North Carolina	12,384	27,303	23,767
North Dakota	15,253	24,644	23,594
Ohio	15,335	25,746	24,296
Oklahoma	12,210	24,070	21,700
Oregon	12,119	26,502	25,097
Pennsylvania	13,850	27,389	25,692
Rhode Island	13,087	29,880	27,515
South Carolina	13,136	26,702	22,560
South Dakota	10,997	24,374	22,561
Tennessee	12,914	24,904	22,937
Texas	13,263	26,207	23,294
Utah	12,812	22,757	21,845
Vermont	20,567	26,603	26,223
Virginia	20,302	34,299	30,651
Washington	14,023	30,310	28,290
West Virginia	15,411	20,321	20,111
Wisconsin	13,655	27,322	25,742
Wyoming	18,092	26,868	25,885

Source: U.S. Bureau of the Census, *American Community Survey, 2007*, table B19301.

Notes: For civilian, noninstitutional population only: use caution when comparing this data to other Census data.
Estimates are only given where the specified population is larger than 65,000.

Units: Income in current (2007) dollars.

Table 7.24: Income of Persons from Specified Sources, 2007

	Hispanic	White	All Races
All persons, 15 years and over	*25874*	*174,890*	*210,019*
Number with income from:			
Earnings	21887	131,853	158,777
Unemployment compensation	622	4,266	5,200
Workers' compensation	225	1,364	1,604
Social Security	2736	36,435	41,897
SSI (Supplemental Security Income)	777	3,501	5,039
Public assistance (total)	340	1,111	1,828
Veterans' benefits	116	2,126	2,533
Survivors benefits	94	2,642	2,906
Disability benefits	170	1,338	1,615
Rents, royalties, estates or trusts	582	8,953	9,894
Educational assistance	753	5,659	7,270
Child support	603	3,922	4,964
Alimony	24	378	411
Mean income, all persons 15 years and older	$27,755	$39,192	$38,174
Mean income from:			
Earnings	$29,544	$42,204	$41,328
Unemployment compensation	3,938	4,266	4,207
Workers' compensation	6,456	7,321	7,431
Social Security	10,217	11,933	11,760
SSI (Supplemental Security Income)	6,153	6,673	6,550
Public assistance (total)	4,010	3,407	3,311
Veterans' benefits	11,509	11,109	11,483
Survivors benefits	8,648	13,332	13,128
Disability benefits	10,532	12,605	12,224
Rents, royalties, estates or trusts	4,577	7,293	7,106
Educational assistance	4,609	6,045	5,846
Child support	4,385	5,277	4,968
Alimony	NA	13,461	13,281

Source: U.S. Bureau of the Census, Current Population Reports, *Annual Social and Economic Supplement 2008*, Person income table PINC-09.

Notes: 'All Races' includes other races not shown separately. Persons 15 years old and older as of March the following year. 'White' as shown is equivalent to 'White alone.'

Units: Number of persons in thousands, mean income in dollars.

Table 7.25: Persons Below the Poverty Level, 1980–2007

	Hispanic	White	All Races
Number Below the Poverty Level			
1980	3,491	19,699	29,272
1985	5,236	22,860	33,064
1990	6,006	22,326	33,585
1995	8,574	24,423	36,425
2000	7,747	21,291	31,139
2001	7,997	22,739	32,907
2002	8,555	23,466	34,570
2003	9,051	24,272	35,861
2004	9,122	25,327	37,040
2005	9,368	24,872	36,950
2006	9,243	24,416	36,460
2007	9,890	25,120	37,276
Percent Below the Poverty Level			
1980	25.7%	10.2%	13.0%
1985	29.0	11.4	14.0
1990	28.1	10.7	13.5
1995	30.3	11.2	13.8
2000	21.5	9.4	11.3
2001	21.4	9.9	11.7
2002	21.8	10.2	12.1
2003	22.5	10.5	12.5
2004	21.9	10.8	12.7
2005	21.8	10.6	12.6
2006	20.6	10.3	12.3
2007	21.5	10.5	12.5

Source: U.S. Bureau of the Census, Current Population Reports: *Income, Poverty, and Health Insurance Coverage in the United States: 2007* (Series P-60-233), table 3.

Notes: 'All Races' includes other races not shown separately. For 2002 and later, 'White' and 'Hispanic' as shown are equivalent to 'White alone' and 'Hispanic alone.'
The 2004 data has been revised to reflect a correction to the weights in the 2005 Annual Social and Economic Supplement.

Units: Number below the poverty level in thousands of persons, percent as a percent of all persons by race.

Table 7.26: Families Below the Poverty Level, 1980–2007

	Hispanic	White	All Races
Number Below the Poverty Level			
1980	751	4,195	6,217
1985	1,074	4,983	7,223
1990	1,244	4,622	7,098
1995	1,695	4,994	7,532
2000	1,540	4,333	6,400
2001	1,649	4,579	6,813
2002	1,792	4,862	7,229
2003	1,925	5,058	7,607
2004	1,953	5,293	7,835
2005	1,948	5,068	7,657
2006	1,922	5,118	7,668
2007	2,045	5,046	7,623
Percent Below the Poverty Level			
1980	23.2%	8.0%	10.3%
1985	25.5	9.1	11.4
1990	25.0	8.1	10.7
1995	27.0	8.5	10.8
2000	19.2	7.1	8.7
2001	19.4	7.4	9.2
2002	19.7	7.8	9.6
2003	20.8	8.1	10.0
2004	20.5	8.4	10.2
2005	19.7	8.0	9.9
2006	18.9	8.0	9.8
2007	19.7	7.9	9.8

Source: U.S. Bureau of the Census, Current Population Reports, *Historical Poverty Tables*, table 4.

Notes: 'All Races' includes other races not shown separately. Families as of March of the following year. For 2002 and later, 'White' and 'Hispanic' as shown are equivalent to 'White alone' and 'Hispanic alone.'
The 2004 data have been revised to reflect a correction to the weights in the 2005 Annual Social and Economic Supplement.

Units: Number below the poverty level in thousands of families, percent of all families by race.

Table 7.27: Poverty Status of Families, by Ethnic Group, 2002, 2003, and 2005

	Mexican	Puerto Rican	Cuban	Central American	South American	Other Hispanic	Total Hispanic
2002							
Poverty status of families							
Total Families	5,832	964	416	676	522	684	9,094
Below poverty threshold	1,221	220	54	122	52	124	1,792
Married-couple families	4,126	538	309	429	367	420	6,189
Below poverty threshold	701	68	34	63	22	39	927
Male householder, no spouse present	567	70	36	83	63	52	872
Below poverty threshold	100	12	9	11	10	7	148
Female householder, no spouse present	1,139	356	71	163	92	212	2,033
Below poverty threshold	421	140	11	48	20	78	717
2003							
Poverty status of families							
Total Families	5,857	985	437	739	531	725	9,273
Below poverty threshold	1,340	208	49	139	61	128	1,925
Married-couple families	4,078	562	338	465	363	421	6,228
Below poverty threshold	749	51	30	69	28	50	976
Male householder, no spouse present	590	81	39	89	44	64	908
Below poverty threshold	121	14	8	5	2	7	157
Female householder, no spouse present	1,188	341	59	185	125	240	2,138
Below poverty threshold	470	143	11	65	31	72	792
2005							
Poverty status of families							
Total Families	6,244	901	429	819	630	845	9,868
Below poverty threshold	1,376	211	39	117	70	134	1,948
Married-couple families	4,371	480	324	546	418	504	6,642
Below poverty threshold	740	39	13	50	26	48	917
Male householder, no spouse present	601	85	27	103	71	84	972
Below poverty threshold	107	17	4	13	4	10	155
Female householder, no spouse present	1,272	336	78	170	141	257	2,254
Below poverty threshold	529	155	22	54	40	75	876

Source: US Bureau of the Census, Current Population Reports, *The Hispanic Population of the United States, 2003*, table 15.2; *2004*, table 15.2; *2005*, 15.2.

Notes: 'Other Hispanic' includes Dominicans.

Units: Number of families in thousands.

Table 7.28: Families Below the Poverty Level by Type of Family and Presence of Related Children, 2004–2007

	Hispanic	White	All Races
2004			
Total Families	*9,537*	*63,227*	*77,019*
Families below poverty level	1,958	5,315	7,854
Married-couple families	939	2,591	3,222
Male householder, no wife present	148	435	658
Female householder, no husband present	871	2,288	3,973
Total families with children under 18 years	*6,625*	*31,212*	*39,710*
Families below poverty level	1,688	3,866	5,847
Married-couple families	781	1,540	1,915
Male householder, no wife present	103	305	443
Female householder, no husband present	805	2,021	3,489
2005			
Total Families	*9,868*	*63,414*	*77,418*
Families below poverty level	1,948	5,068	7,657
Married-couple families	917	2,317	2,944
Male householder, no wife present	155	439	669
Female householder, no husband present	876	2,312	4,044
Total families with children under 18 years	*6,769*	*30,844*	*39,394*
Families below poverty level	1,651	3,682	5,729
Married-couple families	771	1,392	1,777
Male householder, no wife present	102	296	193
Female householder, no husband present	777	1,993	3,493

(continued on next page)

Table 7.28: Families Below the Poverty Level by Type of Family and Presence of Related Children, 2004–2007

	Hispanic	White	All Races
2006			
Total Families	*10,155*	*64,120*	*78,454*
Families below poverty level	1,922	5,118	7,668
Married-couple families	903	2,278	2,910
Male householder, no wife present	139	440	671
Female householder, no husband present	881	2,400	4,087
Total families with children under 18 years	*6,982*	*31,140*	*39,780*
Families below poverty level	1,636	3,773	5,822
Married-couple families	718	1,348	1,746
Male householder, no wife present	106	308	461
Female householder, no husband present	811	2,118	3,615
2007			
Total Families	*10,397*	*63,595*	*77,908*
Families below poverty level	2,045	5,046	7,623
Married-couple families	926	2,265	2,849
Male householder, no wife present	151	451	696
Female householder, no husband present	968	2,330	4,078
Total families with children under 18 years	*7,060*	*30,304*	*38,868*
Families below poverty level	1,759	3,785	5,830
Married-couple families	766	1,408	1,765
Male householder, no wife present	112	324	471
Female householder, no husband present	881	2,053	3,593

Source: U.S. Bureau of the Census, Current Population Reports, *Annual Social and Economic Supplement 2005*, Poverty tables POV44 and POV45; *2006*, tables POV44 and POV45; *2007*, tables POV44 and POV4; *2008*, POV44 and POV4.

Notes: 'All Races' includes other races not shown separately. 'White' as shown is equivalent to 'White alone.'
Figures shown are for families with income below 100% of the poverty level.

Units: Thousands of families.

Table 7.29: Children Below the Poverty Level, 1980–2007

	Hispanic	White	All Races
Number Below the Poverty Level			
1980	1,749	7,181	11,543
1985	2,606	8,253	13,010
1990	2,865	8,232	13,431
1995	4,080	8,981	14,665
2000	3,522	7,328	11,633
2001	3,570	7,527	11,733
2002	3,782	7,549	12,133
2003	4,077	7,985	12,866
2004	4,098	8,308	13,041
2005	4,143	8,085	12,896
2006	4,072	7,908	12,827
2007	4,482	8,395	1,324
Percent Below the Poverty Level			
1980	33.2%	13.9%	18.3%
1985	40.3	16.2	20.7
1990	38.4	15.9	20.6
1995	40.0	16.2	20.8
2000	28.4	13.0	16.2
2001	28.0	13.4	16.3
2002	28.6	13.6	16.7
2003	29.7	14.3	17.6
2004	28.9	14.8	17.8
2005	28.3	14.4	17.6
2006	26.9	14.1	17.4
2007	28.6	14.9	18.0

Source: U.S. Bureau of the Census, Current Population Reports: *Income, Poverty, and Health Insurance Coverage in the United States: 2007*, table B-2.

Notes: 'All Races' includes other races not shown separately. For 2002 and later, 'White' as shown is equivalent to 'White alone.'
The 2004 data has been revised to reflect a correction to the weights in the 2005 Annual Social and Economic Supplement.

Units: Number of persons under 18 who are below the poverty level in thousands of persons, percent of all persons by race.

Table 7.30: Persons 65 Years Old and Over Below the Poverty Level, 1980–2007

	Hispanic	White	All Races
Number Below the Poverty Level			
1980	179	3,042	3,871
1985	219	2,698	3,456
1990	245	2,707	3,658
1995	342	2,572	3,318
2000	381	2,584	3,323
2001	413	2,656	3,414
2002	439	2,739	3,576
2003	406	2,666	3,552
2004	403	2,534	3,453
2005	460	2,700	3,603
2006	472	2,473	3,394
2007	438	2,590	3,556
Percent Below the Poverty Level			
1980	30.8%	13.6%	15.7%
1985	23.9	11.0	12.6
1990	22.5	10.1	12.2
1995	23.5	9.0	10.5
2000	20.9	8.7	10.2
2001	21.8	8.9	10.1
2002	21.4	9.1	10.4
2003	19.5	8.8	10.2
2004	18.4	8.3	9.8
2005	19.9	8.7	10.1
2006	19.4	7.9	9.4
2007	17.1	8.1	9.7

Source: U.S. Bureau of the Census, Current Population Reports: Income, *Poverty, and Health Insurance Coverage in the United States: 2007*, table B-2.

Notes: 'All Races' includes other races not shown separately. For 2002 and later, 'White' as shown is equivalent to 'White alone.'
The 2004 data has been revised to reflect a correction to the weights in the 2005 Annual Social and Economic Supplement.

Units: Number of persons 65 or older who are below the poverty level in thousands of persons, percent of all persons by race.

Table 7.31: Social Assistance and Welfare, 2003

	Hispanic	White	All Races
Percent receiving assistance			
Any program	*27.0%*	*12.3%*	*15.4%*
TANF/General Assistance	2.7	0.8	1.3
Supplemental Security Income	3.0	1.8	2.2
Food stamps	10.9	4.9	6.7
Medicaid	21.8	9.7	12.0
Housing Assistance	5.6	2.4	3.7
Median monthly benefit for families	$259	$249	$255
Median duration of participation, 2001–2003			
Any program	*7.2*	*7.1*	*7.2*
TANF/General Assistance	4.0	4.0	4.9
Supplemental Security Income	22.3	15.0	15.0
Food stamps	7.0	7.4	7.7
Medicaid	7.7	7.6	7.6
Housing Assistance	3.9	3.9	4.0

Source: U.S. Bureau of the Census, *Survey of Income and Program Participation, Dynamics of Economic Well-Being: Participation in Government Porgrams, 2001 Through 2003, Who Gets Assistance?* (Series P70-108), tables A-1 to A-8.

Notes: 'TANF' indicates Temporary Assistance for Needy Families or General Assistance. Median monthly family benefits are calculated only for recipients of TANF, General Assistance, Supplemental Security Income, and food stamps.

Units: Percent of total population; monthly benefit in 2003 dollars; median duration in months.

Table 7.32: Child Support Payments Agreed to or Awarded to Custodial Parents, 2005

	Hispanic	White	All Races
All Custodial Parents	*2,146*	*9,493*	*13,605*
Child support agreed to or awarded	1,062	5,748	7,802
Supposed to receive child support	949	5,038	6,809
Received payments	723	4,005	5,259
Full Payments	421	2,475	3,192
Partial Payments	301	1,530	2,068
Did not receive payments	226	1,032	1,550
Child support not awarded	1,084	3,745	5,803
All Custodial Mothers	*1,854*	*7,644*	*11,406*
Child support agreed to or awarded	943	5,045	7,002
Supposed to receive child support	836	4,447	6,131
Received payments	633	3,568	4,754
Full Payments	377	2,221	2,900
Partial Payments	255	1,347	1,855
Did not receive payments	203	879	1,377
Child support not awarded	911	2,599	4,404
All Custodial Fathers	*292*	*1,849*	*2,199*
Child support agreed to or awarded	119	703	800
Supposed to receive child support	113	590	678
Received payments	90	437	505
Full Payments	44	254	292
Partial Payments	46	183	213
Did not receive payments	23	153	174
Child support not awarded	173	1,146	1,399

Source: U.S. Bureau of the Census, Current Population Reports, *Custodial Mothers and Fathers and Their Child Support: 2005*, table 4.

Notes: 'All Races' includes races not shown separately.

Units: Number of parents in thousands.

Chapter 8

Special Topics

Chapter Eight Highlights

This chapter covers important topics not covered elsewhere in this book, including both the most current data available as well as comparisons of the Hispanic population over time. For almost all tables, corresponding data is provided for the total population of the United States as well as for White persons. This allows for easy comparison between groups. Because 'Hispanic' is not a race or ethnic group, we have included a variety of tables with statistics on some of the ethnic groups that comprise the Hispanic designation (tables 8.10 and 8.16).

The chapter includes information about housing units, including tenure (table 8.01) and affordability (table 8.02). It also includes statistics on geographic mobility (8.03), and on farms and farm operators (tables 8.05 and 8.06).

Also of note are statistics on Hispanic-owned firms in various industries, which are organized in a variety of ways, including by state (table 8.15), by type of industry (tables 8.07, 8.09, and 8.14), by ethnic group (tables 8.10 and 8.16), and by size (table 8.13).

We have also included a summary of results of the 2006 Consumer Expenditure Survey, which tracks annual spending on many types of goods and services, including food, housing, transportation, and entertainment (tables 8.18 and 8.19).

Table 8.01: Occupied Housing Units by Tenure, 1980–2005

	Hispanic Householders	White Householder	All Householders
1980			
All households	4,008	68,810	80,390
Owner-occupied	1,739	46,671	51,795
Percent of total	43.4%	67.8%	64.4%
Renter-occupied	2,269	22,139	28,595
1991			
All households	6,239	79,140	93,147
Owner-occupied	2,423	53,749	59,796
Percent of total	38.0%	67.9%	64.2%
Renter-occupied	3,816	25,391	33,351
2001			
All households	9,814	85,292	106,261
Owner-occupied	4,731	62,465	72,265
Percent of total	48.2%	73.2%	68.0%
Renter-occupied	5,083	22,826	33,996
2005			
All households	11,651	89,449	108,871
Owner-occupied	5,752	65,023	74,931
Percent of total	49.4%	72.7%	68.8%
Renter-occupied	5,899	24,426	33,940

Source: U.S. Bureau of the Census, *Statistical Abstract of the United States, 1999*, table 1214; *2007*, table 955.

Notes: 'All Householders' includes householders of other races not shown separately. Persons of Hispanic origin can be of any race.

Units: Number of housing units in thousands; percent of total units.

Table 8.02: Housing Affordability for Families, 1995, 2002, and 2004

	Hispanic	White	All Races
1995			
Percent that cannot afford a median-priced home			
in their region using conventional, fixed-rate, 30-year financing			
All families	80.8%	47.4%	52.2%
Married couples	73.3	39.9	42.2
Male householder (no wife present)	87.5	69.2	73.2
Female householder (no husband present)	95.7	79.4	84.5
Percent that cannot afford a median-priced home			
in their region using FHA, fixed-rate, 30-year financing			
All families	80.3%	46.1%	51.0%
Married couples	72.3	38.3	40.6
Male householder (no wife present)	87.5	69.6	73.2
Female householder (no husband present)	95.9	79.4	84.6
Percent that cannot afford a modestly priced home			
in their region using conventional, fixed-rate, 30-year financing			
All families	74.7%	39.6%	44.4%
Married couples	65.3	32.2	34.2
Male householder (no wife present)	82.5	59.6	64.1
Female householder (no husband present)	93.1	72.0	77.7
Percent that cannot afford a modestly priced home			
in their region using FHA, fixed-rate, 30-year financing			
All families	72.6%	37.2%	42.1%
Married couples	62.4	29.3	31.4
Male householder (no wife present)	82.5	58.2	62.8
Female householder (no husband present)	92.6	71.3	77.0

(continued on next page)

Table 8.02: Housing Affordability for Families, 1995, 2002, and 2004

	Hispanic	White	All Races
2002			
Percent that cannot afford a median-priced home in their region using conventional, fixed-rate, 30-year financing			
All families	*80.2%*	*46.1%*	*51.1%*
Married couples	73.5	37.3	40.2
Male householder (no wife present)	90.2	73.5	75.7
Female householder (no husband present)	92.2	80.0	84.1
Percent that cannot afford a modestly priced home in their region using conventional, fixed-rate, 30-year financing			
All families	*71.7%*	*38.8%*	*43.6%*
Married couples	63.2	30.3	33.0
Male householder (no wife present)	86.0	64.9	66.9
Female householder (no husband present)	86.6	71.1	76.2
2004			
Percent that cannot afford a median-priced home in their region using conventional, fixed-rate, 30-year financing			
All families	*73.6%*	*44.4%*	*48.7%*
Married couples	66.1	34.8	36.8
Male householder (no wife present)	82.6	69.4	71.2
Female householder (no husband present)	88.6	77.6	81.5
Percent that cannot afford a modestly priced home in their region using conventional, fixed-rate, 30-year financing			
All families	*65.6%*	*37.3%*	*41.6%*
Married couples	56.3	28.0	29.9
Male householder (no wife present)	77.4	60.9	63.2
Female householder (no husband present)	84.0	70.1	74.4

Source: U.S. Bureau of the Census, Current Housing Reports: *Who Can Afford to Buy A House in 1995?*, tables 2-2 and 3-2; *2002*, tables 2-2 and 3-2; *2004*, tables 2-2 and 3-2.

Notes: 'All Races' includes families of all races.

Units: Percent of total families as shown.

Table 8.03: General Mobility, 1999–2000, 2005–2006, and 2006–2007

	Hispanic	White	All Races
March 1999–March 2000			
Total	*32,103*	*221,703*	*270,219*
Non-movers	25,347	187,810	226,831
Moved to:			
Same county	4,254	18,811	24,399
Different county, same state	1,006	7,135	8,814
Different state, same region	335	2,992	4,062
Different division, same region	217	1,076	1,261
Different region	318	2,633	3,105
Abroad	626	1,247	1,746
March 2005–March 2006			
Total	*42,226*	*232,765*	*289,781*
Non-movers	34,429	202,607	249,945
Moved to:			
Same county	5,324	18,681	24,851
Different county, same state	1,222	6,359	8,010
Different state, same region	140	1,132	1,731
Different division, same region	146	915	1,208
Different region	369	2,166	2,740
Abroad	595	905	1,296
March 2006–March 2007			
Total	*44,991*	*236,174*	*294,851*
Non-movers	38,427	209,857	259,685
Moved to:			
Same county	4,841	16,922	23,013
Different county, same state	844	4,962	6,282
Different state, same region	99	909	1,229
Different division, same region	145	791	1,019
Different region	311	2,068	2,479
Abroad	324	666	1,145

Source: U.S. Bureau of the Census, Current Population Survey, *Geographic Mobility: March 1999 to March 2000*, table 2; *March 2005 to March 2006*, table 2; *March 2006 to March 2007*, table 2.

Notes: 'All Races' includes other races not shown separately

Units: Number of persons one year old and over in thousands.

Table 8.04: Selected Characteristics of Farms and Farm Operators, 2007

	Hispanic Farms	All Farms
Characteristics of Farms		
Farms and land in farms		
Number of farms	55,570	2,204,792
Land in farms	17,054,007	922,095,840
Harvested cropland	NA	309,607,601
Farms by size		
1-9 acres	12,139	232,849
10-49 acres	19,687	620,283
50-179 acres	12,169	660,530
180-499 acres	6,215	368,368
500 acres or more	5,360	322,762
Owned and rented land in farms		
Owned land in farms		
Farms	51,680	2,064,225
Acres	10,960,899	571,303,487
Rented or leased land in farms		
Farms	12,774	682,759
Acres	6,093,108	350,792,353
2007 market value of agricultural products sold		
Total	$6,648,073	$297,220,491
Average per farm (in dollars)	119,634	134,807
Crops (including nursery and greenhouse crops)	4,066,957	143,657,928
Livestock, poultry and their products	2,581,116	153,562,563
Farms by value of sales		
Less than $1,000	17,078	499,880
$1,000-$2,499	7,481	270,712
$2,500-$4,999	6,549	246,309
$5,000-$9,999	6,172	254,834
$10,000-$24,999	6,505	274,274
$25,000-$49,999	3,756	163,500
$50,000 or more	8,029	495,283

(continued on next page)

Table 8.04: Selected Characteristics of Farms and Farm Operators, 2007

	Hispanic Farms	All Farms
Characteristics of Farms (continued)		
Farms by North American Industry Classification System		
Oilseed and grain farming (1111)	1,842	338,237
Vegetable and melon farming (11112)	1,385	40,589
Fruit and tree nut farming (1113)	8,871	98,281
Greenhouse, nursery, and floriculture production (1114)	2,341	54,889
Other crop farming (1119)	9,219	519,893
Tobacco farming (11191)	62	9,626
Cotton farming (11192)	319	9,968
Sugarcane farming, hay farming, and all other crop farming (11193, 11194, 11199)	8,838	500,299
Beef cattle ranching and farming (112111)	19,185	656,475
Cattle feedlots (112112)	494	31,065
Dairy cattle and milk production (11212)	581	57,318
Hog and pig farming (1122)	478	30,546
Poultry and egg production (1123)	1,831	64,570
Sheep and goat farming (1124)	2,676	67,254
Animal aquaculture and other animal production (1125, 1129)	6,667	4,777
Characteristics of Farm Operators		
Total principal operators	55,570	2,204,792
Residence		
On farm operated	37,019	1,693,362
Not on farm operated	18,551	511,430
Principal occupation		
Farming	24,933	993,881
Other	30,637	1,210,911
Days of work off farm		
None	14,763	777,747
Any	40,807	1,427,045
1-49 days	7,758	238,479
50-99 days	4,785	115,578
100-199 days	6,393	196,687
200 days or more	21,871	876,301

(continued on next page)

Table 8.04: Selected Characteristics of Farms and Farm Operators, 2007

	Hispanic Farms	All Farms
Characteristics of Farm Operators (continued)		
Years on present farm		
2 years or less	3,339	84,883
3 or 4 years	5,358	138,858
5 to 9 years	12,314	359,545
10 years or more	34,559	1,621,506
Average years on present farm	NA	21.6
Age		
Under 25 years old	298	11,878
25-34 years old	2,700	106,735
35-44 years old	8,211	268,818
45-54 years old	14,995	565,401
55-64 years old	14,332	596,306
65 years old and over	15,034	655,654
Average age	56.0	57.1
Sex		
Male	55,744	1,898,583
Female	16,605	260,452
Principal operator is a hired manager		
Farms	2,930	59,759
Acres	2,703,672	120,672,499

Source: U.S. Bureau of the Census, 2007 Census of Agriculture, Vol. 1 *Geographic Area Series*, Part 51, *U.S. Summary and State Data*, tables 2, 9, 46, 52, and 53.

Notes: 'All farms' includes farms owned/operated by persons of all races.

Units: Farms, farms by size, farms by organization, farms by value of sales, farms by Standard Industrial Classification, in number of farms. Land in farms and harvested crop lands in acres. Market value of agricultural products sold in thousands of dollars. Characteristics of farm operators in number of farm operators.

Table 8.05: Farms and Operators by State, 2002

	Hispanic Operators			White Operators		
	Farms	Operators	Land in Farms	Farms	Operators	Land in Farms
United States	*61,094*	*72,349*	*28,025,352*	*2,077,656*	*2,966,230*	*883,755,206*
Alabama	558	614	85,269	42,407	57,863	8,613,879
Alaska	9	10	3,976	574	825	590,627
Arizona	950	1,200	3,038,456	6,950	11,110	4,846,435
Arkansas	749	837	152,458	45,834	65,838	14,241,472
California	9,784	11,985	2,399,391	75,166	112,321	26,791,340
Colorado	2,110	2,557	1,642,411	31,050	48,283	30,689,204
Connecticut	79	92	7,891	4,178	6,425	354,618
Delaware	46	46	3,281	2,345	3,537	535,686
Florida	2,962	3,696	434,697	42,358	60,195	10,265,971
Georgia	528	591	97,748	47,161	63,239	10,468,416
Hawaii	322	387	39,567	2,367	3,149	1,046,617
Idaho	1,124	1,266	211,690	24,831	37,372	11,328,031
Illinois	450	488	128,934	72,863	99,430	27,284,004
Indiana	445	472	99,372	60,129	85,055	15,041,774
Iowa	499	537	175,610	90,544	124,932	31,708,937
Kansas	559	605	403,554	64,067	87,987	47,110,383
Kentucky	833	887	123,907	85,670	119,703	13,756,749
Louisiana	558	634	102,755	25,475	35,170	7,611,921
Maine	162	198	27,788	7,163	11,051	1,357,281
Maryland	148	164	15,664	11,893	17,740	2,058,069
Massachusetts	159	189	16,376	6,016	9,402	516,536
Michigan	1,020	1,145	165,896	52,977	77,320	10,111,573
Minnesota	599	694	173,808	80,694	111,794	27,472,772
Mississippi	488	563	120,484	37,104	50,069	10,500,522
Missouri	918	1,035	231,675	106,023	153,143	29,788,866
Montana	420	480	829,630	27,066	40,669	55,645,998
Nebraska	403	440	483,821	49,262	69,393	45,856,918
Nevada	175	198	190,857	2,896	4,605	5,170,392

(continued on next page)

Table 8.05: Farms and Operators by State, 2002

	Hispanic Operators			White Operators		
	Farms	Operators	Land in Farms	Farms	Operators	Land in Farms
United States	*61,094*	*72,349*	*28,025,352*	*2,077,656*	*2,966,230*	*883,755,206*
New Hampshire	65	77	8,598	3,334	5,339	441,164
New Jersey	210	239	9,721	9,781	14,715	796,328
New Mexico	4,891	6,039	5,009,435	14,732	21,219	37,459,047
New York	537	604	79,257	37,026	55,896	7,637,736
North Carolina	739	780	156,601	51,705	71,052	8,830,220
North Dakota	180	201	164,636	30,418	40,761	38,782,289
Ohio	942	1,048	153,565	77,387	110,563	14,536,960
Oklahoma	1,870	2,069	495,932	78,451	108,877	32,453,807
Oregon	1,392	1,612	330,022	39,401	62,551	16,272,697
Pennsylvania	494	550	64,699	57,922	84,577	7,727,960
Rhode Island	29	29	3,210	857	1,263	60,873
South Carolina	343	373	57,364	22,592	30,303	4,647,856
South Dakota	302	330	295,370	31,177	43,728	40,846,450
Tennessee	836	927	93,363	86,268	118,922	11,556,118
Texas	17,314	20,988	7,679,717	221,687	317,543	128,788,032
Utah	419	499	151,207	15,174	22,850	7,416,128
Vermont	171	187	29,062	6,543	10,376	1,240,975
Virginia	527	586	107,886	45,906	65,793	8,403,996
Washington	1,551	1,821	361,068	35,268	53,209	12,827,510
West Virginia	218	255	29,037	20,750	28,946	3,574,692
Wisconsin	650	717	117,552	76,928	115,193	15,717,963
Wyoming	357	408	1,221,084	9,286	14,934	32,971,414

Source: U.S. Bureau of the Census, 2002 Census of Agriculture, Vol. 1 *Geographic Area Series, Part 51, US Summary and State Data*, tables 41 and 50.

Notes: Data was collected, by race of operator, with a maximum of 3 operators per farm.

Units: Number of farms and operators; land in acres.

Table 8.06: Farms and Operators by State, 2007

	Hispanic Operators			White Operators		
	Farms	Operators	Land in Farms	Farms	Operators	Land in Farms
United States	*66,671*	*82,462*	*24,600,997*	*2,128,341*	*3,140,754*	*869,916,383*
Alabama	368	407	57,595	45,412	64,715	8,690,034
Alaska	13	13	3,412	660	1,041	567,359
Arizona	1,006	1,293	345,803	7,152	11,355	5,327,179
Arkansas	567	651	120,255	47,343	70,503	13,599,296
California	11,294	14,199	2,325,047	76,211	117,665	24,478,029
Colorado	2,182	2,610	1,004,784	36,519	58,004	31,356,398
Connecticut	84	100	4,080	4,862	7,579	402,976
Delaware	34	35	1,643	2,488	3,767	506,472
Florida	3,662	4,869	438,041	45,203	67,569	9,058,660
Georgia	484	547	102,925	45,369	64,084	9,884,695
Hawaii	539	622	44,225	3,981	5,445	623,373
Idaho	788	929	263,444	25,065	38,804	10,923,421
Illinois	466	553	83,617	76,410	108,345	26,671,675
Indiana	320	362	51,684	60,674	89,356	14,723,199
Iowa	491	551	143,221	92,691	133,506	30,703,559
Kansas	680	780	435,086	65,041	94,707	46,154,779
Kentucky	525	594	78,357	84,112	120,608	13,857,080
Louisiana	492	570	82,162	28,062	39,999	7,931,789
Maine	68	75	6,483	8,064	12,616	1,335,554
Maryland	132	144	15,131	12,532	19,190	2,032,116
Massachusetts	155	198	7,699	7,584	11,787	515,394
Michigan	794	937	102,546	55,291	82,180	9,938,307
Minnesota	440	507	141,104	80,571	116,149	26,800,831
Mississippi	537	599	141,575	36,769	52,218	10,882,133
Missouri	691	736	140,170	106,746	158,187	28,860,944
Montana	297	345	502,722	28,115	43,432	57,493,666
Nebraska	254	288	234,044	47,635	70,502	45,440,306
Nevada	222	260	120,859	2,754	4,420	5,380,200

(continued on next page)

Table 8.06: Farms and Operators by State, 2007

	Hispanic Operators			White Operators		
	Farms	Operators	Land in Farms	Farms	Operators	Land in Farms
New Hampshire	29	35	2,923	4,144	6,717	469,363
New Jersey	182	207	5,177	10,169	15,599	725,945
New Mexico	6,861	8,904	6,232,408	16,368	24,214	36,792,785
New York	328	387	41,097	36,057	56,127	7,132,522
North Carolina	648	738	114,635	50,779	72,262	8,272,825
North Dakota	136	142	228,772	31,606	43,990	39,182,481
Ohio	420	468	69,642	75,547	111,199	13,921,352
Oklahoma	1,104	1,218	318,686	79,048	113,236	33,251,539
Oregon	1,182	1,330	476,530	37,788	61,071	15,792,550
Pennsylvania	454	526	35,962	62,824	92,077	7,771,055
Rhode Island	11	11	1,402	1,198	1,834	67,640
South Carolina	243	277	33,315	23,560	33,261	4,691,625
South Dakota	171	196	224,207	30,453	44,507	40,624,207
Tennessee	642	733	55,316	77,753	112,248	10,813,132
Texas	22,797	28,921	7,261,904	238,436	350,456	128,702,181
Utah	409	473	257,291	16,024	24,369	7,243,497
Vermont	84	94	13,769	6,946	11,050	1,230,099
Virginia	495	551	81,867	45,425	66,911	7,878,628
Washington	2,115	2,604	390,317	38,366	59,947	12,444,778
West Virginia	174	205	21,465	23,529	34,089	3,684,378
Wisconsin	379	412	56,423	78,157	120,197	15,156,499
Wyoming	222	256	1,680,175	10,848	17,660	29,927,878

Source: U.S. Bureau of the Census, 2007 Census of Agriculture, Vol. 1 *Geographic Area Series, Part 51, U.S. Summary and State Data*, tables 50 and 55.

Notes: Data was collected for farms with a maximum of 3 operators, by race of operator.

Units: Number of farms and operators, Land in acres.

Table 8.07: Hispanic-Owned Firms by Major Industry Group, 1992

	All Firms		Firms with Paid Employees			
	Firms	Sales & Receipts	Firms	Sales & Receipts	Employees	Annual Payroll
All industries	*771,708*	*$72,824,270*	*115,364*	*$57,187,370*	*691,056*	*$10,768,112*
Agricultural services, forestry and fishing	31,600	1,464,572	3,985	935,079	19,174	233,781
Mining	1,327	304,926	194	250,485	1,527	33,555
Construction	97,476	8,212,208	20,192	6,447,317	76,882	1,417,290
Manufacturing	18,461	6,157,555	5,209	5,827,194	65,920	1,280,030
Transportation and public utilities	47,797	3,702,744	5,100	2,373,189	35,484	606,617
Wholesale trade	17,727	12,489,034	5,434	11,687,451	37,547	859,658
Retail trade	107,846	17,730,517	27,641	15,116,613	197,626	2,001,152
Finance, insurance, and real estate	49,231	4,831,923	5,087	2,774,196	23,177	472,149
Services	347,297	16,787,257	40,863	11,558,361	231,977	3,836,093
Industries not classified	52,945	1,143,533	1,660	217,485	1,743	27,787

Source: U.S. Bureau of the Census, 1992 Economic Census, *Survey of Minority-Owned Business Enterprises: Hispanic*, table 1.

Notes: 'All firms' includes firms with paid employees and firms with no paid employees. 'Firms with paid employees' indicates firms that file payroll taxes.

Units: Number of firms and employees; sales, receipts, and annual payroll in thousands of dollars.

Table 8.08: Minority-Owned Businesses, 1997

	Hispanic	All Minorities	All Firms in US
All firms	1,199,896	3,039,033	20,821,935
Sales & receipts	$186,274,582	$591,259,123	$18,553,243,047
Firms with paid employees	211,884	615,222	5,295,152
Sales & receipts	$158,674,537	$516,979,920	$17,907,940,321
Employees	1,388,746	4,514,699	103,359,815
Annual payroll	$29,830,028	$95,528,782	$2,936,492,940

Source: U.S. Bureau of the Census, 1997 Economic Census, *Survey of Minority-Owned Business Enterprises*, printed from www.census.gov/epcd/mwb97/us/us.html on July 14, 2006.

Notes: 'All firms' includes firms with paid employees and firms with no paid employees. 'Firms with paid employees' indicates firms that file payroll taxes.

Units: Number of firms and employees; sales, receipts, and annual payroll in thousands of dollars.

Table 8.09: Hispanic-Owned Firms by Major Industry Group, 1997

	All Firms		Firms with Paid Employees			
	Firms	Sales & Receipts	Firms	Sales & Receipts	Employees	Annual Payroll
All industries	*1,199,896*	*$186,274,582*	*211,884*	*$158,674,537*	*1,388,746*	*$29,830,028*
Agricultural services, forestry and fishing	40,040	2,279,397	5,925	1,309,733	25,955	416,702
Mining	1,909	429,446	325	367,442	3,569	97,854
Construction	152,573	21,923,384	31,478	19,146,212	168,873	4,218,419
Manufacturing	25,552	28,684,759	10,173	27,719,404	171,738	4,549,598
Transportation and public utilities	84,554	8,293,935	12,735	5,605,332	79,682	1,587,106
Wholesale trade	31,480	40,386,625	14,125	38,746,137	94,281	2,388,988
Retail trade	155,061	32,280,310	48,713	28,599,447	324,474	3,892,182
Finance, insurance, and real estate	56,629	6,644,826	9,944	4,728,312	34,783	949,006
Services	500,449	39,177,767	70,838	30,406,573	463,889	11,297,362
Industries not classified	151,931	6,174,133	7,909	2,045,945	21,502	432,812

Source: U.S. Bureau of the Census, 1997 Economic Census, *Survey of Minority-Owned Business Enterprises*, printed from www.census.gov/epcd/mwb97/us/us.html on July 14, 2006.

Notes: 'All firms' includes firms with paid employees and firms with no paid employees. 'Firms with paid employees' indicates firms that file payroll taxes.

Units: Number of firms and employees; sales, receipts, and annual payroll in thousands of dollars.

Table 8.10: Hispanic-Owned Firms by Ethnic Group, 1997

	All Firms		Firms with Paid Employees			
	Firms	**Sales & Receipts**	**Firms**	**Sales & Receipts**	**Employees**	**Annual Payroll**
Total Hispanic	*1,199,896*	*$186,274,582*	*211,884*	*$158,674,537*	*1,388,746*	*$29,830,028*
Cuban	125,273	26,492,208	30,203	23,873,193	176,428	4,162,640
Mexican, Mexican American, or Chicano	472,033	73,706,753	90,755	62,270,808	695,372	13,014,996
Puerto Rican	69,658	7,461,069	10,976	5,814,069	61,509	1,496,640
Spaniard	57,160	16,922,913	12,590	15,263,807	76,338	2,045,675
Hispanic Latin American	287,314	40,997,923	42,916	34,798,421	238,612	5,862,668
Other Hispanic	188,458	20,693,715	24,445	16,654,239	140,487	3,247,154

Source: US Bureau of the Census, 1997 Economic Census, *Survey of Minority-Owned Business Enterprises*, printed from www.census.gov/epcd/mwb97/us/us.html on July 14, 2006.

Notes: 'All firms' includes firms with paid employees and firms with no paid employees. 'Firms with paid employees' indicates firms that file payroll taxes.

Units: Number of firms and employees; sales, receipts, and annual payroll in thousands of dollars.

Table 8.11: Minority-Owned Businesses, 2002

	Hispanic	All Minorities	All Firms in US
All firms	1,573,600	19,894,823	22,977,164
Sales & receipts	$221,976,823	$8,303,716,399	$22,634,870,406
Firms with paid employees	199,601	4,712,168	5,526,111
Sales & receipts	$179,556,102	$7,629,211,216	$21,867,386,411
Employees	1,537,801	52,209,027	110,832,682
Annual payroll	$36,733,799	$1,548,757,745	$3,815,069,400

Source: U.S. Bureau of the Census, 2002 Economic Census, *Survey of Business Owners: Hispanic-Owned Firms, 2002* (SB02-00CS-HISP), table 2.

Notes: 'All firms' includes firms with paid employees and firms with no paid employees. 'Firms with paid employees' indicates firms that file payroll taxes.

Units: Number of firms and employees; sales, receipts, and annual payroll in thousands of dollars.

Table 8.12: Hispanic-Owned Firms by Receipts Size, 2002

	All Firms		Firms with Paid Employees			
	Firms	**Sales & Receipts**	**Firms**	**Sales & Receipts**	**Employees**	**Annual Payroll**
All firms	*1,573,600*	*$221,976,823*	*199,601*	*$179,556,102*	*1,537,801*	*$36,733,799*
Less than $5,000	327,851	813,516	1,936	5,478	1,511	79,113
$5,000 to $9,999	301,223	2,064,981	2,933	20,527	1,944	27,691
$10,000 to $24,999	390,932	5,864,973	8,994	155,736	6,402	56,910
$25,000 to $49,999	190,160	6,550,503	15,279	570,888	15,593	159,535
$50,000 to $99,999	138,091	9,725,664	28,767	2,108,651	39,924	533,577
$100,000 to $249,999	112,257	17,481,073	50,678	8,341,111	129,492	2,072,115
$250,000 to $499,999	51,208	17,909,313	36,529	12,907,163	175,666	3,323,380
$500,000 to $999,999	32,694	22,819,305	26,336	18,454,542	228,671	4,900,931
$1,000,000 or more	29,184	138,747,497	28,149	136,992,007	938,599	25,580,548

Source: U.S. Bureau of the Census, 2002 Economic Census, *Survey of Business Owners: Hispanic-Owned Firms, 2002* (SB02-00CS-HISP), table 8.

Notes: 'All firms' includes firms with paid employees and firms with no paid employees. 'Firms with paid employees' indicates firms that file payroll taxes.

Units: Number of firms and employees; sales, receipts, and annual payroll in thousands of dollars.

Table 8.13: Hispanic-Owned Firms by Employment Size, 2002

	Firms	Receipts	Employees	Annual Payroll
All firms	*199,601*	*$179,556,102*	*1,537,801*	*$36,733,799*
No employees	36,765	6,692,253	NA	1,150,889
1 to 4 employees	99,611	23,300,879	202,022	4,568,175
5 to 9 employees	31,498	26,619,230	205,329	4,959,432
10 to 19 employees	18,406	26,973,834	247,761	5,706,638
20 to 49 employees	9,021	29,474,968	267,397	6,390,144
50 to 99 employees	2,790	19,461,192	185,058	4,821,274
100 to 499 employees	1,327	27,218,362	243,972	5,903,075
500 employees or more	183	14,815,385	186,261	3,234,174

Source: U.S. Bureau of the Census, 2002 Economic Census, *Survey of Business Owners: Hispanic-Owned Firms, 2002* (SB02-00CS-HISP), table 9.

Units: Number of firms and employees; sales, receipts, and annual payroll in thousands of dollars.

Table 8.14: Hispanic-Owned Firms by Major Industry Group, 2002

	All Firms		Firms with Paid Employees			
	Firms	Sales & Receipts	Firms	Sales & Receipts	Employees	Annual Payroll
All industries	*1,573,600*	*$221,976,823*	*199,601*	*$179,556,102*	*1,537,801*	*$36,733,799*
Agricultural services, forestry and fishing	9,710	1,303,614	1,156	1,086,655	40,782	442,650
Mining	1,473	718,895	280	669,200	3,142	108,175
Utilities	717	41,459	25	26,687	110	2,079
Construction	212,496	31,439,374	25,139	22,655,674	190,076	5,279,187
Manufacturing	30,948	18,002,370	10,360	17,282,952	125,620	3,746,195
Wholesale trade	34,188	39,337,551	12,432	37,517,653	86,446	2,833,676
Retail trade	151,501	40,466,216	25,958	35,552,989	156,598	3,273,636
Transportation & warehousing	125,750	10,616,280	8,882	5,568,354	54,011	1,338,022
Information	14,516	2,294,001	1,895	1,934,471	13,247	564,919
Finance & insurance	33,282	5,066,488	6,536	3,930,287	24,301	886,627
Professional, scientific & technical services	138,345	15,011,043	19,360	11,523,005	98,418	4,164,421
Health care & social assistance	181,677	13,757,965	20,206	11,208,335	140,477	4,236,792
Services	249,277	10,083,095	19,333	5,328,725	73,720	1,486,277
Industries not classified	1,166	250,584	1,166	250,584	1,517	39,486

Source: U.S. Bureau of the Census, 2002 Economic Census, *Survey of Business Owners: Hispanic-Owned Firms, 2002* (SB02-00CS-HISP), table 2.

Notes: 'All firms' includes firms with paid employees and firms with no paid employees. 'Firms with paid employees' indicates firms that file payroll taxes.

Units: Number of firms and employees; sales, receipts, and annual payroll in thousands of dollars.

Table 8.15: Hispanic-Owned Firms by State, 2002

	All Firms		Firms with Paid Employees			
	Firms	Sales & Receipts	Firms	Sales & Receipts	Employees	Annual Payroll
United States	*1,573,600*	*$221,976,823*	*199,601*	*$179,556,102*	*1,537,801*	*$36,733,799*
Alabama	2,523	740,823	669	659,155	6,698	188,848
Alaska	1,241	171,157	287	149,787	1,985	44,305
Arizona	35,104	4,294,983	5,019	3,434,613	39,363	818,270
Arkansas	2,094	373,797	418	315,842	3,198	63,526
California	427,727	57,169,934	47,615	44,944,183	445,831	9,827,436
Colorado	24,054	5,113,632	4,075	4,465,665	32,465	807,423
Connecticut	9,408	1,276,773	1,281	1,049,725	8,762	224,179
Delaware	879	137,396	142	102,882	960	24,636
District of Columbia	2,162	542,045	424	501,397	3,930	131,383
Florida	266,727	40,894,829	39,956	33,381,832	222,536	5,869,453
Georgia	18,310	4,200,106	2,634	3,466,028	20,412	510,638
Hawaii	3,095	482,647	482	415,895	3,655	98,092
Idaho	2,775	351,849	601	285,941	3,149	65,508
Illinois	39,542	7,401,018	6,577	6,423,606	60,615	1,554,897
Indiana	5,481	786,807	892	646,638	5,824	158,826
Iowa	1,536	288,558	363	250,953	2,956	54,728
Kansas	4,188	674,029	877	570,481	7,585	130,636
Kentucky	2,094	769,587	NA	NA	NA	NA
Louisiana	7,465	1,945,436	1,280	1,755,728	16,319	394,122
Maine	731	112,848	108	92,939	637	15,838
Maryland	15,353	2,398,373	2,086	1,951,452	18,751	599,624
Massachusetts	15,922	2,067,954	2,011	1,647,964	15,319	453,030
Michigan	9,842	3,198,617	1,678	2,990,172	16,021	544,571
Minnesota	3,984	462,777	643	361,805	4,596	97,826
Mississippi	1,326	213,286	256	169,367	2,080	36,739
Missouri	3,652	682,032	722	603,090	5,507	158,942
Montana	964	99,073	NA	NA	NA	NA
Nebraska	1,966	433,790	378	388,387	2,862	63,161
Nevada	9,740	1,638,106	1,342	1,339,407	12,874	332,603

(continued on next page)

Table 8.15: Hispanic-Owned Firms by State, 2002

	All Firms		Firms with Paid Employees			
	Firms	Sales & Receipts	Firms	Sales & Receipts	Employees	Annual Payroll
United States	*1,573,600*	*$221,976,823*	*199,601*	*$179,556,102*	*1,537,801*	*$36,733,799*
New Hampshire	913	194,013	206	160,854	1,742	45,474
New Jersey	49,841	7,245,041	7,533	5,963,794	40,422	1,118,468
New Mexico	29,708	4,678,131	5,204	4,012,036	44,896	891,461
New York	163,639	12,381,637	13,529	9,403,517	70,912	1,929,583
North Carolina	9,043	1,789,068	1,726	1,444,132	11,615	297,825
North Dakota	230	15,855	42	13,242	210	4,566
Ohio	7,109	1,263,422	1,345	1,089,911	11,348	270,941
Oklahoma	5,442	1,140,368	945	1,002,000	8,161	155,622
Oregon	6,360	1,416,236	1,295	1,272,226	8,272	215,581
Pennsylvania	11,023	1,740,151	1,639	1,444,267	10,111	298,186
Rhode Island	3,415	213,718	298	127,479	1,185	27,724
South Carolina	3,015	691,372	681	614,690	5,584	129,794
South Dakota	355	121,877	98	110,634	660	20,422
Tennessee	4,301	1,004,389	885	886,423	7,995	201,715
Texas	319,339	42,191,719	34,398	32,944,672	280,147	6,192,845
Utah	5,177	555,077	895	441,759	5,251	99,301
Vermont	452	37,983	65	29,121	229	5,207
Virginia	18,988	3,453,430	2,430	2,899,027	29,292	799,681
Washington	10,262	1,537,714	2,353	1,319,241	15,852	323,552
West Virginia	648	187,326	248	168,018	1,395	41,136
Wisconsin	3,750	975,457	869	887,415	9,011	243,761
Wyoming	1,320	220,578	315	203,152	3,604	48,560

Source: U.S. Bureau of the Census, 2002 Economic Census, *Survey of Business Owners: Hispanic-Owned Firms, 2002* (SB02-00CS-HISP), table 2.

Notes: 'All firms' includes firms with paid employees and firms with no paid employees. 'Firms with paid employees' indicates firms that file payroll taxes.

Units: Number of firms and employees; sales, receipts, and annual payroll in thousands of dollars.

Table 8.16: Hispanic-Owned Firms by Ethnic Group, 2002

	All Firms		Firms with Paid Employees			
	Firms	Sales & Receipts	Firms	Sales & Receipts	Employees	Annual Payroll
Total Hispanic	*1,573,600*	*$221,976,823*	*199,601*	*$179,556,102*	*1,537,801*	*$36,733,799*
Mexican, Mexican American, or Chicano	698,314	96,534,742	88,943	77,232,402	718,578	15,883,011
Puerto Rican	109,180	12,322,222	11,790	9,567,000	77,150	2,107,133
Cuban	151,614	35,447,828	27,812	30,904,660	206,016	5,928,664
Other Hispanic	599,225	74,455,186	67,807	59,301,349	506,179	12,121,269

Source: U.S. Bureau of the Census, 2002 Economic Census, *Survey of Business Owners: Hispanic-Owned Firms, 2002* (SB02-00CS-HISP), table 3.

Notes: 'All firms' includes firms with paid employees and firms with no paid employees. 'Firms with paid employees' indicates firms that file payroll taxes.

Units: Number of firms and employees; sales, receipts, and annual payroll in thousands of dollars.

Table 8.17: Small Business Administration Loans to Minority-Owned Small Businesses, 2000–2007

	Hispanic-Owned	Total Minority
2000		
Number of loans	3,500	11,999
Amount	$761	$3,634
2002		
Number of loans	4,272	14,304
Amount	$885	$4,228
2003		
Number of loans	6,112	20,183
Amount	$942	$4,215
2004		
Number of loans	7,686	25,413
Amount	$1,151	$5,144
2005		
Number of loans	8,796	29,722
Amount	$1,325	$6,132
2006		
Number of loans	11,215	33,780
Amount	$1,561	$6,607
2007		
Number of loans	11,049	36,320
Amount	$1,482	$6,852

Source: U.S. Census Bureau, *Statistical Abstract of the United States, 2009*, table 743.

Notes: 'Small Businesses' must be independently owned and operated, must not be dominant in their particular industries, and must meet standards set by the Small Business Administration for annual receipts or number of employees.

Units: Number of loans; total amount in millions of dollars.

Table 8.18: Summary of Results of the 2000 Consumer Expenditure Survey

	Hispanic Consumer Units	White Consumer Units	All Consumer Units
Number of consumer units	*9,473*	*96,137*	*109,367*
Average income before taxes	$34,891	$46,260	$44,649
Percent homeowners	47%	68%	66%
Average number in consumer unit:			
Persons	3.4	2.5	2.5
Children under 18 years old	1.2	0.6	0.7
Persons 65 and over	0.2	0.3	0.3
Earners	1.6	1.4	1.4
Vehicles	1.6	2.0	1.9
Average annual expenditures			
Total expenditures	*$32,735*	*$39,406*	*$38,045*
Food	5,362	5,304	5,158
Food at home	3,496	3,066	3,021
Cereals and bakery products	491	462	453
Meats, poultry, fish, and eggs	1,036	780	795
Dairy products	359	336	325
Fruits and vegetables	670	530	521
Other food at home	940	959	927
Food away from home	1,865	2,238	2,137
Alcoholic beverages	285	394	372
Housing	10,850	12,651	12,319
Shelter	6,437	7,312	7,114
Owned dwellings	2,949	4,877	4,602
Rented dwellings	3,307	1,923	2,034
Other lodging	181	512	478
Utilities, fuels and public services	2,170	2,478	2,489
Household operations	465	714	684
Housekeeping supplies	474	507	482
Household furnishings and equipment	1,303	1,640	1,549
Apparel and services	2,076	1,878	1,856

(continued on next page)

Table 8.18: Summary of Results of the 2000 Consumer Expenditure Survey

	Hispanic Consumer Units	White Consumer Units	All Consumer Units
Average annual expenditures (continued)			
Transportation	$6,719	$7,721	$7,417
Vehicle purchases	3,146	3,574	3,418
Gasoline and motor oil	1,244	1,337	1,291
Other vehicle expenses	1,945	2,361	2,281
Public transportation	385	448	427
Health care	1,243	2,198	2,066
Entertainment	1,186	1,980	1,863
Personal care products and services	564	555	564
Reading	59	157	146
Education	363	666	632
Tobacco products and smoking supplies	173	329	319
Miscellaneous	602	804	776
Cash contributions	645	1,260	1,192
Personal insurance and pensions	2,608	3,510	3,365
Life and other personal insurance	189	404	399
Pensions and Social Security	2,420	3,105	2,966

Source: U.S. Department of Labor, Bureau of Labor Statistics, *Consumer Expenditure Survey, 2000*, table 7.

Notes: 'Consumer units' are defined as either: a) members of a household related by blood, marriage, or adoption, b) a single person living alone or with others, but who is financially independent, or c) two or more people living together who share responsibility for at least 2 of the 3 major types of expenses - food, housing, and other expenses. Students living in university-sponsored housing are also considered separate consumer units. 'All consumer units' includes consumer units of all races.

Units: Number of consumer units in thousands; average numbers as shown; average annual expenditures in current dollars.

Table 8.19: Summary of Results of the 2007 Consumer Expenditure Survey

	Hispanic Consumer Units	White Consumer Units	All Consumer Units
Number of consumer units	*14,185*	*101,509*	*120,171*
Income before taxes	$48,330	$65,023	$63,091
Age of reference person	42.5	49.4	48.8
Average number in consumer unit:			
Persons	3.2	2.4	2.5
Children under 18 years old	1.1	0.6	0.6
Persons 65 and over	0.2	0.3	0.3
Earners	1.6	1.3	1.3
Vehicles	1.6	2.0	1.9
Percent of reference persons who are:			
Homeowners	51%	70%	67%
High school diploma only	42	34	35
College graduates	37	60	60
Average annual expenditures			
Total	$41,501	$51,120	$49,638
Food	5,933	6,312	6,133
Food at home	3,424	3,539	3,465
Cereals and bakery products	410	473	460
Meats, poultry, fish, and eggs	890	760	777
Dairy products	368	407	387
Fruits and vegetables	652	610	600
Other food at home	1,104	1,290	1,241
Food away from home	2,508	2,773	2,668
Alcoholic beverages	262	499	457
Housing	15,573	17,169	16,920
Shelter	9,794	10,074	10,023
Owned dwellings	5,419	6,950	6,730
Rented dwellings	4,135	2,389	2,602
Other lodging	239	736	691
Utilities, fuels and public services	3,274	3,476	3,477
Household operations	681	1,029	984
Housekeeping supplies	571	680	639
Household furnishings and equipment	1,253	1,910	1,797
Apparel and services	1,994	1,869	1,881

(continued on next page)

Table 8.19: Summary of Results of the 2007 Consumer Expenditure Survey

	Hispanic Consumer Units	White Consumer Units	All Consumer Units
Average annual expenditures (continued)			
Transportation	8,035	8,996	8,758
Vehicle purchases	2,876	3,357	3,244
Gasoline and motor oil	2,304	2,447	2,384
Other vehicle expenses	2,525	2,662	2,592
Public transportation	330	530	538
Health care	1,486	3,046	2,853
Entertainment	1,674	2,908	2,698
Personal care products and services	526	603	588
Reading	38	129	118
Education	415	952	945
Tobacco products and smoking supplies	165	346	323
Miscellaneous	478	861	808
Cash contributions	1,083	1,899	1,821
Personal insurance and pensions	3,837	5,531	5,336
Life and other personal insurance	109	317	309
Pensions and Social Security	3,729	5,214	5,027

Source: U.S. Department of Labor, Bureau of Labor Statistics, *Consumer Expenditure Survey, 2007*, table 2200.

Notes: 'Consumer units' are defined as either: a) members of a household related by blood, marriage, or adoption, b) a single person living alone or with others, but who is financially independent, or c) two or more people living together who share responsibility for at least 2 of the 3 major types of expenses - food, housing, and other expenses. Students living in university-sponsored housing are also considered separate consumer units. 'All consumer units' includes consumer units of all races. 'White' includes Native Hawaiian and other Pacific Islander, American Indian or Alaska Native, and approximately 1.2 percent reporting more than one race.

Units: Number of consumer units in thousands, average numbers and percentages as shown, average annual expenditures in current dollars.

Guide to Sources

Note: All URLs are valid and accessible as of July 18, 2009. Whenever possible, we have provided a general web address that should still be available when the data sources update, but some sources may move, and the URLs given below may be inaccessible at a later date. Several sources are annual reports and in cases where multiple editions of the report were used, only the most recent edition is cited here. Further details on which editions were used can be found in the **Source** section of individual tables. In addition, several sources are used in multiple chapters. For example, the *Statistical Abstract of the United States* is used as a source throughout this book. In these cases, sources are listed under the most relevant chapter.

Chapter 1: Demographics & Social Characteristics

America's Families and Living Arrangements: 2008, US Bureau of the Census, Current Population Reports.

Containing information drawn from the Annual Social and Economic Supplement, this report presents a variety of information on marriage and families in the US, including marital status, presence or absence of children, children's custodial arrangements, household and family size, and family types. It also contains breakdowns by a variety of other factors, including race and Hispanic origin, employment, health insurance coverage, poverty status, and educational attainment. Prior to 1999, the report was known as *Marital Status and Living Arrangements*. Accessible at http://www.census.gov/population/www/socdemo/hh-fam.html

American Community Survey 2007, US Bureau of the Census.

The American Community Survey (ACS) is a major program conducted by the Census Bureau that collects a monthly sample of the entire US population, including information that was previously only collected in the long form of the Decennial Census. Each month, the ACS sends out surveys to approximately three million household units. Currently, the ACS provides data on a statewide and nationwide level, as well as for all cities and counties with populations 20,000 people, and by 2010, the Census Bureau hopes to provide data for all places, replacing the long form of the Decennial Census. The ACS is already beginning to take precedence over many of the topics covered by the Current Population Survey (CPS) program, due to its much larger sample size and considerable overlap in subject matter. The ACS contains data on population and demographics, as well as labor, unemployment, income, poverty, and a wide variety of other topics. Readers should be cautioned when comparing ACS data to data from other Census programs (such as the CPS), as the groups surveyed may differ. For example, prior to the 2006 edition, the ACS measured only the civilian noninstitutional population. Accessible at http://www.census.gov/acs/www/index.html

The Hispanic Population in the United States, 2006, US Bureau of the Census, Current Population Survey.

This annual report from the CPS is the major source of data on the Hispanic population in the United States, and one of the few sources to provide a breakdown by Hispanic ethnic groups (e.g., Mexican, Puerto Rican, or Cuban). The Hispanic Population in the United States provides data on population, family and household characteristics, income and poverty, employment and labor force status, educational attainment. In addition, this report is the source for data in several other chapters in this book. Accessible at http://www.census.gov/population/www/socdemo/hispanic/tables.html

Married-Couple and Unmarried-Partner Households: 2000, US Bureau of the Census, Special Tabulation from Census 2000 Data.

This report, taken from Census 2000 data, reflects the increasing amount of attention paid by the Census Bureau to unmarried-couple households, including (for the first time) data on households composed of same-sex partners. As more unmarried couples begin to maintain households, the Census Bureau will collect and publish more data on them. More data on same-sex households is also expected to be collected and published by the Census Bureau in the years to come. Accessible at http://www.census.gov/prod/2003pubs/censr-5.pdf

Population Estimates, US Bureau of the Census.

The Census Bureau's Population Estimates program publishes annual estimates of the total population for the nation, states, counties, cities and towns, and other Census-designated places. It also includes data on social and demographic characteristics (such as age, sex, race, and Hispanic origin). The annual estimates are used as input for a variety of calculations and estimates by other programs inside and outside the federal government. Population Estimates data is accessible at the following URLs:

Main page:	http://www.census.gov/popest/estimates.php
National estimates:	http://www.census.gov/popest/states/NST-ann-est.html
State estimates:	http://www.census.gov/popest/states/
Race and Hispanic origin:	http://www.census.gov/popest/race.html
Components of change:	http://www.census.gov/popest/states/NST-comp-chg.html

Projections of the Resident Population by Race, Hispanic Origin, and Nativity, Middle Series, 1999 to 2100; and US Interim Projections by Age, Sex, Race, and Hispanic Origin, 2000-2050, US Bureau of the Census, Population Projections Division.

The Census Bureau periodically releases projections for future populations and demographic characteristics, based on current population counts and trends in migration and fertility rates. The 1990 Decennial Census was used to provide projections for 1999 to 2100. In 2004, the Census Bureau released an interim update based on the results of the 2000 Census. Readers should note that none of the projections take into account events that have occurred since their release. Accessible at http://www.census.gov/population/www/projections/natsum.html and http://www.census.gov/ipc/www/usinterimproj, respectively.

Statistical Abstract of the United States, 2009. US Bureau of the Census.

The *Statistical Abstract* is the summary publication for all the data collected by the Census Bureau, as well as the government's other programs, and collectively presents a thorough profile of the United States and its population, economy, and government. The *Abstract* contains information on just about every possible topic, and is a useful place to start any research project. Each chapter in this book draws some of its information from the *Abstract*. Available at http://www.census.gov/compendia/statab/

Who's Minding the Kids? Child Care Arrangements: Spring 2005, US Bureau of the Census, Current Population Reports.

This CPS report draws from the Survey of Income and Program Participation and is released approximately every 3 years. It contains a wide range of information about child care, including the distribution of care (types of relatives, as well as nonrelatives) and the weekly expenditures on care, both overall and as a percent of the family's income. Accessible at http://www.census.gov/population/www/socdemo/childcare.html

Chapter 2: Health

Abortion Surveillance in the United States-2004, US Department of Health and Human Services, Centers for Disease Control and Prevention, Morbidity and Mortality Weekly Report.

This report contains the annual results of the CDC's surveillance of abortions performed (number and rate), as well as characteristics of the women obtaining them. Note that several states do not report abortion data, so the report is based on an incomplete data set. Accessible at http://www.cdc.gov/mmwr/preview/mmwrhtml/ss5609a1.htm

Births: Final Data for 2006, US Department of Health and Human Services, Centers for Disease Control and Prevention, National Center for Health Statistics, National Vital Statistics System.

This report contains the final (processed) birth statistics for 2005. Released through the CDC's National Vital Statistics Reports, it is accessible at http://www.cdc.gov/nchs/data/nvsr/nvsr57/nvsr57_07.pdf, or through the NCHS at http://www.cdc.gov/nchs/births.htm

Births: Preliminary Data for 2007, US Department of Health and Human Services, Centers for Disease Control and Prevention, National Center for Health Statistics, National Vital Statistics System.

This report contains the preliminary birth statistics for 2007. Note that this data is considered less reliable than the forthcoming final estimates, and figures may be adjusted in that report. Released through the CDC's National Vital Statistics Reports, it is accessible at, http://www.cdc.gov/nchs/data/nvsr/nvsr57/nvsr57_12.pdf or through the NCHS at http://www.cdc.gov/nchs/births.htm

Cases of HIV Infection and AIDS in the United States, by Race/Ethnicity, 2002-2006, US Department of Health and Human Services, Centers for Disease Control, HIV/AIDS Statistics and Surveillance.

This supplement to the annual reports on HIV/AIDS surveillance contains estimates of AIDS cases, including data on how HIV was transmitted and the race/ethnicity of persons with HIV/AIDS. It includes data for the years between 2000 and 2004, and totals dating back to the start of the epidemic. Accessible at http://www.cdc.gov/hiv/topics/surveillance/resources/reports/2008supp_vol13no1/default.htm, or at the main HIV surveillance page at http://www.cdc.gov/hiv/topics/surveillance/index.htm

Deaths: Final Data for 2006, US Department of Health and Human Services, Centers for Disease Control and Prevention, National Center for Health Statistics, National Vital Statistics System.

This report contains the final (processed) death statistics for 2005. Released through the CDC's National Vital Statistics Reports, it is accessible at http://www.cdc.gov/nchs/data/nvsr/nvsr56/nvsr56_10.pdf, or through the NCHS at http://www.cdc.gov/nchs/deaths.htm

Health, United States, 2008, US Department of Health and Human Services, Centers for Disease Control and Prevention, National Center for Health Statistics.

Health, United States is the annual report published by the CDC's National Center for Health Statistics, and serves as a clearinghouse for the Agency's various data-collection programs. It includes excerpts from the National Health Interview Survey (NHIS), the National Vital Statistics System, and other programs from the National Center for Health Statistics (NCHS), as well as programs outside the CDC that collect data relevant to health. With several hundred pages of data covering a wide range of topics, *Health, United States* should be the first step in any search for health data. In addition, tables in the PDF report include links to Excel spreadsheets, which often include more extensive (and often more current) data than that given in the PDF. Accessible at http://www.cdc.gov/nchs/hus.htm

Summary Statistics for the US Population: National Health Interview Survey, 2007, US Department of Health and Human Services, Centers for Disease Control and Prevention, National Center for Health Statistics.

The National Health Interview Survey (NHIS) is the CDC's main source of information on the health of the civilian noninstitutionalized population of the United States. It is an annual survey with a sample size of approximately 35,000 households and 87,500 individuals. This report gives a summary of the overall results of the National Health Interview Survey; several other reports are also available. Accessible through the main NHIS page at http://www.cdc.gov/nchs/nhis.htm

Summary Statistics for US Adults: National Health Interview Survey, 2007, US Department of Health and Human Services, Centers for Disease Control and Prevention, National Center for Health Statistics.

This report gives a summary of the results of the National Health Interview Survey for questions involving adults at least 18 years of age, and is a part of the larger NHIS. Accessible at http://www.cdc.gov/nchs/data/series/sr_10/sr10_240.pdf or through the main NHIS page at http://www.cdc.gov/nchs/nhis.htm

Summary Statistics for US Children: National Health Interview Survey, 2007, US Department of Health and Human Services, Centers for Disease Control and Prevention, National Center for Health Statistics.

This report gives a summary of the results of the National Health Interview Survey for questions involving children's health, and is a part of the larger NHIS. Accessible at http://www.cdc.gov/nchs/data/series/sr_10/sr10_239.pdf or through the main NHIS page at http://www.cdc.gov/nchs/nhis.htm

Chapter 3: Education

College Enrollment and Work Activity of 2008 High School Graduates, US Department of Labor, Bureau of Labor Statistics.

This report contains labor and unemployment data for students who have graduated from high school in the past year (broken down by college enrollment status), as well as those who have recently dropped out of high school without receiving their diplomas. Data is collected during the Current Population Survey for people 16 to 24 years old. Accessible at http://www.bls.gov/news.release/pdf/hsgec.pdf

Digest of Education Statistics 2008, US Department of Education, National Center for Education Statistics.

The *Digest of Education Statistics* is the major report from the US Department of Education, and draws from a variety of other reports and data-collection programs. It provides information on all aspects of education in America, from pre-kindergarten through graduate school, with information on schools, enrollments, student social and demographic characteristics, achievement, teachers, educational finance and funding, and more. Accessible at http://nces.ed.gov/programs/digest

Educational Attainment in the United States, 2008, US Bureau of the Census, Current Population Reports.

This annual report, part of the CPS, tracks Americans' level of educational advancement, providing information based on age, sex, race and Hispanic origin, and a host of other characteristics. The CPS report on educational attainment has been revised and somewhat scaled back for 2007, in part due to the greater role now being played by the ACS, but it remains a useful source of information. Accessible at http://www.census.gov/population/www/socdemo/educ-attn.html

School Enrollment: Social and Economic Characteristics of Students, October 2007, US Bureau of the Census, Current Population Reports.

The Current Population Survey's annual report on school enrollment provides information on age, grade, race and Hispanic origin, income, enrollment status, and educational attainment, and is part of the CPS' larger efforts to track data on education. Accessible at http://www.census.gov/population/www/socdemo/school.html

Chapter 4: Government and Elections

Voting and Registration in the Election of November, 2006, US Bureau of the Census, Current Population Reports.

The official estimates for each presidential and congressional election are contained in this biennial report, which includes information on voter registration and voting, with detailed data on race and Hispanic origin, sex, age, state, income, and educational attainment. Several editions of the report are used for this book. The most recent is accessible at http://www.census.gov/prod/2008pubs/p20-557.pdf. The main page for the reports can be found at http://www.census.gov/population/www/socdemo/voting.html

Chapter 5: Crime, Law Enforcement & Corrections

Annual Survey of Jails and Census of Jail Inmates, US Department of Justice, Bureau of Justice Statistics.

The annual jail census presents tables on trend information for the number and rate of jail inmates. Data collected in the survey is used to generate many of the other reports produced by the Bureau of Justice Statistics. Accessible at http://www.ojp.usdoj.gov/bjs/glance/tables/jailracetab.htm and http://www.ojp.usdoj.gov/bjs/glance/tables/jailrairtab.htm

Capital Punishment 2007, US Department of Justice, Bureau of Justice Statistics, Bureau of Justice Statistics.

This bulletin provides the most current information on prisoners under sentence of death, including time from sentencing to execution and prior legal status. Accessible at http://www.ojp.usdoj.gov/bjs/pub/html/cp/2007/cp07st.htm

Crime in the United States 2007, US Federal Bureau of Investigation, Uniform Crime Reports Unit.

Crime in the United States is the FBI's annual summary of crime data for the nation, state, county, and city levels. The FBI's Uniform Crime Reports division provides a standardized format for tracking offenses, arrests, and law enforcement personnel, and works with over 17,000 law enforcement agencies to produce the nationwide report. Accessible at http://www.fbi.gov/ucr/cius2007/

Criminal Victimization 2007, US Department of Justice, Office of Justice Programs.

This report provides information on victims of crimes, broken down by type of offense, the time and place the crime was committed, and the characteristics of the victims (including sex, race/Hispanic origin, age, housing tenure, household, and marital status). Accessible at http://www.ojp.usdoj.gov/bjs/pub/pdf/cv07.pdf

HIV in Prisons, 2006 and HIV in Prisons and Jails, 2004, US Department of Justice, Bureau of Justice Statistics.

These reports provide data on the incidence of HIV among prisoners, the number of inmates tested, and deaths from AIDS. The reports are accessible at http://www.ojp.usdoj.gov/bjs/pub/html/hivp/2006/hivp06.htm and http://www.ojp.usdoj.gov/bjs/abstract/hivp04.htm, respectively.

***Prison and Jail Inmates at Midyear 2006*, US Department of Justice, Bureau of Justice Statistics.**

This prisoner report contains state-by-state breakdowns of incarceration rates based on race and Hispanic origin. Accessible at http://www.ojp.usdoj.gov/bjs/pub/pdf/pjim06.pdf

Prisoners in 2007, US Department of Justice, Bureau of Justice Statistics.

The BJS' annual report on prisoners in the United States provides counts and rates for prisoners by state, type of facility, offense category, sex, race, and Hispanic origin. Accessible at http://www.ojp.usdoj.gov/bjs/pub/pdf/p07.pdf

Sourcebook of Criminal Justice Statistics, 2003 and Online, US Department of Justice, Bureau of Justice Statistics.

The *Sourcebook of Criminal Justice Statistics* collects data from over 200 sources on many topics relating to criminal justice in the United States, including crime statistics, victims, arrests, prisons, sentencing, and public opinion. While the *Sourcebook* began with regular annual editions, since 2003 updates have been added as new data becomes available. Accessible at http://www.albany.edu/sourcebook.

Chapter 6: Labor, Employment & Unemployment

Employment and Earnings, 2007, US Department of Labor, Bureau of Labor Statistics.

The major annual report from the CPS on topics relating to labor, employment, and unemployment, *Employment and Earnings* contains information on a wide range of topics, including unemployment rates, employed persons by industry and occupation, weekly earnings, employment status (full-time and part-time), and union affiliation, with further breakdowns based on age, sex, race and Hispanic origin, and educational attainment. The CPS' main page at the Bureau of Labor statistics, http://www.bls.gov/cps, contains links to individual tables in this report, and several other useful reports, as well as featuring a tool to create custom tables or download raw data files. Earlier versions of the report were known as the *Handbook of Labor Statistics*.

Employment and Unemployment in Families, 2008, US Department of Labor, Bureau Labor Statistics.

This is the major report from the Bureau of Labor Statistics concerning employment in families, including data on marital status and presence of children under 18. It is accessible at http://www.bls.gov/news.release/pdf/famee.pdf

Geographic Profile of Employment and Unemployment, 2003, US Department of Labor, Bureau of Labor Statistics.

The *Geographic Profile* provides labor information for Census-designated regions and divisions, the 50 states (plus the District of Columbia), 50 major metropolitan areas, and 17 central cities. The full report is accessible at http://www.bls.gov/opub/gp/laugp.htm

Geographic Profile of Employment and Unemployment, 2008 Annual Averages, US Department of Labor, Bureau of Labor Statistics.

While the full *Grographic Profile* is released several years after the dates of its data, the program also produces more current preliminary estimates at the statewide level. The statewide estimates are accessible at http://www.bls.gov/lau/ptable14full2008.pdf

Work at Home in 2004, US Department of Labor, Bureau of Labor Statistics.

This BLS report presents data on individuals working from home, including information on industry and occupation, the number of hours worked, race and Hispanic origin, sex, marital status, and educational attainment. Accessible at http://www.bls.gov/news.release/pdf/homey.pdf

Chapter 7: Earnings, Income, Poverty & Wealth

Annual Social and Economic Supplement 2008, **US Bureau of the Census, Current Population Reports.**

The Current Population Survey is a joint program between the Census Bureau's Population division and the Bureau of Labor Statistics. The *Annual Social and Economic Supplement* (ASEC, formerly known as the *March Supplement*) presents much of the data from the Current Population Survey on income for individuals, families, and households, including information on household characteristics, health insurance coverage, and employment status. The detailed ASEC is based on a sample of approximately 76,000 households, and collects much of the same information as the American Community Survey, although the two programs are distinct. Because the ACS collects much of the same data (with a larger sample size), the *Annual Social and Economic Supplement* is losing prominence in favor of the ACS, but it is still one of the Census Bureau's central programs collecting income and demographic data. Data from the *Annual Supplement* is accessible at the following URLs:

CPS Main Page:	http://www.census.gov/cps
Person Income:	http://pubdb3.census.gov/macro/032007/perinc/toc.htm
Family Income:	http://pubdb3.census.gov/macro/032007/faminc/toc.htm
Household Income:	http://pubdb3.census.gov/macro/032007/hhinc/toc.htm
Poverty:	http://pubdb3.census.gov/macro/032007/pov/toc.htm
Health Insurance Coverage:	http://pubdb3.census.gov/macro/032007/health/toc.htm

Data in the *Annual Supplement* has been released under different names in the past, including *Money Income of Households, Families and Persons in the United States*, and *Money Income of Households in the United States*. Some older data can also be found on the CPS' website under "historical income-tables." Finally, much of the data in the social and demographic tables in Chapter 1 was also drawn from the *Annual Supplement*.

Custodial Mothers and Fathers and Their Child Support: 2003, **US Bureau of the Census, Current Population Reports.**

This report from the CPS tracks the number of custodial parents receiving child support, and a variety of details about the parents and support. Data is given separately for custodial mothers, custodial fathers, and all custodial parents. Accessible at http://www.census.gov/population/www/socdemo/childcare.html

Income, Poverty, and Health Insurance Coverage in the United States, 2007, **US Bureau of the Census, Current Population Reports.**

This annual report contains a summary of the data on a wide range of measures relating to income, poverty, and health insurance coverage (see the above description for the Annual Social and Economic Supplement). Accessible at http://www.census.gov/prod/2008pubs/p60-235.pdf or through the CPS' main page at http://www.census.gov/cps

Measuring the Effect of Benefits and Taxes on Income and Poverty: 1992, **US Bureau of the Census, Current Population Reports.**

This report provides a breakdown of the amount of household income received from a variety of sources, including Social Security, food stamps, housing assistance, subsidized school lunches, Medicare, and Medicaid, as well as the overall percent of households receiving income from each source. This report series is not currently maintained; much of the data collected has been absorbed into the CPS' *Annual Supplement*. Accessible at http://www.census.gov/hhes/www/poverty/prevcps/p60-186rd.pdf

Participation in Government Porgrams, 2001 Through 2003, Who Gets Assistance?, US Bureau of the Census, Survey of Income and Program Participation.

The Survey of Income and Program Participation (SIPP) investigates the effectiveness of federal, state, and local government programs by collecting information on income and program participation of individuals and households, including cash and noncash income, taxes, assets, liabilities, and participation in government transfer programs. The SIPP report used in this chapter measured participation in a variety of government aid programs, including the median benefit awarded and duration of program participation. Accessible at http://www.bls.census.gov/sipp/p70s/p70-108.pdf

Chapter 8: Special Topics

US Summary and State Data, US Bureau of the Census, Census of Agriculture, 2007, Vol. 1 Geographic Area Series, Part 51.

The Census of Agriculture is performed every 5 years, and is comparable in scope for farm and agricultural data to the Decennial Census for population and demographic data. The Agricultural Census presents a wealth of information on all aspects of farming, and should be considered the authoritative government source on the topic. Data from the 2007 Census is accessible at http://www.agcensus.usda.gov/Publications/2007/Full_Report/usv1.pdf

Consumer Expenditure Survey, 2007, US Department of Labor, Bureau of Labor Statistics.

The Consumer Expenditure Survey is the major BLS program tracking household spending in a variety of areas, including food, housing, apparel, transportation, health care, entertainment, reading, education, and insurance, as well as information on income, household size, housing tenure (homeowners and renters), and number of vehicles. Accessible at http://www.bls.gov/cex

Survey of Minority-Owned Business Enterprises: Black-Owned Firms [HISPANIC, ASIAN], US Bureau of the Census, Economic Census, 2002.

The Economic Census is performed every 5 years, and is comparable in scope for business data to the Decennial Census for population and demographic data. The Economic Census presents a wealth of information on all topics related to business, industry, occupations, sales, receipts, employers and employees, taxes, and more, and should be considered the authoritative source on the topic. Data from the 2007 Economic Census is still being processed; results will be available between October 2009 and August 2010. Data from the 2002 Census is accessible at http://www.census.gov/econ/census02

Geographic Mobility: March 2005 to March 2006, US Bureau of the Census, Current Population Survey.

This annual report from the CPS estimates the number of people who have moved in the past year, as well as the type of move (within the same county, or to a different county, state, Census region, or out of the country), with detailed breakdowns by age, sex, and race or Hispanic origin. Accessible at http://www.census.gov/population/www/socdemo/migrate.html

Who Can Afford to Buy A House in 2002? US Bureau of the Census, Current Housing Reports.

This report from 2002 measured the percentage of families who could afford a median-priced or modestly-priced house using several different types of mortgages and financing, with detailed breakdowns by marital status and race/Hispanic origin. Accessible at http://www.census.gov/hhes/www/housing/hsgaffrd/hsgaffrd.html

Glossary

[ip]
Essential
Topics
Series

AGE ADJUSTMENT

A method of creating an overall rate in order to account for observed differences resulting from different age distributions in populations. The raw rates for each age group are combined (using a weighted average) to produce an overall rate that would apply if the population in question had the same age distribution as a reference population (usually the overall population of the United States).

AGGRAVATED ASSAULT *see* **CRIME.**

AMERICAN COMMUNITY SURVEY

A monthly sample of the civilian, non-institutionalized population that tracks much of the information previously only measured by the Decennial Census. Currently the ACS provides data on a nationwide and statewide level, as well as for cities and counties with populations over 65,000. For the 2007 edition (released in 2009), ACS coverage will expand to all communities with populations greater than 20,000. By 2010, the Bureau of the Census hopes to use the ACS to track all the information currently collected in the long form of the Decennial Census. *See also* **civilian noninstitutional population.**

ARSON *see* **CRIME.**

AVERAGE *see* **MEAN, MEDIAN.**

BED DAY *see* **DISABILITY DAY.**

BIRTH *see* **LIVE BIRTH.**

BODY MASS INDEX (BMI)

An estimate of body fat used to determine whether a person is a healthy weight, overweight, obese, or underweight. It is obtained by dividing a person's weight in kilograms by the square of their height in meters (kg/m^2). In general, a BMI over 25 is considered overweight, and a BMI over 30 is considered obese.

BURGLARY *see* **CRIME.**

CAUSE OF DEATH

For the purpose of national mortality statistics, every death is attributed to one underlying condition, based on information reported on the death certificate and utilizing the international rules (International Classifications of Disease) for selecting the underlying cause of death from reported conditions.

CIVILIAN LABOR FORCE

All persons, excluding members of the Armed Forces, who are either employed or unemployed.

Employed persons are those persons 16 years old and over who were either a) "at work" – those who did any work at all as paid employees, in their own business or profession, on their own farm, or worked 15 or more hours as unpaid workers on a family farm or in a family business; or b) "with a job but not at work" – those who did not work during the reference period, but had jobs or businesses from which they were temporarily absent due to illness, bad weather, industrial dispute, vacation, or other personal reasons. Excluded from the employed are persons whose only activity consisted of work around the house or volunteer work for religious, charitable, and similar organizations.

Employed persons are classified as either **full-time workers**, those who worked 35 hours or more per week, or **part-time workers**, those who worked less than 35 hours per week.

Unemployed persons are those who were neither "at work" nor "with a job, but not at work" *and* who were both looking for work and available to accept a job. Also included as unemployed are persons who are waiting to be called back to a job from which they have been laid off. The unemployed are divided into four groups according to reason for unemployment:

- Job losers (including those who have been laid off)

- Job leavers who have left their job voluntarily

- Re-entrants, who have worked before and are re-entering the labor force

- New entrants to the labor force looking for work

Discouraged workers, those who do not have a job and have not been seeking one, not considered to be part of the labor force.

CIVILIAN NONINSTITUTIONAL POPULATION *see **POPULATION**.*

CIVILIAN POPULATION *see **POPULATION**.*

COLLEGE

A postsecondary school which offers a general or liberal arts education, usually leading to an associate's, bachelor's, master's, doctoral, or first professional degree. Junior colleges and community colleges are included. *See also **institution of higher education**, **university**.*

COMMUNITY HOSPITAL

All non-federal short-term hospitals, excluding hospital units of institutions, whose services are available to the public. **Short-term hospitals** are those where the average length of stay is less than 30 days.

CONSUMER EXPENDITURE SURVEY

A survey of current consumer expenditures, reflecting the buying habits of American consumers. Begun in 1979 and conducted jointly by the US Bureau of Labor Statistics and the US Bureau of the Census, the survey consists of two parts: an interview panel survey in which the expenditures of consumer units are obtained in five interviews conducted every three months, and a diary (or recordkeeping) survey completed by the participating households for two consecutive one-week periods. It should not be confused with the **Consumer Price Index**, which measures the average change in prices of consumer goods and services *See also* **consumer unit.**

CONSUMER UNIT

An entity used as the basis of the **Consumer Expenditure Survey**. A consumer unit comprises either:

• All the members of a particular household who are related by blood, marriage, adoption, or other legal arrangements;

• A person living alone or sharing a household with others, or living as a roomer in a private home or lodging house or in a permanent living quarters in a hotel or motel, but who is financially independent;

• Two or more persons living together who pool their income to make joint expenditure decisions, and share responsibility for at least two of the three major types of expenses – food, housing, and other expenses.

A consumer unit may or may not be a household. Students living in university housing are usually counted as separate consumer units.

CRIME

A crime is an action which is prohibited by law. Their are two major statistical programs which measure crime in the United States. The first is the **Uniform Crime Reporting** (UCR) program, administered by the FBI. The Bureau receives monthly and annual reports from most police agencies around the country (covering nearly 300 million people in America). These reports contain information on eight major types of crimes (collectively called **serious crime**), which are known to police. Serious crime consists of four **violent crimes: murder** and **non-negligent manslaughter** (which includes willful felonious homicides and is based on police investigations rather than determinations of a medical examiner), **forcible rape** (which includes attempted rape), **robbery** (which includes stealing or taking anything of value by force or violence, or by threat of force or violence, and includes attempted robbery), and **aggravated assault** (which includes intent to kill), as well as four **property crimes: burglary** (which includes any unlawful entry to commit a felony or theft and includes attempted burglary and burglary followed by larceny), **larceny** (which includes theft of property or articles of value without use of force, violence, or fraud, and excludes embezzlement, con games, forgery, etc.), **motor vehicle theft** (which includes all cases where vehicles are driven away and abandoned, but excludes vehicles taken for temporary use and returned by the taker), and **arson** (which includes any willful or malicious burning or attempt to burn, with or without the intent to defraud, of a dwelling house, public building, motor vehicle, aircraft, or personal property of another).

The second approach to the measurement of crime is through the **National Crime Victimization Survey** (NCVS – formerly known as the National Crime Survey), administered by the Bureau of Justice Statistics. The survey is based on a representative sample of approximately 49,000 households containing about 100,000 persons age 12 and over. Although the categories of crime are similar to those used by the FBI in the UCR, the NCVS is based on reports of victimization directly by victims, as opposed to crimes reported to police as in the UCR. As might be imagined, not all crimes are reported or known to police, so NCVS estimates of crime tend to be significantly higher than UCR figures. The NCVS also differs from the UCR in that only crimes whose victims can be interviewed are included (hence there are no homicide statistics), and only victims who are 12 years old or older are counted. The two central concepts in the NCVS are victimization, which is the specific criminal act as it affects a single victim, and a criminal incident, which is a specific criminal act involving one or more victims. Thus, in regard to personal crime there are more victimizations than incidents.

DEATH *see* *CAUSE OF DEATH, INFANT MORTALITY.*

DISABILITY

The presence of a physical, mental, or other health condition which has lasted six or more months and which limits or prevents a particular type of activity. *See also* **work disability.**

DISABILITY DAY

A day on which a person's usual activity is reduced because of illness or injury. There are four types of disability days (which are not mutually exclusive):

a) A **restricted-activity** day, a day on which a person cuts down on his or her usual activities because of illness or an injury.

b) A **bed-disability** day, a day on which a person stays in bed more than half of the daylight hours (or normal waking hours) because of a specific illness or injury. All hospital days are bed-disability days. Bed-disability days may also be work-loss days or school-loss days.

c) A **work-loss day**, a day on which a person did not work at his or her job or business for at least half of his or her normal workday because of a specific illness or injury. Work-loss days are determined only for employed persons.

d) A **school-loss day**, a day on which a child did not attend school for at least half of his or her normal school day because of a specific illness or injury. School-loss days are determined only for children 6 to 16 years of age.

EMPLOYED PERSONS *see* *CIVILIAN LABOR FORCE.*

EMPLOYMENT STATUS *see CIVILIAN LABOR FORCE.*

ENROLLMENT

The total number of students registered in a given school unit at a given time of year, generally in the fall. *See also full-time enrollment, part-time enrollment.*

ETHNICITY *see RACE*

FAMILY

A type of household containing two or more persons (including the householder) related by birth, marriage, or adoption living together. All such related persons in one housing unit are considered as members of one family. (For example, if the son or daughter of the family householder and that son's or daughter's spouse and/or children are members of the household, they are all counted as part of the householder's family.) However, non-family members who are not related to the householder (such as a roomer or boarder and his or her spouse, or a resident employee and his or her spouse who are living in), are not counted as family members but as unrelated individuals living in a family household. For Census purposes, a housing unit can contain only one household, and a household can contain only one family.

Families are classified by type according to the sex of the householder and the presence of a spouse and children. The three main types of family households are: **married couples**, in which a husband and wife live together (with or without other persons in the household); **male householder, no wife present**, in which a male householder lives together with other members of his family but without a wife; and **female householder, no husband present**, in which a female householder lives together with other members of her family but without a husband. *See also household.*

FAMILY INCOME *see INCOME.*

FARM

As defined by the Bureau of the Census (and adopted by the Department of Agriculture), a farm is any place from which $1,000 or more of agricultural products were sold, or would have been sold during a given year. Control of the farm may be exercised through ownership or management, or through a lease, rental or cropping arrangement. In the case of landowners who have one or more tenants or renters, the land operated by each is counted as a separate farm. This definition has been in effect since 1974.

FARMLAND

All land under the control of a farm operator, including land not actually under cultivation or not used for pasture or grazing. Rent-free land is included as part of a farm only if the operator has sole use of it. Land used for pasture or grazing on a per head basis that is neither owned nor leased by the farm operator is not included except for grazing lands controlled by grazing associations leased on a per acre basis.

FARM INCOME

Gross farm income comprises cash receipts from farm marketings of crops and livestock, federal government payments made directly to farmers for farm-related activities, rental value of farm homes, value of farm products consumed in farm homes, and other farm related income such as machine hire and custom work.

FULL-TIME ENROLLMENT

The number of students enrolled in higher education courses with a total credit load equal to at least 75% of the normal full-time course load.

FULL-TIME WORKERS *see CIVILIAN LABOR FORCE.*

HATE CRIME

A hate crime, also known as a bias crime, is a criminal offense committed against a person, property, or society that is motivated, in whole or in part, by the offender's bias against a race, religion, disability, sexual orientation, or ethnicity/national origin.

HEALTH LIMITATION OF ACTIVITY

A characteristic of persons with chronic conditions. Each person identified as having a chronic condition is classified by the extent to which his or her activities are limited by the condition as follows:

• Persons unable to carry on a **major activity** (the principal activity of a person of his or her age sex group): for persons 1–5 years of age, it refers to ordinary play with other children; for persons 6–16 years of age, it refers to school attendance; for persons 17 years of age and over, it usually refers to a job, housework, or school attendance.

• Persons limited in the amount or kind of major activity performed.

• Persons not limited in major activity, but otherwise limited.

• Persons not limited in activity.

HEALTH MAINTENANCE ORGANIZATION (HMO)

A prepaid health plan delivering comprehensive care to members through designated providers, having a fixed monthly payment for health care services, and requiring members to be in the plan for a specified period of time (usually one year). HMOs are distinguished by the relationship of the providers to the plan. HMO model types are: **Group** – an HMO that delivers health services through a physician group controlled by the HMO, or an HMO that contracts with one or more independent group practices to provide health services; and **Individual**

Practice Association (IPA) – an HMO that contracts directly with physicians in independent practice, and/or contracts with one or more associations of physicians in independent practice, and/or contracts with one or more multispecialty group practices, but is predominantly organized around solo single specialty practices.

HIGHER EDUCATION *see* *INSTITUTION OF HIGHER EDUCATION.*

HISPANIC ORIGIN

An aspect of a person's ancestry. The Bureau of the Census in many of its survey asks persons if they are of Hispanic origin. There are four main subcategories of Hispanic origin: Mexican, Puerto Rican, Cuban, and other Hispanic. Hispanic origin is not a racial classification. Persons may be of any race and of Hispanic origin. Hispanic origin is used interchangeably with Spanish and Spanish origin.

HOME OWNERSHIP *see* *TENURE.*

HOSPITAL *see* *COMMUNITY HOSPITAL.*

HOSPITAL DAY

A hospital day is a night spent in a hospital by a person admitted as an inpatient.

HOUSEHOLD

The person or persons occupying a housing unit. There are two main types of households: **family households**, which consist of two or more persons related by birth, marriage, or adoption living together; and **non-family households**, which consist of a person living alone, or together with unrelated individuals. *See also householder, family.*

HOUSEHOLD INCOME *see* *INCOME.*

HOUSEHOLD TYPE *see* *HOUSEHOLD.*

HOUSEHOLDER

The person in whose name a housing unit is rented or owned.

HOUSING UNIT

A house, apartment, mobile home or trailer, group of rooms, or single room occupied as a separate living quarter, or, if vacant, intended for occupancy as a separate living quarter. Separate living quarters are those in which the occupants live and eat separately from any other persons in the building and which have direct access from the outside of the building or through a common hall.

Both occupied and vacant housing units are counted in many surveys; however, recreational vehicles, boats, caves, tents, railroad cars, and the like are only included if they are occupied as someone's usual place of residence. Vacant mobile homes are included if they are intended for occupancy on the site where they stand. Vacant mobile homes on dealers' sales lots, at the factory, or in storage yards are excluded. Vacant units held for seasonal use or migratory labor are also excluded.

See also **Occupancy Status**, **Tenure**.

HOUSING TENURE *see* **TENURE**.

INCOME

The term 'income' has different definitions depending on the context in which it is used. Like many government statistical terms, income can be viewed hierarchically.

Personal income is the current income received by persons from all sources, minus their personal contributions for social insurance. Persons include individuals (including owners of unincorporated firms), nonprofit institutions serving individuals, private trust funds, and private non-insured welfare funds. Personal income includes transfers (payments not resulting from current production) from government and business such as Social Security benefits, public assistance, etc., but excludes transfers between persons. Also included are certain non-monetary types of income, chiefly estimated net rental value to owner occupants of their homes, the value of services furnished without payment by financial intermediaries, and food and fuel produced and consumed on farms.

Disposable personal income is personal income less personal tax and non-tax payments. It is income available to persons for spending and saving. Personal tax and non-tax payments are tax payments (net of refunds) by persons (excluding contributions for social insurance) that are not chargeable to business expenses, and certain personal payments to general government that are treated like taxes. Personal taxes include income, estate and gift, personal property, and motor vehicle licenses. Non-tax payments include passport fees, fines and penalties, donations, tuition and fees paid to schools and hospitals mainly operated by the government.

Money income is a smaller, less inclusive category than personal income. Money income is the sum of the amounts received from wages and salaries, self-employment income (including losses), Social Security, Supplemental Security Income, public assistance, interest, dividends, rents, royalties, estate or trust income, veterans payments, unemployment and workers' compensation payments, private and government retirement and disability pensions, alimony, child support, and any other source of money income which was regularly received. Capital gains or losses and lump sum or one-time payments, such as life insurance settlements, are excluded. Also excluded are non-cash benefits such as food stamps, health benefits, housing subsidies, rent-free housing, and the goods produced and consumed on farms. Money income is reported for households and various household types, as well as for unrelated individuals. It is reported in aggregate, median, mean, and per capita amounts. Money income is also used for determining the poverty status of families and unrelated individuals. Family money income includes only the amount received by all family members 15 years old and over and excludes income received by household members not related to the householder.

INFANT MORTALITY

The deaths of live-born children who do not reach their first birthday. Infant mortality is usually expressed as a rate per 1,000 live births.

INSTITUTION OF HIGHER EDUCATION

An institution which offers programs of study beyond the secondary school level terminating in an associate, baccalaureate, or higher degree. *See also* **college**, **university**.

JAIL

A facility, usually operated by a local law enforcement agency, holding persons detained pending adjudication and/or persons committed after adjudication to a sentence of one year or less. *See also* **prison**.

LABOR FORCE STATUS *see* **CIVILIAN LABOR FORCE.**

LARCENY *see* **CRIME.**

LIMITATION OF ACTIVITY *see* **HEALTH LIMITATION OF ACTIVITY.**

LIVE BIRTH

The live birth of an infant, defined as the complete expulsion or extraction from its mother of a product of conception, irrespective of the duration of the pregnancy, which, after such separation, breathes or shows any evidence of life such as heartbeat, umbilical cord pulsation, or definite movement of voluntary muscles, whether or not the umbilical cord has been cut or the placenta is attached. Each such birth is considered live-born.

MARITAL STATUS

All persons 15 years of age and older are classified by the Bureau of the Census according to marital status. The Bureau defines two broad categories of marital status: **Single** – all those persons who have never been married (including persons whose marriage has been annulled), and **ever married**, which is composed of the now married, the widowed, and the divorced. **Now married** persons are those who are legally married (as well as some persons who have common law marriages, and some unmarried couples who live together and report their marital status as married), and whose marriage has not ended by widowhood or divorce. The now married are sometimes further subdivided into four categories: married, spouse present; separated; married, spouse absent; and married, spouse absent, other. **Married, spouse present** covers married couples living together. **Separated** includes those persons legally separated or otherwise absent from their spouses because of marital discord (such as persons who have been deserted or who have parted because they no longer want to live together but who have not obtained a divorce). Separated includes persons with a limited divorce. **Married, spouse absent** covers those households where the husband and wife were not counted as members of the same household, or where both husband and wife lived together in group quarters. **Married, spouse absent, other**, includes those married persons whose spouse was not counted as a member of the same household, besides those who are separated. Included are persons whose spouse was employed and living away from home, absent in the armed forces, or was an inmate of an institution. **Widowed** includes widows and widowers, women and men, respectively, whose spouses have died and who have not remarried. **Divorced** includes persons who are legally divorced and have not remarried.

MARRIED COUPLES *see FAMILY.*

MARRIED PERSONS *see MARITAL STATUS.*

MEAN

The arithmetic average of a set of values. It is derived by dividing the sum of a group of numerical items by the total number of items. Mean income (of a population), for example, is defined as the value obtained by dividing the total or aggregate income by the population. Thus, the mean income for families is obtained by dividing the aggregate of all income reported by persons in families by the total number of families. *See also median.*

MEDIAN

In general, a value that divides the total range of values into two equal parts. For example, to say that the median money income of families in the United States in 1985 was $27,735 indicates that half of all families had incomes larger than that value, and half had less. The median is less susceptible to distortion by extremely large or small values, and in many situations is preferred over the mean. *See also mean.*

MEDICAID

A federally-funded but state-administered and operated program which provides medical benefits to certain low-income persons in need of medical care. The program, authorized in 1965 by Title XIX of the Social Security Act, categorically covers participants in the Aid to Families with Dependent Children (AFDC) program, as well as some participants in the Supplemental Security Income (SSI) program, along with others deemed medically needy in each participating state. Each state determines the benefits covered, rates of payment to providers, and methods of administering the program.

MEDICARE

A federally-funded nationwide health insurance program providing health insurance protection to people 65 years of age and over, people eligible for social security disability payments for more than two years, and people with end-state renal disease, regardless of income. The program was enacted July 30, 1965, as title XVIII, Health Insurance for the Aged, of the Social Security Act, and became effective on July 1, 1966. It consists of two separate but coordinated programs: hospital insurance (Part A), and supplementary medical insurance (Part B).

METROPOLITAN AREA

Roughly, a population concentration of at least 50,000 inhabitants, generally consisting of a central city with a dense population and a surrounding area whose economy is closely linked with the city. The US Office of Budget and Management (OMB) designates which areas are considered metropolitan. The definitions are frequently altered and updated to reflect changes in the population. The most recent definition, **Core-Based Statistical Area (CBSA)**, was adopted in June, 2003. Past categories used the the OMB are **Metropolitan and Micropolitan area, Consolidated Metropolitan Statistical Area (CMSA), Metropolitan Statistical Area (MSA), Primary Metropolitan Statistical Area (PMSA), Standard Consolidated Statistical Areas (SCSA), Standard Metropolitan Statistical Area (SMSA), and New England County Metropolitan Area (NECMA).**

Tables that refer to metropolitan or non-metropolitan areas use the definition that was in effect at the time for the source used. Readers seeking a more detailed explanation should consult the original source or the Office of Budget and Management (www.whitehouse.gov/omb).

MOBILE HOME see *HOUSING UNIT.*

MODESTLY PRICED HOME

A home that is less expensive than 75% of the owner-occupied homes in that area of residence (often used as a measure of affordability).

MONEY INCOME see *INCOME.*

MURDER see *CRIME.*

NATIONAL CRIME VICTIMIZATION SURVEY

Formerly the **National Crime Survey**, a twice-yearly survey of 49,000 households containing over 100,000 inhabitants 12 years of age and older. Administered by the Bureau of Justice Statistics, the survey measures criminal victimization by surveying victims directly. It differs from the **FBI Uniform Crime Report** (UCR) which is based on crimes reported to police. *See also crime.*

OCCUPATION

The kind of work a person does at a job or business. Occupation is reported for a given survey period, or **reference period** (most frequently the week including March 12). If the person was not at work during the reference period, occupation usually refers to the person's most recent job or business. Persons working at more than one job are asked to identify the job at which he or she works the most hours, which is then counted as his or her occupation.

Occupations are classified according to the the federal Office of Management and Budget's Standard Occupational Classification system (SOC).

OWNER-OCCUPIED HOUSING UNIT *see* **TENURE**.

PART-TIME ENROLLMENT

The number of students enrolled in higher education courses with a total credit load of less than 75% of the normal full-time credit load.

PART-TIME WORKERS *see* **CIVILIAN LABOR FORCE**.

PERSONAL INCOME *see* **INCOME**.

POPULATION

The number of inhabitants of an area. The total population of the United States is the sum of all persons living within the United States, Puerto Rico, Guam, and the US Virgin Islands, plus all members of the Armed Forces living in foreign countries. Other Americans living abroad (e.g., civilian federal employees and dependents of members of the Armed Forces or other federal employees) are not included.

The **resident population** of the United States is the population living within the geographic United States. This includes members of the Armed Forces stationed in the United States and their families, as well as foreigners working or studying here. It excludes foreign military, naval, and diplomatic personnel and their families located here and residing in embassies or similar quarters, as well as Americans living abroad. Resident population is often used as the denominator when calculating birth and death rates, incidence of disease, and other rates.

The **civilian population** is the resident population excluding members of the Armed Forces. However, families of members of the Armed Forces are included.

The **civilian non-institutional population** is the civilian population not residing in institutions. Institutions include correctional institutions; detention homes and training schools for juvenile delinquents; homes for the aged and dependent (e.g., nursing homes and convalescent homes); homes for dependent and neglected children; homes and schools for the mentally and physically handicapped; homes for unwed mothers; psychiatric, tuberculosis, and chronic disease hospitals; and residential treatment centers.

POVERTY STATUS

Although the term "poverty" connotes a complex set of economic, social, and psychological conditions, the standard statistical definition provides for only estimates of economic poverty. These are based on money income before taxes and exclude the value of government payments and transfers such as food stamps or Medicare; private transfers, such as health insurance premiums paid by employers; gifts; the depletion of assets; and borrowed money. Thus the term poverty as used by government agencies classifies persons and families in relation to being above or below a specified income level, or **poverty threshold**. Those below this threshold are said to be in poverty, or more accurately, as below the poverty level. Poverty thresholds vary by size of family, number of children, and age of householder, and are updated annually. Poverty status is also determined for unrelated individuals living in households, but not for those living in group quarters nor for persons in the Armed Forces. The poverty threshold is revised each year according to formula based on the **Consumer Price Index**, which measures the average change in prices of consumer goods and services.

PRISON

A confinement facility having custodial authority over adults sentenced to confinement for a period of more than one year. Prisons are usually run by state or federal authorities. *See also jail.*

PRIVATE SCHOOL *see SCHOOL.*

PROPERTY CRIME *see CRIME.*

PUBLIC SCHOOL *see SCHOOL.*

RACE

The Bureau of the Census in many of its surveys (most notably in the decennial censuses of population) asks all persons to identify themselves according to race. The concept of race as used by the Bureau reflects the self-identification of the respondents, and is not meant to denote any clear cut scientific or biological definition.

Although it is often reported with racial categories, **Hispanic origin** is not a racial category. Persons may be of any race and of Hispanic origin. Those who describe themselves as Hispanic (or Mexican, Cuban, Chicano, etc.) in response to a question about race are included by the Bureau in the racial classification "other." *See also **Hispanic origin.***

RAPE *see CRIME.*

REFERENCE PERSON

Most frequently, the person who responds to a government survey. Most surveys done by the federal government are based on households and begin by asking the initial respondent the name of the person in whose name the housing unit is owned or rented (this person is designated as the **householder**). Usually the householder is the reference person. Other household members are defined in relation to the householder.

REGION

The Bureau of the Census has divided the United States into four regions. This division is the primary geographic subdivision of the nation for statistical reporting purposes. As a result, almost all federal agencies, along with many private data collectors, have adopted the regional subdivision and use it for presenting statistical data. The four regions are the Northeast (Maine, New Hampshire, Vermont, Massachusetts, Rhode Island, Connecticut, New York, New Jersey, Pennsylvania); the Midwest (Ohio, Indiana, Illinois, Michigan, Wisconsin, Minnesota, Iowa, Missouri, North Dakota, South Dakota, Kansas, Nebraska); the South (Delaware, Maryland, District of Columbia, Virginia, West Virginia, North Carolina, South Carolina, Georgia, Florida, Kentucky, Tennessee, Alabama, Mississippi, Arkansas, Louisiana, Oklahoma, Texas); and the West (Montana, Idaho, Colorado, Wyoming, New Mexico, Arizona, Utah, Nevada, Washington, Oregon, California, Alaska, Hawaii). All regional data in this book conforms to these definitions.

REGULAR SCHOOL *see SCHOOL.*

RELATIVE STANDARD ERROR

A measure of an estimate's reliability derived by dividing the **standard error** by the estimate itself. Estimates with a high relative standard error are considered unreliable, and are frequently not presented in reports.

RENTER-OCCUPIED HOUSING UNIT *see TENURE.*

RESIDENT POPULATION *see POPULATION.*

ROBBERY *see CRIME.*

RURAL *see URBAN.*

SCHOOL

Elementary and secondary schools are divisions of the school system consisting of students in one or more grade groups or other identifiable groups, organized as one unit with one or more teachers giving instruction of a defined type, and housed in a school plant of one or more buildings. More than one school may be housed in one school plant, as in the case where elementary and secondary programs are housed in the same building.

Regular schools generally are those which advance a person toward a diploma or degree. They include public and private nursery schools, kindergartens, graded schools, colleges, universities, and professional schools.

Public schools are controlled and supported by local, state, or federal government agencies.

Private schools are controlled and supported mainly by religious organizations, private persons, or private organizations.

SCHOOL ENROLLMENT *see ENROLLMENT.*

SELF-EMPLOYMENT INCOME

A type of money income which comprises net income (gross receipts minus operating expenses) received by persons from an unincorporated business, profession, and/or from the operation of a farm as a farm owner, tenant, or sharecropper. *See also **money income.***

SEPARATED PERSONS *see **MARITAL STATUS.***

SERIOUS CRIME *see **CRIME.***

SINGLE-PERSON HOUSEHOLDS *see **HOUSEHOLD.***

SINGLE PERSONS *see **MARITAL STATUS.***

STANDARD ERROR

An estimate of the variation of a statistic, obrained by dividing the standard deviation by the square root of the sample size. See also ***relative standard error.***

SUBURBAN *see **URBAN.***

TAXES

Compulsory contributions exacted by a government for public purposes (except employee and employer assessments for retirement and social insurance purposes, which are classified as insurance trust revenue). All tax revenue is classified as general revenue and comprises amounts received (including interest and penalties, but excluding protested amounts and refunds) from all taxes imposed by a government.

TENURE

A concept relating to housing units. All occupied housing units are classified as being either owner-occupied or renter-occupied. A housing unit is **owner-occupied** if the owner or co-owner lives in the unit, even if the unit is mortgaged or not fully paid for. All other housing units are considered to be **renter-occupied**, regardless of whether or not cash rent is paid for them by a member of the household. *See also **housing unit.***

UNEMPLOYMENT *see **CIVILIAN LABOR FORCE.***

UNIFORM CRIME REPORTING (UCR) PROGRAM

A program administered by the FBI which collects reports from most police agencies in the nation (covering nearly 300 million people in America) on serious crimes known to police (violent crime and property crime), arrests, police officers and related items. The Bureau issues monthly and annual summary reports based on the program. *See also **crime.***

UNIVERSITY

An institution of higher education consisting of a liberal arts college, a diverse graduate program, and usually two or more professional schools or faculties and empowered to confer degrees in various fields of study. *See also **higher education.***

URBAN

Urban, suburban, and **rural** populations refer, respectively, to people living in the central city of a **metropolitan area**, outside the central city in a metropolitan area, or in a non-metropolitan area. Readers seeking a more detailed explanation, and the definition of metropolitan area that was in effect at the time, should refer to the original source. See also *suburban*, *rural*, *metropolitan area*.

VICTIMIZATION *see CRIME.*

VIOLENT CRIME *see CRIME.*

VOTING-AGE POPULATION

All persons over the age of 18 (the voting age for federal elections) in a given geographic area comprise the voting-age population. The voting-age population does include a small number of persons who, although of voting age, are not eligible to vote, such as resident aliens, and inmates of institutions. The voting-age population is estimated in even-numbered years by the Bureau of the Census.

WAGES AND SALARIES

A type (subgroup) of money income that includes civilian wages and salaries, Armed Forces pay and allowances, piece rate payments, commissions, tips, National Guard or Reserve pay (received for training periods), and cash bonuses before deductions for taxes, pensions, union dues, etc. *See also money income.*

WIDOWED PERSONS *see MARITAL STATUS.*

WORK DISABILITY

A health condition which limits the kind or amount of work a person can do, or prevents working at a job. A person is limited in the kind of work he or she can do if the person has a health condition which restricts his or her choice of jobs. A person is limited in amount of work if he or she is not able to work at a full-time (35 hours or more per week) job or business.

WORK-LOSS DAY *see DISABILITY DAY.*

Index

ORDER FORM

Title	Qty	Edition	Price	ISBN Number	Standing Order	
					YES	NO
State & Municipal Profiles Series						
Almanac of the 50 States 2009		Hardcover	$95	978-0-929960-53-1	☐	☐
		Paperback	$85	978-0-929960-52-4	☐	☐
California Cities, Towns & Counties 2009		Paperback	$129	978-0-911273-48-9	☐	☐
		CD	$129	978-0-911273-49-6	☐	☐
Connecticut Municipal Profiles 2009		Paperback	$89	978-0-941391-32-0	☐	☐
		CD	$89	978-0-941391-33-7	☐	☐
Florida Cities, Towns & Counties 2009		Paperback	$129	978-0-941391-34-4	☐	☐
		CD	$129	978-0-941391-35-1	☐	☐
Massachusetts Municipal Profiles 2009		Paperback	$119	978-0-911273-44-1	☐	☐
		CD	$119	978-0-911273-45-8	☐	☐
The New Jersey Municipal Data Book 2009		Paperback	$129	978-0-911273-46-5	☐	☐
		CD	$129	978-0-911273-47-2	☐	☐
North Carolina Cities, Towns & Counties 2009		Paperback	$129	978-0-941391-36-8	☐	☐
		CD	$129	978-0-941391-37-5	☐	☐
Essential Topics Series						
Energy, Transportation & the Environment: A Statistical Sourcebook and Guide to Government Data 2009		Paperback	$85	978-0-929960-57-9	☐	☐
		CD	$85	978-0-929960-61-0	☐	☐
American Profiles Series						
Black Americans: A Statistical Sourcebook and Guide to Government Data 2009		Paperback	$85	978-0-929960-55-5	☐	☐
		CD	$85	978-0-929960-59-3	☐	☐
Hispanic Americans: A Statistical Sourcebook and Guide to Government Data 2009		Paperback	$85	978-0-929960-56-2	☐	☐
		CD	$85	978-0-929960-60-9	☐	☐
Asian Americans: A Statistical Sourcebook and Guide to Government Data 2009		Paperback	$85	978-0-929960-54-8	☐	☐
		CD	$85	978-0-929960-58-6	☐	☐

Offer and prices valid until 12/31/09

Purchase orders accepted from libraries, government agencies, and educational institutions.

Prepayment required from all other organizations.

Order Subtotal _____

(Required ONLY for shipments to California) CA Sales Tax _____

Shipping & Handling _____

Total _____

Please complete the following shipping and billing information. If paying by credit card or PO please call **(877)544-4636** or fax your completed order form to **(877)544-4635**. To pay by check, please mail this form and your payment to the address below.

Information Publications, Inc.
2995 Woodside Rd., Suite 400-182
Woodside, CA 94062

U.S. Ground Shipping Rates	
Order Subtotal	Shipping & Handling
$0-129	$9
$130-260	$15
$261-400	$19
$401-500	$22
>$500	Call

Call for Int'l or Express Shipping Rates

Shipping Information (UPS/FedEx tracking number sent via email)

Organization Name		
Shipping Contact		
Address (No PO Boxes, please)		
City	State	Zip
Email Address (req'd if want tracking #)	Phone #	

Payment Information (mark choice)	☐ **Check**	☐ **Credit Card** ☐ Visa ☐ MC ☐ AMEX		☐ **Purchase Order** (attach PO to this form)
	Check #	CC#		PO #
		Exp Date		

Credit Card Billing Information   ☐ Check if same as Shipping Address

Name on Credit Card		
Billing Address of Credit Card		
City	State	Zip
Signature		

ORDER FORM

Title	Qty	Edition	Price	Extended Price	Standing Order	
State & Municipal Profiles Series					YES	NO
Almanac of the 50 States 2008		Hardcover	$89		☐	☐
Almanac of the 50 States 2008		Paperback	$79		☐	☐
California Cities, Towns & Counties 2008		CD	$119		☐	☐
		Paperback	$119		☐	☐
Connecticut Municipal Profiles 2008		CD	$85		☐	☐
		Paperback	$85		☐	☐
Florida Cities, Towns & Counties 2008		CD	$119		☐	☐
		Paperback	$119		☐	☐
Massachusetts Municipal Profiles 2008		CD	$109		☐	☐
		Paperback	$109		☐	☐
The New Jersey Municipal Data Book 2008		CD	$119		☐	☐
		Paperback	$119		☐	☐
North Carolina Cities, Towns & Counties 2008		CD	$119		☐	☐
		Paperback	$119		☐	☐
Essential Topics Series						
Energy, Transportation & the Environment: A Statistical Sourcebook and Guide to Government Data 2008		Paperback	$77		☐	☐
American Profiles Series						
Black Americans: A Statistical Sourcebook and Guide to Government Data 2008		Paperback	$77		☐	☐
Hispanic Americans: A Statistical Sourcebook and Guide to Government Data 2008		Paperback	$77		☐	☐
Asian Americans: A Statistical Sourcebook and Guide to Government Data 2008		Paperback	$77		☐	☐

Offer and prices valid until 12/31/08

Order Subtotal _____

Purchase orders accepted from libraries, government agencies, and educational institutions.
Prepayment required from all other organizations.

(Required ONLY for shipments to California) **CA Sales Tax** _____

Shipping & Handling _____

Total _____

Please complete the following shipping and billing information. If paying by credit card or PO please call **(877)544-4636** or fax your completed order form to **(877)544-4635**. To pay by check, please mail this form and your payment to the address below.

Information Publications, Inc.
2995 Woodside Rd., Suite 400-182
Woodside, CA 94062

U.S. Ground Shipping Rates

Order Subtotal	Shipping & Handling
$0-$89	$7
$90-$119	$9
$120-$240	$14
$241-$400	$19
$401-$500	$22
>$500	Call

Call for Int'l or Express Shipping Rates

Shipping Information (UPS/FedEx tracking number sent via email)

Organization Name		
Shipping Contact		
Address (No PO Boxes, please)		
City	State	Zip
Email Address (req'd if want tracking #)	Phone #	

Payment Information (mark choice)

☐ Check	☐ Credit Card ☐ Visa ☐ MC ☐ AMEX	☐ Purchase Order (attach PO to this form)
Check #	CC#	PO #
	Exp Date	

Credit Card Billing Information ☐ Check if same as Shipping Address

Name on Credit Card		
Billing Address of Credit Card		
City	State	Zip
Signature		

2995 WOODSIDE RD., SUITE 400-182
WOODSIDE, CA 94062

WWW.INFORMATIONPUBLICATIONS.COM

TOLL FREE PHONE 877-544-INFO (4636)
TOLL FREE FAX 877-544-4635

• Since 1980, A Trusted Ready Reference Resource for Easy-To-Use Federal, State and Local Information •